The Archers

THE TRUE STORY

ABOVE: 'Thank Goodness for Eddie Grundy,' said the *Evening Standard* in January 1996. 'Life in Ambridge, fictional home of the Archers may seem to be all sex, drugs and parish strife at present, but at least things never change for the lovable rogue from Grange Farm . . .' The programme celebrated its forty-fifth anniversary with a whisky and temazepam overdose for Kate Aldridge.
Press Association: Rebecca Naden

BELOW: Recording in Studio 2, Broad Street, Birmingham, in the early Fifties. Norman Painting (Phil Archer), Pamela Mant (Christine) and Harry Oakes (Dan).
Camera Press: Tom Blau

The Archers

THE TRUE STORY

The History of Radio's Most Famous Programme

William Smethurst

MICHAEL O'MARA BOOKS LIMITED

First published in Great Britain in 1996 by
Michael O'Mara Books Limited
9 Lion Yard, Tremadoc Road
London sw4 7nq

A CIP catalogue record for this book is available
from the British Library

ISBN 1-85479-689-5

1 3 5 7 9 10 8 6 4 2

Designed and typeset by Martin Bristow
Printed and bound by The Bath Press, Bath

ACKNOWLEDGMENTS

My grateful thanks go to Godfrey Baseley, who kindly allowed me to reproduce excerpts from the original character notes of *The Archers* written by him in 1949. My thanks also go to those members of the cast and production team, both past and present, who allowed me to see cuttings and photographs that they have collected over the years, and shared with me their memories of the programme.

DEDICATION

To Jock Gallagher, who saved the programme from being axed in the early Seventies, and whose support for me during my time as editor was unswerving.

Contents

A PROGRAMME ON WHICH
THE SUN NEVER SETS

IT IS THE LONGEST-RUNNING radio serial in the world. It has a large and loyal following in Holland, Belgium, and in Northern France – where in the Eighties the *International Herald Tribune* discovered it to be the most *chic* programme heard in Paris. It is broadcast daily by the British Forces Network from Cologne, Gibraltar, and Cyprus. It has many listeners in Israel. You cannot hear it in Central Asia, Afghanistan, or Iran (which might account for the troubled history of that region in recent years) but many a Nepalese hill farmer learned his colloquial English by listening to it. It is heard in Brunei – a listening must, no doubt, for the head hunters – and has a devoted following in Hong Kong. It is broadcast in Belize in South America, and since the Falklands War it has been beamed out over the South Atlantic, to puzzle the penguins and confuse the Argentine. It is received via satellite by a number of British embassies, and by the larger of Her Majesty's ships at sea, and in 1996 there were plans to transmit it via satellite to Medicine Hat in Canada. Its famous signature tune 'Barwick Green' is heard, the BBC has claimed, some forty-eight times every twenty-four hours as the Earth turns. It is the last remembrance of Empire: the programme on which the sun never sets. It is that most remarkable phenomenon, *The Archers*, an everyday story (well, a sort of everyday story) of countryfolk.

How did it happen? How did it start?

Its first trial episodes were first heard on the Midland Home Service in Whit Week, 1950, but – appropriately for a mighty oak – its seed was long in germination. To find the origins of *The Archers* we must go back first to 1948, and then, even earlier, to the dark days of Hitler's war, and the threat to the asparagus growers of the Vale of Evesham . . .

1

A Farming
Dick Barton

IN THE SPRING OF 1948 the BBC in London was busy planning a new and ambitious drama serial. It was to be what Americans called a 'soap opera' and it was hoped to attract a huge, new audience for BBC radio. In America radio soaps were so popular that they were now being transferred to television – but nobody in BBC radio, in 1948, was worrying about television. Only a few thousand households, all of them in the London area, were equipped to watch the murky, flickering, 14-inch TV screens, and there was little for them to view apart from *Muffin the Mule*. Every January the national broadcasting awards were entirely devoted to radio. Every week magazines were filled with stories of radio programmes and radio stars. The nation was gripped by the amazing *Adventures of PC49* and by the jollity of Wilfred Pickles and Mabel.

Soon, drama chiefs believed, listeners would be gripped by a new domestic serial drama. It would be very different from the BBC's previous attempt at a family series, *The Robinson Family*, or from the serials that had been attempted from time to time on Radio Luxembourg. It would be broadcast on the Light Programme five days a week.

In the spring and early summer meetings were held. Stories were devised. Characters were created and given names. The new series, the very best that the drama brains of BBC London could invent, would be about a doctor in general practice, and about his wife. It would be called *Mrs Dale's Diary*.

In Birmingham, meanwhile, a BBC regional programme assistant – middle-aged, slightly balding, wearing thick glasses and a flamboyant bow tie that indicated an artistic temperament – was less concerned with entertaining people than with feeding them. The war had been over for three years, but Britain was still a place of rationing and austerity. People were tired and hungry. What spare resources there were – food, petrol, dollars – were being diverted to support the Berlin Airlift. Bread rationing had been introduced – something that had never happened during the war, not even in the most bleak days of the Battle of the Atlantic. The 'Victory Loaf' of wartime was darker and less pleasant to eat than ever.

The BBC man who was worrying about all this was Godfrey Baseley. He was a butcher's son from Alvechurch in Worcestershire, and had worked as a butcher himself for several years, before trying his hand as an actor. He had drifted into broadcasting, eventually playing Mr Mayor in the BBC Midlands edition of *Toytown*. By the end of the war he was on the BBC's Midland Region staff, titled 'programme assistant' but effectively in charge of farming and countryside programmes. Each week he produced a lively series called *Down on the Farm* in which reporters Raymond Glendenning, Wynford Vaughan Thomas, and Gilbert Harding paid visits to a farm outside Stratford-upon-Avon and tried to explain what was happening in agriculture to a wide general audience.

The most important part of his job, though, in the early summer of 1948, was to make programmes that would encourage small farmers to modernize and increase their output.

It was a frustrating task. Week after week he made programmes full of earnest, good advice. Audience research showed that farmers were not listening to them. 'They didn't trust the Ministry of Agriculture,' he later explained. 'During the war small farmers had been forced to do a lot of very stupid things. In the Vale of Evesham, for example, ministry officials had tried to make the small growers plough up their asparagus beds – beds that had taken years and years to establish – to grow potatoes. That sort of thing wasn't forgotten.'

In despair he abandoned making actual programmes, and arranged for progressive, large-scale farmers to tour the country giving lectures in village halls. But small farmers did not bother to attend, or if they did, they did not do anything about it.

He arranged a meeting in Birmingham to discuss the problem. It took place on 3 June, and was attended by prominent farmers and by officials from the Ministry of Agriculture. The venue was the Council Chamber of Birmingham City Hall and the meeting was considered important enough to be chaired not by Baseley, but by the newly-appointed Controller of BBC Midland Region, John Dunkerley.

Dunkerley told the gathering what they knew already: Britain's food rationing would only be eased if more food could be produced at home. There would be twenty horses for every combine harvester bringing in the 1948 harvest – what could be done to persuade small farmers to modernize their methods? What could be done to make them listen to the BBC's agricultural advice programmes?

During the discussion that followed a farmer from Lincolnshire, Mr Henry Burtt of Dowsby, famously stood up and said what was to become, in the history of *The Archers*, an immortal line.

'What we need,' he said, 'is a farming *Dick Barton*.'

Dick Barton – Special Agent was an adventure thriller broadcast in fifteen-minute episodes every night on the Light Programme. Each episode ended with Dick and his chums Snowy and Jock in a situation of the most desperate danger.

'Everybody laughed, including myself,' Godfrey Baseley said later.

The meeting in Birmingham City Hall ended. Baseley went back about his business, compiling daily market reports from the nation's stockyards, devising gardening programmes (one of them with the young Percy Thrower) and trying, with little success, to persuade farmers of the virtues of tractors and artificial insemination for their cows. It was only after some time that he began to think about Farmer Burtt's comment.

A farming Dick Barton . . .

He thought about the drama that existed in a farmer's life when a cow lost her calf; the bitterness and misery – lost money and wasted effort – over a sugarbeet crop that failed; 'the importance,' he was to say later, perhaps less convincingly in terms of popular dramatic appeal, 'of the February price review.'

The next time he was in Lincolnshire he called on Farmer Burtt, and Farmer Burtt pointed to a hundred-acre field of blackcurrants and said: 'If I were to find blackbud rearing its ugly head among those acres of bushes, I would be as horrified as Dick Barton if he found himself in a pit full of crocodiles.'

Godfrey Baseley drove back to Birmingham. In his mind he started to create a drama serial. He started to think up the characters – the situations. His fiction would be set in a Midland village, he decided, and because the target audience would be small farmers, the principal characters would also be small farmers. 'I knew the entertainment would have to be directed at the wives,' he later recalled. 'If the farmers' wives started to listen, then the husbands would have to listen – and then they'd start taking in the things I wanted them to hear.'

He took the idea to his boss Denis Morris. They had worked together since before the war, when Morris had been a senior producer in BBC Midland Region and Baseley had been a hopeful newly-married actor from Bromsgrove, desperate to earn his living away from the butchering trade. In the early years of the war BBC Midlands had closed down and the Baseleys had suffered two years of hardship before Morris, who was then head of the Ministry of Information in Birmingham, had given him a job. 'I had to stand on street corners in Birmingham shouting out the ministry propaganda stuff,' Baseley later remembered. 'I did it for so long I started to believe what I was saying.'

Now they were both back in the BBC. Baseley described his idea for 'a farming *Dick Barton*'. Morris – well used to Baseley's enthusiasms – suggested that perhaps he might like to put something down on paper.

'I was not a writer. I couldn't do it. I wrote a script but it was terrible and I threw it in the waste paper bin. That night at home I wished I'd kept it, but I knew it would be gone by the morning, the cleaners would have chucked it away with all the other rubbish. Next day I found that my secretary Norma had rescued the script. She'd taken it out of the waste paper basket and I found it smoothed out on my desk.'

So was this to be the very first episode of *The Archers*? Rescued, saved – as so many programmes over the years have been saved – by the intelligence of a BBC production secretary?

Well, no.

'I read it again,' Baseley confessed. 'It was still no good.'

He chucked it back into the bin. He had, in the past, worked with a Midland writer, Ted Mason, who had become a scriptwriter on *Dick Barton*. He contacted Mason and described his idea. Mason suggested a meeting. He also suggested that his fellow *Dick Barton* writer, Geoffrey Webb, should become involved. 'They could both see the writing on the wall for Dick Barton,' remembered Baseley.

The meeting took place in Broadcasting House, in Broad Street, Birmingham, one day in 1949. By this time Baseley had already invented, in full detail, the principal characters. They were designed, he told Webb and Mason, 'to reflect every aspect of farming in a Midland village'. Each had a biography, typed by Godfrey Baseley and carefully bound in brown covers with the character's name stencilled, again by Baseley, in black ink.

Ted Mason and Geoffrey Webb opened the folder with the name PHILIP ARCHER on its cover. Philip Archer, they read, had been born in 1928, and had studied at the local Farm Institute, where he had showed ability in the engineering side of things. He was handsome in a quiet sort of way – the sort of young man who would dance well, be a fairly good tennis player, and whose scarf might stream out at the back as he rode his motorbike. He was a member of the Young Farmers' Club. His religion was Church of England, and he was a fairly regular attender who would go with his mother.

One can hardly read the words without feeling a loss of innocence. How long has it been, how long, since the male heart-throbs of the teenage generation were good tennis players whose scarves streamed out in the wind as they rode their BSA motorbikes? How long since heroes were chaps who went to church with their mothers?

But England at the end of the Forties had values that are not easily recognized today. Early in 1948 *Dick Barton* had been given a code of conduct. Violence had to be 'restricted to clean socks on the jaws' said one of eleven guidelines. 'Sex plays no part in his adventures,' said another. At the London Olympics a huge message behind the Olympic flame read: THE IMPORTANT THING IN THE OLYMPIC GAMES IS NOT WINNING BUT TAKING PART. There were horrors in the world (in Korea, British 29th Brigade was suffering heavy casualties) but a hero could still go to church with his mother. Nobody had yet heard of Bill Haley and the Comets, or Elvis the Pelvis Presley.

The two *Dick Barton* writers opened the file marked DORIS ARCHER. Inside it revealed that Doris's full name was Doris Evelyn Rebecca, and that she was the daughter of William and Lisa Forrest (William being a gamekeeper) and that she had five brothers and sisters. Her eldest brother, Charles, had been killed in the First World War, and the next eldest, William, was a gamekeeper on a big estate in Scotland, and was married to a Scots girl – and they had three sons,

A classic photograph of Brookfield Farm in 1953, taken by *Picture Post*'s famous photographer,
Bert Hardy. Dan Archer (Harry Oakes) and Tom Forrest (Bob Arnold).
Hulton Deutsch: Bert Hardy

aged 30, 28, and 27. Doris Archer's sister Mary, said the file, had married a butler, and she and her husband owned a small hotel in London, and had a boy called Charles and a daughter called Mary Elizabeth . . .

What can have happened to William and his Scottish wife? To Mary who married the butler, and to her children Charles and Mary Elizabeth – who are, we are told, the same ages as Phil and Christine now?

Where are the Scots boys? They never seem to visit Ambridge – they certainly didn't come back to their Aunt's funeral. In fact, neither Phil nor Christine have mentioned any of their cousins in living memory. Even when Phil and Jill go up to London we never hear of them staying at their cousins' hotel, which seems odd.

Was there a terrible family row? Or have birthday cards and Christmas cards been passing back and forth all these years? Does the mantelpiece over the Aga at Brookfield have occasional invites on it – to cousin Mary Elizabeth's silver wedding, perhaps, or to the wedding of one of the Scots boys' children?

We never hear anything about it. These characters, these people, were briefly known about in 1949. Geoffrey Webb and Edward J. Mason knew them as creatures of flesh and blood. Their names, though, were not transcribed to the continuity files. They dropped from sight. Like flowers born to blush unseen, they went about their lives, unheard of, unknown, un-talked-about – that is until now, when we can welcome them back into the Archer family.

Another early character cannot be welcomed back. At the time no newspaper headlines screamed CAST STUNNED AS ARCHERS STAR SACKED because the character – Doris's youngest sister, Gertrude by name – was killed off before the programme actually started. Only four lines of type, later inked out, tell us that she was something of a recluse and might be considered by some to be not quite all there, and that she did her job very efficiently and was a constant reminder of an age that was fast passing in the country – the age of Squiredom.

Characters and stories were discussed. Baseley and the two *Dick Barton* writers went to the BBC club bar and talked on into the evening. Next morning, when Baseley reached his office, he found a script lying on his desk.

It was '*The Archers*; Episode One'.

Denis Morris wanted five scripts to look at. 'I asked them to write four more scripts. I had to say to them, "There's no money. You're doing this for love."'

The scripts were written. Denis Morris read them but he did not respond as quickly as Baseley would have liked. 'He took a long time. I got very impatient,' Baseley admitted. In fact it took the best part of a year. Morris, during these months, was trying to get London to support the project. He was not successful. Eventually he agreed to find the money for five pilot episodes from his own resources, and to broadcast them in the Midland Region.

In 1950 Norman Painting was a young contract writer and actor working in an office near to Baseley. It was a time when the top radio show was *Much Binding in the Marsh*, the top film was *Passport to Pimlico*, and a new fictional character called Dan was becoming the hero of every British schoolboy – not Dan Archer, but Dan Dare in the new comic *Eagle*. Painting was told by Baseley that he was in the running to be a writer, researcher or even producer of the new 'agricultural drama serial'. Painting remembered how the name Archer had been chosen. Baseley, he said, believed that to be successful the name of the programme should begin with an open vowel. He had the same conviction about the village they would occupy – hence Ambridge.'

On Friday, 12 May 1950 the actors who had been cast by Baseley met at 6.30pm to read through the first five scripts. Daniel Archer was played by Harry Oakes; Doris Archer by Nan Marriott Watson; Philip Archer by Norman Painting; Christine Archer by Pamela Mant; Jack Archer by Denis Folwell; Peggy Archer by June Spencer; Walter Gabriel by Robert Mawdesley; and Simon Cooper by Eddie Robinson.

On the Saturday the cast rehearsed and on Sunday they recorded the scripts. The sound engineer allocated to the job was a young 'Jeep' (BBC Forties slang for a Junior Programme Engineer) called Tony Shryane. He had become infected by Baseley's enthusiasm. 'When the first notes of the now-famous signature tune came through the loudspeaker we all crossed our fingers,' he later recalled. 'Would it be a success or would it not?'

The next day most of the actors involved were back in the same studio to record a serialization of George Eliot's *The Mill on the Floss* and Godfrey Baseley was back making farming and 'outdoor' programmes. In London, in due course, BBC programme chiefs listened to the effort from Birmingham, sent down to them on huge acetate discs. There was little enthusiasm. The regions were forever trying to extend their independence and increase their budgets. Nobody in the Broadcasting House drama department wanted to lose control of drama commissioning. Who was this Midland agricultural programme assistant, this man Baseley, who thought he could make a daily drama serial? All anybody in London knew was that he had recently made a regional documentary series called *Midland Roads and Rivers*. His voice was heard, on occasion, telling farmers the price of yearling calves in Leominster stockmarket. His 'outdoor' programmes had a tendency to become lyrical, and he occasionally recited poetry. Didn't he know about *Mrs Dale's Diary*? Who had been foolish or mischievous enough to give him the money for five pilot programmes?

They listened to the huge, slowly revolving black discs. They noted that the five episodes were to be broadcast in the Midland Region. They decided to wait, without bated breath, for some sort of reaction from listeners.

Whit Monday, 1950, was the day petrol rationing ended. Motorists danced round their cars and tore up their ration books. There was glorious sunshine from Kent to Lincolnshire (Godfrey Baseley later remembered it being a wet day, with folk forced to stay at home and listen to the wireless, but the records say otherwise).

In the evening, listeners to the national BBC news heard an excited voice tell them of a new post-war phenomenon – not exactly of traffic jams, but of traffic moving in a steady stream that extended 'for a full ten miles on main arterial roads outside London'. Then listeners in the Midlands heard an announcer say: 'Tonight Midland Region has pleasure in bringing to the air its new farming family. We present . . . The Archers, of Wimberton Farm, on the fringe of the village of Ambridge.'

The signature tune 'Barwick Green' played. A cow mooed lustily, indicating its heavily pregnant condition. A voice – Dan Archer though listeners did not yet know it – said: 'Well, Simon, what do you think?' and farm labourer Simon said a line that was to become so typical of the future: 'Ah well – 'er might and 'er mightn't,' – thus putting us instantly into a state of suspense over Daffodil's prolonged and evidently painful labour.

Wimberton Farm was not the only name that sounds unfamiliar to modern ears. When Dan and Doris went to market they went to Oldchester instead of Borchester. But Walter Gabriel's famous catchphrase – 'Well me old pal, me old beauty' – was there, and all the familiar story ingredients, with Dan worrying about how to tackle white fly on his tomatoes; Doris fretting over daughter Christine's extravagant ways ('Twenty pounds for a holiday in Paris when we've just bought you a piano for your birthday? Oh Chris!'); and high domestic drama with young Peggy Archer leaving her no-good husband Jack for the first, but certainly not for the last time: 'I'm leaving him. Jack and I are finished. We don't get on. And don't try to change my mind because this time I mean it.'

'Barwick Green' played again, and the first episode was over. An estimated fifty thousand listeners turned to their other activities, or stayed listening, perhaps to hear on the nine o'clock news about the French foreign minister's startling proposal for a 'common market' of European coal and steel that would include Germany but not Britain.

A few days later the actors received letters from Baseley, thanking them for their efforts. 'The team spirit was excellent,' he said. 'I only hope the powers that be will be pleased, so that we shall all meet again on the job before long.'

There was a long silence from London. There was a rumour that the project was dead. Then there was a rumour that the Ministry of Agriculture was pleading on Baseley's behalf; then that the Director-General had ruled against the programme, saying that *Mrs Dale's Diary* was quite enough: 'No more family programmes unless there's a war,' he was supposed to have said.

In fact, the Controller of the Light Programme, T.W. Chalmers, had sent Denis Morris in Birmingham a gloomy note saying that the Director of Home Broadcasting was not keen to give national coverage to yet another family programme. Chalmers did, though, ask for a general plan of the serial with an analysis of characters.

Godfrey Baseley sent him one.

The weeks passed. A newspaper statistic (a cloud on the horizon so small that

Tony Shryane was a young 'Jeep', (Forties slang for a Junior Programme Engineer) when Godfrey
Baseley asked him to be the sound operator on the first trial episodes of *The Archers* in Whit
Week, 1950. He went on to produce *The Archers* for more than 25 years, and to produce Radio 4's
long-running favourites *My Word* and *My Music*. Shryane started his BBC career as a 'night page'
in the Birmingham studios, where he was paid 12s 6d a week and 2s 6d dress allowance.

Camera Press: Tom Blau

hardly anybody noticed it) revealed that production of television sets in the UK
had increased by 225 per cent in the previous year. England was beaten 1-0 by the
US in the World Cup in Brazil. Frank Sinatra sang in London. Then North
Korea invaded South Korea and American troops were forced to flee. British
troops were sent eastward from Hong Kong and told by C-in-C Far East Land
Forces to 'Shoot quickly, shoot straight, and shoot to kill.'

Was this the war that the Director-General had said must come before he
would authorize 'another family programme'?

On 16 September, a memo finally arrived on the desk of Denis Morris. *The
Archers*, it said, was to be given a trial three-month run on the Light Programme.
The memo did not exude enthusiasm. There was no hurry about starting the
programme, said T. W. Chalmers. He added that before he committed himself
he would like to have a precise estimate of the cost.

2

A Three-Month Run

THERE FOLLOWED WEEKS of grim bargaining. In truth, London did not want the programme and was reluctant to pay for it. Denis Morris in Birmingham had no funds for a drama serial. Baseley was told he would have to add the new programme to his existing job, without dropping any of his other programme commitments. He was to be responsible for 'policy, acceptance of scripts and any other trouble that might arise' said a memo, and it was reckoned that this task (which in the late Nineties is considered a full-time job for at least two people) would take him one day a week. Tony Shryane, the sound engineer who had worked on the pilots and had become enthusiastic for the project, was given the additional and unpaid role of 'junior producer'. The only full-time member of the production team was to be a single clerk/typist employed for £6 a week. Baseley had chosen 'Barwick Green' for the pilot programmes but was dissatisfied with it, and asked for a new theme to be specially composed and recorded. It was estimated that this would cost between £250 and £350 and the proposal was turned down flat.

Baseley worked out his budget. Using the strictest economies, he estimated that he could deliver the programme – scripts, actors and production staff – for £55 a week.

The BBC in London studied this and were upset by his extravagance. They said he could have £47 a week. (It is interesting, if not strictly fair, to compare this with the £200,000 a week it costs to make *EastEnders* in the late Nineties.)

Baseley agreed. London, sensing that he was planning unlawful economies, told him that he must not attempt to pay any of the repertory artistes less than ten guineas a week. It was an instruction that was apparently ignored and in the first three months the actors were paid between £9 and £12 a week. To stop petty jealousy, or perhaps to deceive London, they were told by Baseley that they were all on the same money. The ploy backfired when Norman Painting, sitting in the Broad Street canteen, discovered that he was getting £2 a week less than Harry Oakes ('Twelve pounds a week isn't to be sneezed at,' said Harry, putting the cat among the pigeons) and that another member of the cast was getting only £9. He threatened not to renew his contract and there was a showdown with Baseley in the Midland Light Orchestra's studio. Painting declared that he intended to quit the tinsel world of acting and live in a garret where he would write the plays he had always felt were in him. 'You stupid young fool!' Godfrey Baseley bellowed, banging one of the Midland Light Orchestra's grand pianos. 'You've got a job here for ten years if you want it!'

This was in March 1951, when *The Archers* was two months old, and showing strange – and to BBC drama chiefs in London, baffling – signs of being a success. In the autumn of 1950, however, *The Archers* was just a pilot farming serial that a few people had heard broadcast in Whit Week. In October, a middle-aged part-time actress, who ran a little shop in Wolverhampton and had recently done a radio version of Arnold Bennett's play *The Card* (playing opposite Wilfred Pickles), received a letter from the BBC in Birmingham: 'Dear Mrs Berryman, You may have heard that after Christmas there's a possibility of a daily serial play ("The Archers") coming from the Midland Region, on similar lines to that of "Mrs Dale's Diary".'

Gwen Berryman – who was not a Mrs at all, but a plain Miss – was told by Baseley that she was being considered for the part of Mrs Archer, the only character it was intended to re-cast after the trial episodes. If she got the part, the letter said, it would mean recording on Saturday, Sunday and Monday mornings. She was invited to an audition. 'I don't want the character to have any accent at all,' wrote Baseley, 'but I want her to be recognized as a country woman in her manner and speech.'

On Friday, 3 November 1950, Gwen Berryman, clutching her character notes, went as 'nervous as a kitten' to audition for the part of Doris. She was up against seven other actresses. On the audition panel were Tony Shryane – she knew him as the studio manager on *The Card* – the two writers Geoffrey Webb and Edward J. Mason, and a puckish man she had seen occasionally around the BBC canteen – Godfrey Baseley.

Tony Shryane soothed her, Baseley frightened her. He wore horn-rimmed glasses and a floppy bow tie and spoke, she afterwards recalled, with 'alarming precision and authority'. He demanded that she read the script as if she were president of the Women's Institute. Then he told her to speak as though she was talking to her husband out in the farmyard. He gave her advice on how to sound like a countrywoman without using an accent.

Gwen went home, to the house that she shared with her brother Trevor. A letter came offering her the part of Doris, but she decided to turn it down. Godfrey Baseley, she said, hadn't liked her. At the auditions he had said – not once, but several times – that he really wanted an older voice for Doris. Gwen didn't fancy working for somebody who didn't like her; she'd rather stay in Wolverhampton and run her little shop.

Then she heard that Tony Shryane, not Godfrey Baseley, was to be the producer, so she changed her mind and accepted the part, blissfully unaware that, although Tony would have the title of producer, it would be Godfrey Baseley – 'God' as the cast were soon to call him – who made the decisions.

The very first picture of the cast. It was taken in the Broad Street studios, Birmingham, on Thursday, 28 December 1950, the day the introductory programme *Announcing The Archers* was broadcast. Back row, left to right: Godfrey Baseley (creator), Tony Shryane (producer), Leslie Bowmar (Fairbrother), June Spencer (Peggy Archer), Denis Folwell (Jack Archer), Monica Grey (Grace Fairbrother), Eddie Robinson (Simon Cooper); Front row: Christine Wilson (programme assistant), Robert Mawdesley (Walter Gabriel), Pamela Mant (Christine Archer), Gwen Berryman (Doris Archer), Harry Oakes (Daniel Archer), Norman Painting (Philip Archer) and Deirdre Alexander (programme secretary).

Mirror Syndication International

In the wider world, as Christmas 1950 approached, Sir Stafford Cripps resigned and was replaced in the cabinet by Hugh Gaitskell, and Scottish Nationalists stole the Coronation Stone from Westminster Abbey. For Baseley, Tony Shryane, and the two writers, however, the real world became grey and insubstantial; the pastures and people of Ambridge acquired a firm, technicolor reality. There was a moment of alarm when London suddenly took a creative interest. An executive noted that the intention was to call the programme after the name of the family. But was this wise when it actually dealt with the wider aspects of country life? The writer went on to suggest calling it 'Little Twittington'.

The change of name was rejected and future generations of listeners were saved from 'Little Twittington'. Stories were mapped out. The characters were fleshed out. Walter Gabriel was to be an old-fashioned stubborn farmer – the sort of chap who cared nothing for new herbicides and pesticides, or for Ministry Advisers – the sort of chap whose sloppy habits could be contrasted to the virtuous behaviour of Farmer Dan. His farm implements were to be old-fashioned, his buildings falling down. Godfrey Baseley told the writers that although Walter was a silly old rascal he had to be a loveable character underneath, and have his little jokes in his own funny way.

Robert Mawdesley had played Walter Gabriel in Whit Week, and was to continue playing him. June Spencer later said that her main memory of the early recordings was of hearing Robert produce his famous gravelly voice. 'We were all stunned and then wildly enthusiastic.'

Norman Painting was told that his character, Phil, was to be a representative of the bright young generation.

The first scripts were written and just before Christmas Godfrey Baseley called the cast together for the first time. He made them improvise, talk to each other in character. Using a microphone, and recording the conversations on disc, he interviewed them in character. He put them into situations and made them react in the way they thought their characters would react, but without a script to help them – in short, he used techniques that would be considered new and revolutionary in television drama in the Seventies.

The result was a remarkable 'documentary'. Baseley made Ambridge sound totally real. He assumed that Borchester was a real town, and Brookfield a real farm (there had been second thoughts, always the best, about the names Old-chester and Wimberton) and that he, Godfrey Baseley, a well-known BBC Midlands agricultural reporter, was able to go there with his OB unit (he called it a 'mobile recording vehicle') and talk to the inhabitants. The programme was called *Announcing The Archers* and was broadcast on Thursday, 28 December 1950. Baseley was heard taking tea at Brookfield Farm – 'We're rare ones for tea, here!' said Dan – and was introduced to farmhand Simon, who called Dan 'Gaffer' and said he was going to mend a hedge where sheep were getting through. Then Dan took Mr Baseley into Ambridge to visit Walter Gabriel, and said that Mr Baseley was going to put them on the wireless, and Walter wheezed and snorted and said: 'Wireless! I don't hold with these new-fangled nonsenses.' A minute or two later Baseley popped his head round a haystack to discover dashing young heart-throb Phil murmuring sweet nothings to lovely young Grace, the daughter of Squire Fairbrother.

'I've . . . sort of . . . bumped into a bit of romance, eh?' said Baseley coyly, and Phil and Grace both assured him that they were really just good friends.

It was the mixture of fiction and reality that was so startling. Phil Archer was a made-up character, wasn't he? But Godfrey Baseley was real, surely, so how could they be talking to each other?

'I do hope you enjoy eavesdropping on these countryfolk,' said Baseley earnestly, signing off. Yes, it was all real. It was all true. It was all happening, out there somewhere, beyond the Vale of Evesham. Three years later girls would write tearful letters to Phil Archer, offering to marry him after Grace's death. Thirty years later money would be sent for a wreath at Polly Perks' funeral.

That same day the programme acquired its first press feature. The Birmingham *Evening Dispatch* photographed the cast, said that recordings had taken place in secret (the hand of Baseley, no mean publicist) and said: 'Every effort is being made to produce a true picture of life in an agricultural community.'

On 30 December, two days before the first episode was broadcast, the *Daily Mirror* asked: 'What's Mrs Dale going to say about this?' and went brutally on to stoke up a nascent rivalry between the two programmes. 'Listeners who tune in to *The Archers*,' it said, would not find 'suburban small talk or over-the-fence gossip'. It went on to make one of the most faulty predictions ever: 'Cliff-hanging suspense and tricks of that sort will be out.' The BBC Midlands publicity office – comfortably unchanging over the years – was no doubt responsible for the totally false statement: 'The Archers are here in response to the many requests from countryfolks for a daily serial centred on their own lives.'

The article summed up: 'Eventually, one of these radio families will have to go. So the real test is whether Britain's housewives will stay loyal to the Dales or draw a bow for the Archers.'

Programme chiefs in Broadcasting House, London, made it clear which serial they wanted the housewives of Britain to choose. *Mrs Dale's Diary* went out at 11am – an established 'coffee-break' time, but *The Archers* was given the terrible programme slot of 11.45am, when self-respecting housewives were out shopping, doing their chores or preparing lunch. But it had made it. Two and a half years after Farmer Burtt called for 'a farming *Dick Barton*', the programme was to be heard nationally. It was New Year's Day 1951. Britain's housewives – listening in to the Light Programme as they fretted over the not very festive lunch they were about to serve – heard an announcer say for the very first time: '*The Archers*. An everyday story of countryfolk,' and then describe Britain's new farming family as 'children of the soil . . . like most work-a-day folk they have their joys and troubles . . .'

Doris Archer wished her husband Dan a Happy New Year. Dan said 'Thanks, Mother,' and Jack Archer, their elder son and future pub-owner, piped up with: 'How about some more of that rich and ripe old cooking port, Dad?'

Eavesdropping on the Archer family had begun.

3

In the Shadow
of The Dales

PROVINCIAL, COCKY, not really professional drama – but from its first
episode *The Archers* had a remarkable air of self-confidence. Tony Shryane's
name was on the scripts as producer but it was Godfrey Baseley who, for the first
two months, directed every episode, every line in every episode, every inflection in
every word, every sound effect. Gwen Berryman, who had been frightened of him
from the start, was more than once reduced to tears. He complained that her voice
was too high – she sounded too much like Pamela Mant who played Christine –
and was forever pressing the talkback and barking, 'Use your lower register! Get it
down! Make her older!' Already she was talking of leaving the programme.

The actors were encouraged to know their characters down to the smallest
detail. Walter Gabriel had been born on 25 August 1896. The first cry of baby
Daniel Archer had come six weeks later. Dan's two elder brothers were John
Benjamin (known as Ben), who had married a woman called Simone Delamain
(an early example of the tendency for exotically-named Frenchwomen to feature
in *The Archers*) and Frank, who had emigrated to New Zealand and married a
girl called Laura.

Young Doris Forrest had gone into service as a girl with the squire's wife,
Lettie Lawson-Hope, and had started walking out with Dan in 1918, just as the
Great War ended. They were married two years later, on 17 December 1920, and
two years after that their first child, Jack, was born. Hard times on the land, in
the Twenties, had accounted for the delay of six years before the birth of a second
son, Philip; and three years after that a daughter, Christine.

In the Second World War Jack had met a pretty young ATS girl called Peggy
Perkins (who said she was a socialist) and eventually he had married her. Philip
had only just managed to scrape a scholarship for the County Farm Institute.
Christine was the clever one. She had won a scholarship and got her HSC with
distinction in biology and a credit in chemistry, and now she was an outside milk
sampler for the Min. of Ag.

Now the children were all grown up. The New Year's Eve party in the parlour
at Brookfield – which opened the first episode – was already a tradition spanning

two generations. Dan and Doris were middle aged; the great events of their lives were, it seemed, over.

Not that they were without problems. Listeners to the first episode soon realized that Jack was quite a worry. He had not settled easily after the war and now he was scratching a living on a smallholding, and quarrelling with his pretty London wife. Christine was a worry too, always chasing after unsuitable men.

Philip, however, was as steady as a rock. He was farm manager for Mr Fairbrother, and already, at twenty-two, earning £1 a week more than the national weekly average. He was friendly with Fairbrother's daughter, Grace, who everybody said was a nice young girl and would make him a good wife. (She was at the New Year's party at Brookfield. 'I hope you'll always be here,' she said, looking round presciently, with tears in her voice.)

Doris didn't dare to be too hopeful about a wedding, though: Grace was also being pursued by Lieutenant Alan Carey, a tanks officer who had been wounded in Korea and was, like Jack, having a hard time adjusting to peacetime life.

In the meantime, should poor Boxer, the shire horse, be sold off so that Dan could buy a Massey Ferguson tractor? And should Dan get the Brookfield dairy herd attested, which would give him an extra 4d. a gallon for his milk?

The first scene of the first episode ended with a line that tempted fate: 'Time we all packed it all up and went to bed,' said Dan, inviting the humour of the critics. But 1951 was an age less cruel than that in which modern script editors have to work. The housewives of Britain (the programme's success depended on the housewives, as Baseley and the *Daily Mirror* knew full well) went on listening to the first episode, and then to the second, and were still listening by the end of the week. In due course they heard how Phil was spotted by Grace in the wood with willowy blonde blue-eyed Jane Maxwell – 'It was only a rabbiting party!' said a bewildered Phil – and how Christine, returning home from the cinema (*Tilly of Bloomsbury*) with a chap called Keith Latimer, saw saboteurs running away from an iron-ore exploration site on the Fairbrother estate.

They heard that Dan hated pyjamas and always wore a night-shirt, and had ambitions to be vice-president of the tennis club. They heard how Walter Gabriel had been left a sheep farm in Australia (worthless, of course) by his Uncle Nat, and how his son, Nelson, had been promoted to corporal in the RAF.

In February 1951 Peggy had a baby, Anthony William Daniel, and a new character arrived in Ambridge: Peggy's mum, Mrs Perkins.

'Cliff-hanging suspense and tricks of that sort will be out,' the *Daily Mirror* had firmly predicted, but cliffhangers abounded when a cousin of Peggy's called Bill Slater (a poor worker, sacked from Brookfield) – was killed in a fight outside the Bull, and when Philip, impetuously running after Grace (she had found him and Jane Maxwell kissing in the poultry farm office) jumped on the running board of her car, hit his head on a tree branch and was . . . stunned? maimed? killed?

February 1951 saw the arrival in Ambridge of Peggy's mum, Mrs Perkins, played by actress
Pauline Seville, seen here being welcomed to the Broad Street studios by Gwen Berryman.
Pauline Seville was around twenty-five years younger than the part she was playing, which led
to difficulties when newspapers and magazines demanded pictures of her in character.
Camera Press: Tom Blau

Everyone had to listen to the next episode to find out.

At Brookfield Farm, as the weeks progressed, there was drama when first the sugarbeet factory complained about dirt tare, and said that Dan had not topped his beet properly, and then the dairy complained that Brookfield milk was low on butterfat content.

Were the cunningly-disguised messages to small farmers getting through? Godfrey Baseley, and many others, certainly hoped so. Even as the first episodes of *The Archers* were being broadcast, in January 1951, Britain's negotiations to buy meat from the Argentine had collapsed and the meat ration had been reduced to its lowest level ever. The meat allowance for an entire week, the BBC announced, was henceforth to be the equivalent of five ounces of imported lamb chops.

At the end of January there were two big talking points in the BBC canteen in Broad Street, Birmingham, the haunt of Midlands BBC journalists. One was the decision by the Director-General that no men with 'dialect voices', and no women with any kind of voices, would in future be allowed to read the news. (A BBC statement said, 'People do not like momentous events such as war and disaster to be read by the female voice.')

The other talking point was *The Archers*, the agricultural drama programme being done by Godfrey Baseley and a gang of actors in Studio 2. Its audience was rumoured to have reached two million. The actors themselves were full of the story that their 'trial period' of three months was about to be extended by a further three months. Sitting in the canteen with them, writer Geoffrey Webb said that if they survived six months they could easily last for two or even three years. Three years of steady work!

Then there was a rumour that the programme was not only to be continued, it was to be moved to a better slot. The rumour was accurate. Early in February Godfrey Baseley called the cast together and announced that *The Archers* was to be moved to the Light Programme's peak-listening time of 6.45pm.

The programme it was to replace, the programme that would be killed to make way for it, was *Dick Barton – Special Agent*.

Suddenly everything was different. *Archers* storylines – which nobody in London had previously commented on, or, in all probability, even read – were now subject to detailed scrutiny. The Assistant Head of the Light Programme, John MacMillan, came to Birmingham and said the programme should be all about Dan Archer and Brookfield Farm, with less of the domestic unpleasantness that was coming from Jack and Peggy's marriage. The microphone, he said, need not move down to the smallholding so often. Baseley said that Peggy and Jack represented the longings and desires of millions of people. MacMillan said that in that case there should at least be no 'indelicacies', and the injunction was faithfully noted in the minutes of the meeting.

In future London would examine every script before recording as a check for indelicacies. They did not expect to find buggery in the barn or sodomy in the sheep pens, this being 1951, but they soon found cause for alarm. In early summer a stern memo winged its way to Birmingham. Two lines of conversation between Dan and Doris, must, London said, be expunged. The lines were from a scene just before the Ambridge coach outing. Doris's line was: 'Would you like another cup of tea before we go?' and Dan's coarse reply was: 'No. No thanks, Doris. You know what I'm like on coaches.'

At that first script conference MacMillan made it clear that no 'American-isms' should be used if there was a suitable English equivalent, and the meeting decided that the amount of agricultural information should be 15 per cent of the script. The first object of the programme, said MacMillan firmly – already ditching the agriculture and the education – was to entertain.

The obsession with percentages would be a continuing feature through the programme's early years. Percentages of farming information, romance, and 'country lore', were varied by successive script conferences, rather like the secret ingredients of cough syrup or cola drinks. In future the microphone should spend 30 per cent of its time at Brookfield, declared a script meeting on Hallo-ween night 1951, held in a Birmingham pub called the Hope and Anchor. The amount of natural history and folk lore – heads whispering over the beer glasses agreed – should vary between 10 and 15 per cent.

For the most part Godfrey Baseley suffered interference from London in grudging silence. He called London chiefs the 'hierarchy', and tried to ignore them. A memo from London described Ambridge's vicar as 'a musical comedy character', and asked for a new vicar who would be 'worldly-wise'. Baseley did not agree, but said, mildly enough, that he would watch the situation. He was more waspish when he received a memo from a London programme chief who had been in the West of England. The programme chief said that the local 'yokels' were being scornful of *The Archers*. They had accused the programme of making a mistake about the age at which a heifer could give birth to a calf. Would Baseley care to comment? Baseley responded tersely, that in the Midlands it was regular practice for heifers to mate at 15–18 months old. This was absolutely authentic, he said, and it was time the yokels in the West grew up.

Baseley knew, from his own sources, that the 'yokels' were actually BBC staff in the West Region studios at Bristol.

4

Success!

On Easter Monday, 2 April 1951, the move was made to 6.45 in the evening. Within weeks the audience had doubled to four million.

There was a transformation in the stature of the cast. Some of them – Harry Oakes who played Dan, and Pamela Mant who played Christine – were well-established Midlands actors and rather resented being described in newspapers as 'unknowns', or, even worse, as semi-amateurs. It had been the war, many of them claimed, that had forced them to take on other work – selling insurance or painting porcelain in the Potteries. But as far as the press was concerned, *Archers* actors were country bumpkins shooting their way to stardom. In the May issue of *Radio Review* they were featured alongside Peter Sellers – 'the young bachelor comedian-impressionist'. A columnist wrote: 'When the new family serial took over the 6.45pm daily spot from *Dick Barton* many people thought it would prove a flop. To follow an all-action serial with a story about everyday life and people on a farm seems a little like anti-climax. Well the doubters have been proved wrong . . .'

The cast found themselves invited to a BBC cocktail party given by the Head of Midland Region, John Dunkerley. They were horribly ill at ease. 'Thank you for the use of the Hall!' said Denis Folwell, embarrassingly, in his Jack Archer voice. Then they found that they had been given their own reserved table in the canteen that they shared with Midland news reporters. There might not be flowers and champagne in Miss Berryman's dressing room – but she no longer had to queue up for her toad-in-the-hole. It was Godfrey Baseley's idea. He wanted his radio family to learn to behave like a family even when away from the microphone.

In the event they learned too well. Those who liked a quick snorter sloped off to the bar leaving the non-lunchtime-drinkers waiting hungrily for their delayed lunch. The news people thought the actors were being snooty and rude. The canteen staff were annoyed at the extra work, and served them very slowly.

The cast suffered. Godfrey Baseley, after only token resistance, abandoned the experiment.

Baseley, anyway, had enough on his plate. Incredible though it seems now, he was still masterminding a daily serial drama in his spare time. And his assistant, his 'junior producer' Tony Shryane, was still supposed to be doing a job elsewhere as a sound engineer. Programme Operations department was complaining steadily and bitterly about Shryane being sent to record cows mooing when he ought to have been tweaking the microphones for the Midland Light Orchestra.

By late spring the situation had become impossible. They had, Denis Morris said, hit a nasty staffing problem. Godfrey Baseley, it was felt, was big enough to cope with two, or possibly even three, jobs at once. But Tony Shryane was collapsing from overwork. It was essential that he should be made full-time producer of *The Archers*. Would London pay for his replacement in Programme Operations?

London had no real choice. *The Archers* was proving hugely successful. Nobody expected *Mrs Dale's Diary* to be produced by a London sound engineer. They found the money for a replacement sound man but added hopefully that if there was any likelihood that the staffing problems might become easier perhaps there was just the possibility that they could let Shryane go back to his present job.

Well, yes, and Ambridge pigs might fly. Even in 1951 they must have been aware that the BBC manager had not been born who would surrender a post, however temporary.

The audience was rising, week by week. The national newspapers wanted stories. They wanted quotes. 'There's no doubt about it, we're all caught up in country fever,' Baseley said in a press handout, 'and I've never known a group of actors and actresses get so caught up in the parts they play.' Soon the newspapers wanted pictures, but not pictures of actors round a microphone. They wanted pictures of Farmer Dan milking his cows, and lovable rogue Walter Gabriel making eyes at Mrs Perkins, and Doris in the scullery at Brookfield Farm – and, of course, dashing young Phil Archer, the madcap romantic hero of Godfrey Baseley's imagination, canoodling with lovely Grace Fairbrother, even if it was at the poultry unit.

Baseley said no. He had chosen the actors with great care so that the character he imagined would be projected through their voices. Every listener, he said, had a mental image of the characters. It would be a terrible mistake for the nation to discover that homely Doris Archer was Miss Berryman of Wolverhampton. Or, indeed, that Jack Archer was two years older than his mother.

Baseley was overruled. *Radio Times* wanted pictures. BBC Radio chiefs in London insisted that it should have them. They were starting to get edgy about the growing popularity of television, which was spreading across the nation like some awful disease. A transmitter was about to start up in the Manchester area. A service would start in Scotland in 1952. It was being predicted that viewing would double within two years. Already, Roy Plomley was getting massive newspaper coverage with his TV show *We Beg to Differ* with its lively panel of Joyce Grenfell, Gilbert Harding, Bernard Braden and Barbara Kelly. Even worse, Arthur English was compèring a hugely successful variety show called *The Top Hat*, in which chorus girls called The Toppers showed their legs.

Had radio chiefs been able to peer over time's horizon and espy the lovelies of the Black and White Minstrels, or glimpse, through the gauze, the luscious limbs of Pan's People, they might have given up the fight there and then. But in 1951 it was still possible to believe that television was just a passing phase. It seemed worth the effort of launching a counter attack with photographs of Dan in his cowshed, and Doris in her farm kitchen.

On 1 April 1951, a Sunday, the cast were photographed in character, on location on a farm in Worcestershire. The photographer made Gwen Berryman roll up her sleeves, assuring her that the plumpness of her elbows proved she was a country wife. 'The number of times I had to wear one of those wrap-round pinnies and roll up my sleeves!' Gwen said later.

The pictures were published and, apart from Jack, who looked not two years but ten years older than his mother, the reality of Ambridge was confirmed.

'Perhaps the most important thing in its favour is that it is authentic,' Baseley told the newspapers, 'and behind us is every rural organization of importance, ready to help in presenting a true picture of the countryside and to bring a breath of fresh air every day to tired and weary townsfolk.'

Tony Shryane was reported to have made authentic sound effect recordings in Women's Institute meetings, village churches, riding schools, parks and country estates, railway stations, farms, cattle markets and skittle alleys. '*The Archers* employ an ornithologist,' the BBC Midlands Press Office quoted him as saying, 'who comes to the studio each month and listens to the various bird noises, so that we are always sure of hearing the right bird song at the right time of year.' (This wise and sensible practice was later dropped, with devastating results in 1984 when the springtime dawn chorus was broadcast in September).

Godfrey Baseley's energy and imagination knew no bounds. This first year saw the first 'topical insert' in which characters in Ambridge were heard chatting about the budget only hours after its provisions had been announced. The Head of Light Entertainment in London had not been told about this radical experiment in drama topicality and heard it only on his car radio. Unlike future London heads, who were to react unpleasantly to being taken unawares by Birmingham, he sent a telegram of congratulation.

At the end of November the Ambridge carol service was recorded in a village church, with villagers singing along with Dan and Doris, quite untroubled by Equity, the actors' union, who some thirty years on would object so violently to real villagers singing in church when Doris died.

In early December Baseley was quoted at length in the press, musing on the first 250 episodes. He was determined that London should get as little credit as possible. 'Although the programme is now an established part of the Light Programme, it is still a one hundred per cent Midland production,' he declared stoutly. 'The actors, the authors, the producer, and the editor, are all Midlanders.'

He admitted to having made mistakes during the first year. A heifer had given birth to a calf much earlier than nature permitted (Had the 'yokels' been

Picture Post's famous photographer Bert Hardy was fascinated by *The Archers* to such an extent that he photographed himself 'in Ambridge' talking to Christine Archer (Pamela Mant). Many of his atmospheric pictures are published now for the first time.
Hulton Deutsch: Bert Hardy

right all along?), there had been chrysanthemums in the summer show when really they should have waited to the autumn, and there had been the terrible business of the sugarbeet yield at Brookfield – forty tons to the acre instead of forty tons for the whole farm!

But there was also cause for quiet satisfaction. 'During the year we set about big schemes,' said Baseley, 'such as the love affair between Christine and Basil Grove, and the ironstone story, but we find that what is really wanted is the straightforward story of the daily happenings in the countryside. During the New Year we shall do our utmost to give you what you want.'

On Boxing Day Baseley decided that what the listeners wanted was for the entire programme – the Brookfield Christmas party – to be broadcast live. It featured Dan and Doris singing old favourites like 'Down the Vale' and 'The Old Rustic Bridge by the Mill'. The piano was at one end of Studio 2 and the microphones for speech at the other end. When Dan said, 'Right ho, Phil, ready when you are,' Norman Painting had to dash from one end of the studio to the other, while six million people at home waited.

The cast held a Christmas party in the boardroom in Broad Street. With the formality of the times, the actors invited members of the production team as guests – Mr and Mrs Baseley were the guests of Harry Oakes, and Mr and Mrs Webb were the guests of Norman Painting. Eddie Robinson's guest was a Miss V. Hodgetts, who was joining the programme as continuity girl. Miss Hodgetts – Valerie – was nineteen years old and straight out of secretarial college, living at home with her mum and dad. At the party she drank a Christmas toast with Tony Shryane, her new boss.

They chatted, perhaps, about the romance of Phil and Grace. Nobody in the boardroom, eating austerity sausage rolls and mince pies, was aware that a romance of their own was getting under way: the romance of a continuity girl who, in the best Hollywood tradition, would marry the producer.

At the end of 1951 the programme had over five million listeners. It was, beyond any question of doubt, a huge success.

5

'G'd evenin' all'

GODFREY BASELEY HAD PRESSED, in the autumn of 1951, for an omnibus compilation to be heard at the weekend. The response from London had been glacial. The rise in the programme's popularity though, was meteoric, and at the beginning of 1952 he got his way. The first Omnibus was broadcast on Saturday, 5 January at 7.30pm. To set the scene for new listeners, Baseley came up with the idea that the first programme should be introduced by one of the characters. He selected Tom Forrest, the Ambridge gamekeeper, a man who was always out and about watching over his pheasants and taking an interest in village affairs.

Bob Arnold, who played Tom, had auditioned for the programme in 1950, but Godfrey Baseley found his rich Cotswold voice – he was a butcher's boy from Burford – a bit too distinctive, and Bob had had to wait until the programme was a month old, in February 1951, before joining the cast. (It was a delay that would cost him dear, in later years, when Norman Painting and June Spencer, the two original cast members, were always given the places of honour at celebratory events, while he, a latecomer, was placed on the far table next to the kitchens.)

Now Baseley wanted Bob's 'warm, friendly burr' to set the Ambridge scene. The chat was so warmly received that it was repeated a week later, on 12 January. 'G'd evenin' all,' said Tom, a bit like PC Dixon. 'Here I am again, Tom Forrest, come to tell you what's bin goin' on in this little village of Ambridge since you was here last Saturday.'

He went on to talk about the 'touch of snow' freezing on the trees and hedges round the village. Every listener wanted snow in Ambridge at Christmastide, even if the rest of the nation was sodden with rain. (A cunning way to account for the anomaly, used later by Norman Painting when he wrote scripts, was for one character to comment on the snow and another to say, 'And would you believe they haven't had any snow at all in Penny Hassett!')

On 12 January, with the news bulletins full of the tragic crash of Britain's prototype Vickers Valiant bomber, Tom talked about badgers and stoats and weasels, and how he had just followed an old fox's track as far as Peggy's fowls. 'Get down Judy! Can't you see I'm talking?' he ad-libbed suddenly. But to whom? A frolicsome village maiden? He went on to tell listeners that 'young Jack' was still down

35

in Cornwall – he'd run off in a sulk to start a business with his old wartime chum Barney Lee – and Peggy was left running the smallholding.

But the real doings, said Tom, saving the juiciest gossip for the last, was about the letter that Doris and Mrs Perkins had found in a library book – 'and they just couldn't help reading it . . . well, you know how it is yourself, don't you?' – a letter revealing that Dick Raymond, Christine's boyfriend, was married. Doris and Mrs Perkins didn't know what to do. They didn't dare tell 'old Dan, because they think he'd worry himself to death . . .'

The Tom Forrest narration, two minutes or so of countryside lore and village gossip, was quickly established. Anthony Cornish, the senior radio drama producer at Pebble Mill who in later years directed the programme when Tony Shryane went off to the Channel Islands for his annual holiday, called Tom Forrest the Greek Chorus – in many ways the most essential part of the drama. The narrations remained popular for twenty-five years. In the late Seventies Phil Drabble took over writing them and, because he was not involved in the actual scripts, the element of gossip was reduced to just the final line – 'Over at Home Farm last week Jennifer was having a bit of trouble with young Debbie' – and they didn't work quite as successfully. In the late Eighties a more drastic experiment took place when other characters in the village were allowed to take a turn, but that didn't work at all. Eventually the narrations were dropped. Which all goes to show the folly, as Ambridge folk would say, of changing things that are working perfectly well.

In 1952 the news from the wider world was all very depressing. Britain was testing its first atomic bomb, and the Americans the first hydrogen bomb. The French were trying the stop the Viet Minh from taking Saigon, and warning that all South East Asia would fall to the communists if they failed. George VI died – and in Ambridge the 'topical insert' was kept deliberately low-key: 'You've heard the news?' 'It's like losing a member of the family.' Many lives were lost in the floods in Lynmouth, and in a massive rail crash in Harrow.

But every Saturday night, after sombre news bulletins read by grave, all-male, non-dialect voices, listeners to the Light Programme could feel their stress slide away as Tom Forrest said, 'G'd evenin', yes, it's me Tom Forrest again,' and told them about the frost being just right for rabbiting.

'What did you think about Walter putting Peggy's kids to bed? I wonder what the old rascal will be up to next! Fancy him going to the pictures with Phil and Chris,' he said on 19 January, still ad-libbing to Judy: 'All right Judy, I'm coming! You know,' – breathlessly to the listeners – 'she gets a bit restless when I stops.' In view of the moral climate of the BBC in the Fifties, we must assume Judy was a gundog.

The Omnibus rapidly acquired a further three million listeners. *The Archers* formula, it seemed, was irresistible. But what was it, exactly? What was the magic that Godfrey Baseley could summon out of Dan and Doris that London drama chiefs could not, despite their most strenuous efforts, coax out of poor Mrs Dale and husband Jim? Would it help if Doctor Dale read bits out loud from the *BMA Journal*?

In newspapers and magazines Godfrey Baseley and his two writers solemnly repeated their dedication to agriculture. The secret of *The Archers*, said Baseley (speaking at a time when the cheese ration was being reduced to one ounce a week) was 'the fascination and important facts of farming, that help to make it the vital economic factor in modern life'. The Ministry of Agriculture was certainly behind the programme. At one storyline meeting sixteen heads of division waited on Baseley and his writers, and fell over themselves to offer 'full facilities at any of their research stations, laboratories and experimental farms'.

Did Godfrey Baseley ever reflect that, so short a time ago, he had been a regional 'programme assistant', unheard of by these heads of division who now so eagerly caught the train to Birmingham in the hope of winning his good opinion? At the meeting with the sixteen ministry chiefs, Baseley stressed 'the necessity of the editor having the final selection of material' and they all said they understood.

Nevertheless, chunks of advice for farmers were produced by the Ministry, and were dutifully inserted into scripts. Dan was heard reading out loud, slowly, the Ministry's latest advice on eradication of the warble fly. Christine Archer was overheard lecturing her mother on Milk Marketing Board hygiene regulations. Phil shared with the nation the morsels of information he gleaned from the *Pig-breeder's Weekly*.

In March 1952 the *Daily Graphic* carried the result of an opinion poll. Asked to choose between the nation's two top soaps, *The Archers* and *Mrs Dale's Diary*, 78.3 per cent voted for *The Archers*. *Daily Graphic* writer Jonah Barrington couldn't understand it: 'A daily serial with the momentum of a steam roller,' he declaimed in amazement, 'and rather less glamour than a corn-chandler's catalogue. A background of damp raincoats and wet gumboots, its earthy atmosphere, its daily narratives of small-holders, mangle-wurzels, vets, pigs and leaking roofs . . .' How, he asked, could such a programme be steadily gaining the mass affections of British listeners? 'Only a Harley Street psychologist,' he said, 'could faithfully analyse the reason.'

The reason was clear enough to anyone who examined the reality of *Archers* stories as compared to the public perception. A myth was growing up – a myth that would persist, stubbornly, against all the evidence, for the next thirty years. *The Archers*, said the myth, was not a melodrama like *Dick Barton*. It did not rely on false cliffhangers, the way poor Mrs Dale did. *The Archers* was 'an everyday story of countryfolk'. It was about real people. 'We want to give a true picture of rural England, of the daily round of thousands of small farming communities throughout the country,' Geoffrey Webb told the *Daily Mirror*. 'And there'll be no *Dick Barton* stuff either.'

Well, there are tales of homely rural joy, certainly, in the early stories: Walter Gabriel trying to make a television set for Mrs Perkins; Dan elected vice-president of the Ambridge Tennis Club and taking Doris for a week's holiday in Aberystwyth; Doris reduced to tears after being accused of trying to buy votes (she had been nominated as president of Ambridge Women's Institute) by giving away bottled gooseberries.

But there were other stories, stories of a darker hue, *Dick Barton* stories – and without any BBC guidelines over violence and sex.

Phil overturned his tractor and was nearly crushed, and had an operation to save an eye. Christine had love affairs with three men in rapid succession before developing a very strange friendship – they didn't talk about lesbians in 1952, but they knew funny business when they heard it – with a certain Lady Hydleberrow who hated seeing her with boys, insisted on calling her Felicity, and wanted to take her away to Ethiopia. Peggy fended off the passionate advances of Jack's old wartime chum Barney Lee before collapsing with diphtheria. Millions of people were astonished to hear how a mysterious Irish thriller writer, who had moved into Ambridge under a false identity, was not Major Smith, an embezzler from the Pay Corps, as they had been led to expect, but secret-service agent Mike Daly MC who, during the war, had been smuggled out of Dachau concentration camp by British Intelligence, and was now hiding in Ambridge to confuse the Queen's enemies.

Then Reggie Trentham's girlfriend Valerie Grayson was revealed as another secret-service agent, and Mike Daly tried to tempt her to join him on 'special work'. Soon after, a mysterious lady called Baroness Czorva arrived, and told him that 'a certain party' was waiting for him overseas . . . and poor Tom Forrest had hardly got over all this when a mysterious housekeeper at the lodge called Madame Garonne was revealed as a notorious diamond smuggler.

And Jack was mucking about with Elsie Catcher the schoolmistress, then being packed off to the county hospital for nervous and mental disorders. And squire's son Clive Lawson-Hope was trying to seduce Grace. And then a jet plane crashed in the village . . .

'An everyday story of countryfolk,' said the BBC announcer, every night, without a hint of shame, and amazingly everybody believed him, and thought they were listening to a farming programme just because, in between the tales of spies and diamond smugglers, there were interludes in the kitchen at Brookfield Farm, and people telling them about the milk yields possible from Friesian cows fed on high-protein concentrates.

When, years later, 'The Voice of America' commissioned a survey to discover why the BBC World Service was so trusted to tell the truth, a listener in South East Asia told them: 'BBC World Service tells us who won the prizes in the Chelsea Flower Show. Nobody can think of any reason why they should lie about such a thing.' It was the same with events in Ambridge. Stories of passion, betrayal, and sabotage were mixed up with dramas about dirt tare on sugarbeet, and problems with cows' milk butterfat content: things that nobody would ever *make up*.

Nothing like it had ever been done before.

In the spring of 1952 programme chiefs in London found themselves pondering over a piece of information that two years previously would have seemed a fantasy. *The Archers* had more listeners than *Mrs Dale's Diary*. It had overtaken the BBC's flagship drama. The professionals of Portland Place had been beaten by their country cousins.

The listening figures were marked confidential but the BBC Midland Press Office had other ideas. Next day every national newspaper carried the story. '*Mrs Dale's Diary*, for years the BBC's top daily serial, has been pushed into second place by the family farming programme, *The Archers*,' said the *Daily Mirror*. 'This BBC secret was revealed by the Midland Region last night – to the surprise of the London HQ, for listener figures, compiled by the research unit, are usually given only to one hundred and twenty BBC heads of departments. Now, says the Midland Region, six million a day listen to *The Archers*. "This means they have exceeded the *Dale* figure by about a million," adds the Midland announcement.'

The story further rubbed salt into London's wounds: '*The Archers* is a Midlands serial, but is so good that it gets a daily national broadcast with an omnibus edition on Saturdays. *Mrs Dale's Diary* is a London programme with a daily national broadcast . . .'

By midsummer the listening figure was eight million. An article in *Reveille* said *The Archers* was the second most popular programme on radio, without saying which was the most popular.

The actors were becoming stars. More precisely, the characters were becoming stars. Ellis Powell who played Mrs Dale was a star, but she was famous as Ellis Powell not as Jim the doctor's wife. The folks of Ambridge were something different. They had become real in the imagination of their listeners. Harry Oakes was an actor from the Potteries who did not know 'one end of a pitchfork from the other until this lark started', but to listeners he was Dan Archer, farmer. During the summer of 1952 it was Dan and Doris, not Harry Oakes and Gwen Berryman, who were asked to open fêtes. They also handed out school prizes, crowned carnival queens, opened Christmas bazaars and toured factories. At a shoe factory in Northampton Gwen Berryman was knowledgeable about leather cutting, her father having been involved in the business, and a worker was overheard wondering if Doris Archer had been given a briefing like they gave the King when he visited Northampton. At a flower show and garden party at Droitwich, in August 1952, Norman Painting made his appearance wearing dark glasses (Phil was recovering from an eye operation) and was led around by Pamela Mant, who was indistinguishable from Christine in the crowd's mind. The public was touched and sympathetic, and the *Droitwich Guardian* carried a front page photograph of the scene. The producer of a radio record programme wanted Dan Archer – Farmer Dan, not actor Harry Oakes – to present a show, introducing various renderings of 'Down the Vale' and 'The Old Rustic Bridge' – a 1952 version of *Top of the Pops*. Birmingham managers were in favour of the idea, but London emphatically was not. An urgent teleprinter message said: 'Not in favour of the Archers presenting record programmes in character. It would embarrass us with other characters including the Dale family, PC49, Archie Andrews and Christopher Blaze.'

It was not always easy for the cast to maintain their characters outside the studio. Harry Oakes did not know what to reply when, going home one night, a stranger accosted him and told him he ought to put his money into Friesians instead of Shorthorns. Robert Mawdesley (gravel-voiced old Walter) was a Cambridge graduate, ex-RAF, and an ex-BBC announcer. June Spencer was a city girl from Nottingham. Norman Painting was an Anglo-Saxon scholar from Leamington Spa, even if he did live in a converted barn in the countryside. The part of Simon, the rustic farmhand, was played by Eddie Robinson, the manager of a Black Country employment exchange. Denis Folwell – apart from being older than Gwen, his fictional mother – was an ex-army officer and theatre director. Pauline Seville, who played cockney Mrs Perkins, was an attractive actress from Leicester who looked as though she was hardly out of her teens. (Pauline also took her turn, like June Spencer, at playing naughty Irish barmaid Rita Flynn.)

The only central member of cast whose life remotely matched that of her character was Pamela Mant. Pamela, like Christine, was an excellent horse-woman, and lived in an old gypsy caravan under the shadows of Tewkesbury Abbey.

They were actors, however, and they did their stuff, painful though it was at times. Gwen Berryman recalled visiting a town's new swimming pool and being required to clamber up to the top of the diving platform. Water soaked into her gloves so that when she took them off at the mayoral lunch she had navy blue hands. In the afternoon she and Harry Oakes (Dan and Doris, as far as the public was concerned) were leading a procession in a Land-Rover. Walter and Mrs P were behind them in a pony and trap, and behind them came Mr Fairbrother on a tractor. Gwen later told the story of how the noise of the tractor startled the pony, which bolted. The Land-Rover driver was determined to stay at the head of the procession so drove 'at terrific speed and Dan fell flat on the floor with his feet waving in the air. . .'

In Stevenage, when Gwen went to open a fête, everybody sang 'Happy Birthday to You' as she walked in, much to Gwen's surprise because it wasn't her birthday at all – but, of course, it was Doris's.

It was very confusing. A woman overheard actor John Franklin speaking and said: 'You are Mike Daly in *The Archers*, aren't you? Oh, I am pleased to meet you. All my family said you were fiction, but I knew you must be real.' A vicar wrote to the programme asking if a member of the Archer family could open his church fête – 'send Phil or Dan or even the Vicar . . . the Vicar could take his fee for his church expenses if he wished . . .' A man on a bus passing Broad Street studios was overheard by Tony Shryane to say to his friend, 'That's where the

Grace Archer (Ysanne Churchman, standing on the log) and Christine (Pamela Mant) are given
advice on their proposed new riding school by Fairbrother (Leslie Bowmar). *Picture Post* said:
'The growing popularity of the show confirms editor Godfrey Baseley's statement that "every
Britisher has his roots in the soil".' Soon after the photograph was taken Pamela Mant left
the programme for what were described as personal reasons (*see* Chapter 6).
Hulton Deutsch: Bert Hardy

Archers are,' and his friend replied quite seriously, 'How do they get all the cows
in there?'

This dramatic authenticity did not make things easy for the writers. 'When
we wrote *Dick Barton*,' Geoffrey Webb recollected, 'I'd ring Mason and say "I'm
ending my twenty-episode story with Barton, Snowy and Jock flying back across
the Atlantic from the Brazilian jungle. The engines of the plane have just caught
fire. Will you carry on from there?" With *The Archers* it's different. These are real
people – not fabulous characters of the imagination. We might argue about what
would happen if Philip Archer found Bill Slater kissing Philip's girlfriend,
Grace. Would Philip set about Bill? Would he turn on his heels and walk away in
disgust? Or would he merely say, "I wonder if I could have a word with you
Grace, when you can speak again?"'

Accuracy of characterization, consistency of factual detail – these were elements that were clearly making the programme work. There was a great fuss when a mistake was made over Dan's sheep – he had three hundred one week, and only a hundred the next. As a result Godfrey Baseley insisted that each writer bought a toy farm with model sheep and cows and pigs. Each little sheep was to represent a certain number of real sheep. The experiment was only partially successful. 'Mason has four children and I have two,' Geoffrey Webb recalled later, 'and we found the stock situation on the farms changing from day to day, depending on how many toy cows and sheep went to school in their pockets.'

Throughout the summer and autumn of 1952 the cast were out opening fêtes and being fêted. Ironically, the only place in England were they were not super-stars was the studio. Each week they came back from their travels – Gwen Berryman and Harry Oakes used to rehearse their duets in the car – back to the small, tatty studio in Broad Street, Birmingham. Broadcasting House was not imposing. It was a shabby jumble of offices and studios built over a car showroom. When they walked up the narrow stairs, past Midlands news reporters who were less than adulatory, their celebrity status slowly seeped away. At the top of the stairs they found Godfrey Baseley waiting for them. He also had a model farm which he kept in his office. Unlike the writers he was sensitive on the subject. 'It's not just a toy,' he said sharply to a reporter. 'By keeping this up to date I've got an accurate check on the stock position.' No small child or naughty actor, we can safely assume, dared to sneak off with Godfrey's little sheep in his pocket.

Godfrey Baseley and his model farm, his sharp tongue, and his relentless perfectionism . . . Gwen Berryman was very unhappy. At one point she made some suggestions about her character, and the way the future storyline ought to develop. She was slapped down in no uncertain manner. 'Whenever Godfrey Baseley was around,' she confessed, 'he was so demanding, he made me feel that *The Archers* was the only thing that mattered to him and that, somehow, I was letting him down by not sharing his obsession.' Gwen wanted time off – longer than the regular fortnight's holiday – to look after her mother who was ill. 'Such needs seemed to be beyond his comprehension,' she said, 'and I often dissolved into tears.'

Gwen resigned. Not once, but several times. It made no difference to Godfrey Baseley. She had to un-resign herself without being cosseted or coaxed. 'It was usually Tony Shryane or Norman Painting who calmed me down and persuaded me to carry on,' she said.

The 500th episode was marked by a party given by the Controller Midland Region, John Dunkerley, and the Controller of the Light Programme, Kenneth Adam. There was an article in *Radio Times* by a real farmer. He said that the girl who helped his wife with the housework stamped her foot with annoyance every time the programme ended just at the exciting part. His wife, he wrote, could see budding romance weeks ahead. He himself had one criticism: 'The Archers are a gossipy lot. Much of farming is one man on one job, and if he is talking he cannot be working. How that scrounging but lovable old gasbag Walter Gabriel ever makes a living is a mystery.'

The production office was swamped with Christmas cards, many addressed to characters by name, often sent just to 'Brookfield Farm, Ambridge', but delivered by the Royal Mail as conscientiously, no doubt, as letters sent to Father Christmas. And there were the fan letters. Right from the beginning, there had been letters of appreciation. 'I enjoy listening to the serial play of country life *The Archers*,' said an earnest correspondent at the end of January 1951. 'The play is so instructive. There are lots of things young men and women who intend to learn farming could learn from it . . .' But now the letters were of a different kind. One read: 'Dear Philip Archers, I am 9 years old and lived 110 North Station Road Colchester. and If grace wont marry you I will. Will you say happy birthday to christine please. And my love from Diana xxxxxxx'

6

Romance
of the Decade

IT WAS 1953, Coronation Year. Sweet rationing was abolished and there were adverts everywhere for Rowntree's Fruit Gums. The Ford Popular was launched at a cost of £390 including purchase tax: the cheapest four cylinder car in the world. Levi jeans went on sale – with the slogan 'America's finest Overall'. In America itself, John Fitzgerald Kennedy wed Miss Jacqueline Lee Bouvier, and a real life soap opera began to unfold.

In Birmingham, the man who wove the fantasy of Britain's favourite programme faced his first major crisis with an actress. Godfrey Baseley could control life in Ambridge, but not in the real world. Poring over his little farm he was free to decide that Dan should be troubled by swine fever at the piggery in May and should make silage at Brookfield for the first time in June (plenty of Min. of Ag. handouts to be read out here). He could have poor Tom Forrest viciously mauled by a poacher and then forced to flee his little cottage when a fire broke out in the Squire's wood. He could have Walter Gabriel's sheep killed by dogs, and, on the slightest whim, strike down Nelson Gabriel with a terrible disease so that Walter had to give very nearly all his blood to his son. In the studio he could dominate the cast and make Gwen Berryman cry. He couldn't, though, stop June Spencer from deciding to leave the programme.

She and her husband wanted to raise a family. She said she might be willing to return to the programme in due course, but for the moment the pressure of two and a half days a week in the studio, and the constant attention of newspapers and fans, was too much.

Baseley tried to make her change her mind. She refused. When he realized that she really was leaving, and not just hoping for another five shillings a week, he decided on a course of action that would stop any other artiste from thinking they could drop out for a little rest.

Peggy Archer, he said, must die.

She must be struck down, killed off, leaving weak 'grasshopper-mind' Jack to cope with two daughters and little baby Anthony Daniel. It would provide wonderful story material for Dan and Doris, who would inevitably have to shoulder

Britain's great romantic couple of the Fifties – Grace Archer (Ysanne Churchman) and Phil
the young pig farmer (Norman Painting) have a tryst in a Borchester teashop.
Hulton Deutsch: Bert Hardy

the burden. On a more serious level, he argued, it would add to the programme's credibility to have a major bereavement in Ambridge. It was already being felt that the nightly cliffhangers – 'Watch out Dan! Dan the tree's falling, it's going to crush you!' – were in danger of losing credibility when the next day's episode always started with Dan saying, 'Phew, Tom, that was a bit close.'

In fact, the false cliffhangers never did lose credibility, not in *The Archers* nor anywhere else: the ability of people to be kept in suspense over the fate of a character they know perfectly well is going to survive, intact and unharmed, is one of the most curious aspects of mankind's response to drama. In the spring of 1953, though, there was no doubt that suspense for listeners would be heightened, and Godfrey Baseley's authority over the rest of the cast greatly enhanced, if, just once, a cliffhanger on the lines of 'It's Peggy! She's being gored to death by a mad bull!' was followed next day by 'Oh dear, too late, Peggy's dead.'

Baseley and his two writers plotted the death. The storyline was written. It was copied, in strict confidence, to the Controller of the Light Programme, H. Rooney Pelletier, in London. Had he read it carelessly, or been too busy with other matters to read it at all, history would have been changed, and Jennifer, Lilian and Tony would have grown up without a mum, and Jack Woolley would never have won his bride in the autumn of his years, and June Spencer would have had to go and act with the RSC, or be a Bond Girl, or do voice-overs for telly . . .

But the Controller, Light Programme, did read the storyline. He sent it instantly to the Director of Home Service Broadcasting, the man who was next in the BBC's hierarchy to the Director-General himself.

Only a year ago it would have been incredible for the Director of Home Service Broadcasting to concern himself over the possible demise of one of Godfrey Baseley's farming characters. But by 1953 events in Ambridge were having a curious, and not altogether welcome, effect on the nation at large. Franklin Engelmann – Head of Light Programme Presentation with a responsibility for vetting scripts – had already sent round a memo noting that Jack Archer's mental health problems had resulted in doctors up and down the country reporting an increase in men who believed they were heading for a mental collapse. 'I hope that this doesn't snowball,' Engelmann had written to Birmingham.

Now a memo came about Peggy. To have a death in *The Archers*, said the Controller, Light Programme, to John Dunkerley, would be very unfortunate. The memo went on to suggest that they might perhaps employ another actress.

Godfrey Baseley was denied his death. The role of Peggy was taken by Thelma Rodgers, who had already played the small part of Elsie Catcher, the village schoolmistress lusted over from time to time by weak Jack. There was a deluge of complaint from listeners – and a further deluge of complaint in 1962 when Thelma left and June Spencer returned.

Godfrey Baseley had forgiven her. She had, in fact, spent much of the intervening years playing the Irish lass Rita Flynn.

Two other major cast changes were made in 1953. The death of Robert Mawdesley in September led to a re-casting that at first seemed impossible. To kill Walter Gabriel was unthinkable, but Robert Mawdesley's gravelly-voiced performance was impossible to imitate. The part, eventually, went to Chris Gittins, who had valiantly but unsuccessfully tried to imitate Mawdesley's voice when he was in his final illness. The response from the public was muted. The new Walter was soon to be described as being 'now as lovable an old rogue as ever'.

A third cast change also caused little public comment, though it caused great frustration to Godfrey Baseley. Pamela Mant, who had played Christine since the trial episodes in 1950, left for what were described as personal reasons. (Baseley told the *Sun* in 1972: 'Do you remember Mike Daly, a crazy Irishman always after the girls? . . . Well, in real life he ran away to South Africa with our first Christine, and left us in a spot.')

Various actresses were auditioned for Christine but none were considered suitable. Then Denis Folwell remembered a young woman who had asked for his autograph at a Whitsun fête in Louth, and who had a voice exactly like Pamela Mant's – they had joked about it at the time – and luckily he also remembered her name and where she lived. The story has the aura of a press-office publicity release about it – what on earth was Denis Folwell doing knowing, let alone remembering, the name and address of a nineteen-year-old autograph hunter at a Whitsun fête? – but perhaps that was how it was, for certainly the part was given to Leslie Saweard, a young teacher who had trained as an actress, and who slipped perfectly into the role of Christine.

By the end of 1953 the principle that characters could be re-cast, that the public would quickly adapt to new voices, had been established. Attempts to find exact voice matches were abandoned: it was recognized as more important to get good actors who could subtly re-invent the characters, than poor actors who could only produce pale shadows of the past.

It was a year of hectic activity. Topical inserts marked the deaths of Queen Mary and Stalin. The programme began to be broadcast on the BBC's General Overseas Service and several special 30-minute episodes were written and recorded to bring the new audience up to date. In May and June the cast spent every weekend at Coronation events – a Coronation Year Rally at Harpenden; a Coronation Year Carnival at Fazeley where the cast, it was announced, 'would crown the Queen'; a Coronation Year Horse Show and Dog Show at Silsoe in Bedfordshire. There were dozens of invitations to street parties – 'myself and Mrs Ellis said that I was to ask you if you would like to come down to Brighton on that evening . . .' said one. Norman Painting received many letters, at this time, from unknown young ladies. 'It was an occupational hazard,' he wrote later in his book, *Forever Ambridge*, 'for someone playing the lusty young romantic lead . . .'

Phil and Grace. Coronation Eve found them roasting potatoes on the bonfire on Lakey Hill until four o'clock in the morning. She told him she was going to go to Ireland for a year to train in horse management. Devastated, he told her she was crazy. She held a farewell party at the Country Club and they quarrelled bitterly. Mrs P offered to lend him some money, so that he could speed up his new pig-breeding scheme and afford to marry her straight away.

The nation was enthralled. The letters poured in.

Four admirers from Merthyr Tydfil wrote: 'We listen every night at 6.45 patiently waiting for your entrance. We are really dying to hear you in a "Love Scene" . . . *a full five minute* scene; please try to do something about it . . .'.

Many of the letters had a pig theme running through them: 'I am pleased you have made it up with Grace again perhaps when you have sold all your little pigs you will have enough money to get married,' wrote a listener from Walsall. 'Well we all hope your pigs are progressing and that they will do well and get a good price for them. It takes a lot of money to get married on . . .' said one listener wisely, while another wrote sternly: 'If Grace Fairbrother wants to go away for a year why be mardy about it she is right when she says get on with your pigs . . .'

And so they kept coming: 'This is just a word of warning – if you marry Grace Fairbrother you will regret it to the last day of your life. She is utterly self-ish, bad tempered and altogether detestable – she was a perfect little fiend to her father when he married again and when his baby was coming, and most unsym-pathetic when your eyes were bad . . . you'd do much better to marry Margery (who helps with the pigs) or even kind little Mary Jones, who at least has a heart and is kind to her old father.'

'Unless you wish to lose much of your profit on the pig sales, you must ask Grace to advance the date a few days and reclaim a year's marriage allowance . . .'

Pigs, of course, meant bacon, and pork chops. Although Britain had emerged from the long years of rationing, memories of enforced vegetarianism were still sharp, and supplies of fresh meat were a topic of national interest.

Up and down the country, girls mooned over Phil. It was an awesome achievement by the writers, and by actor Norman Painting at the microphone, for in his publicity photographs and personal appearances he was a most unlikely heart-throb, even for 1953, with his chubby cheeks and Bunterish spectacles. Per-haps his wavy hair, brushed back the way hair was in the 'Brylcreem' adverts, helped. The girlhood of England had no complaints. Even small girls loved him. 'My little girl loves your programme and insists on being called Philip, she does not answer to any other name,' wrote one despairing mother. A thirteen-year-old girl showed signs of impatience:

> We've listened thro' Rita, Jane
> Maxwell and Mary,
> Grace Fairbrother, Anne Trentham,
> It's getting quite dreary,
> So we are all switching over to
> Mrs Dale's Diary

It was an older girl (one hopes) who wrote: 'In your edition of *The Archers* tonight you spent 63*s.* on nylons for your sister and Miss Fairbrother, if you can afford that much for a sister and friend, how about me?'

The romance was spun out for months. Grace went off to Ireland and Phil missed saying goodbye to her – he was busy helping shepherd Len Thomas, whose wife in Wales had been killed in a car crash – and from one end of Britain to the other the romantics sobbed. While Grace was away his hot blood was roused by Anne Trentham, the pretty cousin of Reggie Trentham. Phil might be a farmer, but he was a man of passion – there had already been romantic encounters with flighty Rita Flynn, Jane Maxwell, and Mary the pig assistant. He was the Lothario of the pig-breeding world, a fantasy male for girls who had no Beatles or Rolling Stones to idolize.

Would Grace return from Ireland? Would it all be all right in the end?

As 1953 drew to a close, the nation waited to find out.

7

Fame

IN JANUARY 1954 the cast of *The Archers* travelled south to London to attend the *Daily Mail* National Radio Awards, the most glamorous night of the broadcasting year.

The ceremony was held at the Scala Theatre and went out between 9 and 10pm on the Light Programme. In a night of glitter, Norman Painting was intrigued to see Gilbert Harding (Personality of the Year) groom his moustache with a little comb as he waited to go on stage. Then it was the turn of *The Archers*. They had been nominated in the 'Most Entertaining Programme' category. In the event they shared the award with *Take It From Here*, the Dennis Norden and Frank Muir comedy starring Dick Bentley, June Whitfield and Jimmy Edwards, and featuring 'The Glums'.

Sydney Torch and his Orchestra played and the cast of *The Archers* went forward to receive their silver microphone. Richard Dimbleby impressed the actors by knowing their real names as well as their character names – a feat of memory not matched by poor Harry Oakes who, at the champagne reception afterwards, was overcome by the grandness of it all and called the Director-General Sir Ian Isaacs instead of Sir Ian Jacob. But if Farmer Dan was embarrassed so was Doris: Gwen Berryman found herself wearing a dress virtually identical to that of Lady Jacob.

It was a night of great satisfaction for Godfrey Baseley and his two writers. They had beaten off poor Mrs Dale and Jim. They had beaten *The Goon Show* which was delighting – or infuriating – the nation with Major Bloodnok, Eccles and the manic boy scout Bluebottle. They had also triumphed over the strangest success of 1953, *Educating Archie*, that extraordinary radio show about a ventriloquist's dummy which featured a former stand-up comic at the Windmill Theatre called Tony Hancock (there were rumours that he was to be given his own half-hour comedy show).

The *Archers* cast were lionized. London couldn't see enough of them and Tony Shryane arranged for a week's recordings to be done from Broadcasting House so that they could all make personal appearances. Television was eager to share the glamour of the radio world, and invited several members of the cast to appear as the joint 'celebrity guest' on *What's My Line*. They finished recording *The Archers* one afternoon and set off for the Shepherd's Bush Empire Theatre. Only then did Godfrey Baseley in Birmingham – ceaselessly worrying over his storylines and scripts, still making several other programmes a week for the Home Service and the Light Programme – discover what was happening.

He picked up the phone and vetoed the entire venture. The television producer in Shepherd's Bush was stunned. How on earth, he pleaded, could he find another guest celebrity at such short notice? Godfrey couldn't care less. The idea that Dan and Doris, and Phil Archer, small farmers from a Midland village, would be 'celebrities' on a television show was ludicrous, he said. People would listen to *The Archers* next day and know full well that they hadn't been to London.

The *Archers* actors arrived at Shepherd's Bush. To their surprise they were not taken to make-up or to a hospitality suite, but were led instead into an empty dressing room. There they sat for over an hour. There was a problem, they were told, and they wondered, uneasily, what it could be. Eventually the door opened and in came H. Rooney Pelletier, Controller of the Light Programme.

In the mid-Fifties Harry Oakes and Gwen Berryman (calling themselves Dan
and Doris Archer) were happy to open Conservative Association fêtes up and down the
country – until Labour MP Edwin Gooch complained to the BBC's Board of Governors.
They are seen here at a fête in Norfolk.
North Norfolk News

Godfrey Baseley had won. Pelletier's job was to release the actors from their confinement, and tell them that instead of becoming television stars they must return to Birmingham to face the wrath of their maker. He apologized to them. They should never, he said, have been invited to appear on television. They should never have been allowed to record for a week at Broadcasting House. They were creatures of the soil, of the fields and the hedgerow: the city was not for them. To ease their disappointment he promised that a short film would be made of them 'in character and on location' to be shown on television, but it never happened.

Before returning to Birmingham the actors were allowed to watch *What's My Line* from the back of the circle. They saw bandleader Cyril Stapleton – summoned at the last minute – appear as Eamonn Andrews' guest celebrity. A girl held up the placard announcing his name for viewers at home. When she put the placard down the theatre audience gasped – for on the back, plainly visible, was written THE ARCHERS.

'I was really very cross,' said Gwen Berryman, 'because the trouble was created by Godfrey Baseley again raising the argument about us not being seen so as not to destroy the listeners' illusions.' Gwen went on with some asperity: 'As almost everyone in the cast had already been pictured in almost every newspaper in the country I could not see that there were many illusions left.'

There were stories in the press. '*The Archers* banned from the TV screen' said the *Daily Mirror*. The matter was taken up in the higher reaches of Broadcasting House. Baseley's objection to television appearances was overruled, and Dan and Doris appeared, later in the year, on *What's My Line*, much to the satisfaction of Gwen Berryman.

The cast were getting used to stardom. It would be several years before they achieved a basic salary of £20 a week as actors, but they were making substantial amounts from personal appearances. There was, though, a problem. Many personal appearances had a strange, and in the eyes of Member of Parliament Edwin Gooch, sinister similarity. He believed he had spotted a common link between the organizations that booked the *Archers* cast in the summer of 1954: the Conservative Association fête at Thoresby; the Conservative Association fête at Cromer; the Monmouthshire Conservative Association fête at Caerleon; the Conservative Association fête at Ludlow.

Keen-eyed Mr Gooch, Labour member for North Norfolk, complained to the BBC's Board of Governors. The chairman, Sir Alexander Cadogan, looked at the list himself and admitted, wriggling more than a little: 'There is a danger that such actions might appear to associate the programme itself with party politics.'

The cast were summoned to a solemn meeting by Midland Region Controller John Dunkerley. They were told they must not appear at political fêtes as cast members of *The Archers*. They protested that they would just as happily accept cash from the socialists – it wasn't their fault, they said, that the socialists didn't ask them.

No, it was Godfrey Baseley's fault. His character notes, written back in 1949, show: Dan Archer, religion Church of England, politics Conservative; Doris Archer, religion Church of England, politics Conservative; Walter Gabriel, religion Church of England, politics Conservative; Philip Archer, religion Church of England, politics Conservative, inclined towards left.

Making Phil into a Tory wet scarcely redressed the right-wing balance. Labour clubs up and down the country noted the general tenor of Ambridge's political philosophy, and preferred to ask Wilfred Pickles to open their fundraising events.

Dunkerley told the cast that they could open fêtes providing they did so as actors, using their real names, and not mentioning *The Archers* as a programme. And so it came to pass. At the Thoresby Conservative Association fête, the poster had the names of the actors under the heading 'famous radio stars' but no mention at all of *The Archers*.

The poster did, however, have in large letters the words ARCHERY DEMONSTRATION and a silhouette of an archer in its centre.

In Ambridge, Dan transferred his pullets from free range to deep litter and Phil got his pig-breeding scheme under way. A new love interest was introduced, to fill the gap while Grace simmered gently in Ireland. Clive Lawson-Hope, who had failed to seduce Grace, started hanging round Christine. But what would a handsome squire's son want with a tenant farmer's daughter? Millions of listeners – including the curious daughters of all those tenant farmers that Godfrey Baseley was targeting – listened to find out. Eventually Lawson-Hope proposed. Was he serious, or was he just up to his tricks? Christine suspected tricks. (It was ever thus, tenant farmers up and down the country must have told their daughters.) She turned him down. He went to Africa.

Showing the proper proprieties for a Fifties lover, a young, dashing horse-owner called Paul Johnson asked Dan if Christine could ride for him at a two-day show at Belverston. Dan and Doris discussed the matter at length. In the end they agreed that Christine could go away for two days.

Elsewhere in the village, too, romance was in the air. Carol Grey, a cool, glamorous young woman from Surrey, had bought Dan's smallholding and turned it into a market garden. A 'bearded young wanderer with a green caravan', John Tregorran, was already living in the village. Carol, in her car, knocked him off his scooter. He took her to the woods and she was bitten by an adder. The passion between them, hot and cold over the years, would survive endless arguments, misunderstandings, and marriages to others. For the thousandth edition John proposed to her and she turned him down – but not, listeners noted, with conviction.

Grace sent Phil a set of fishing rods, came back from Ireland, and when Phil proposed to her said 'yes.'

At the end of the year the *Daily Mail* National Radio Awards for 1955 were announced. The most promising new programme was *Hello Playmates* with Arthur Askey, David Nixon and Irene Handl; the personality of the year was Jean Metcalf; the most popular musical entertainer was Cyril Stapleton – and the outright winner as 'Most Entertaining Programme' was *The Archers*.

They had won for two years running. Was it the stories of Hereford cattle, deep-litter poultry, and pig-breeding schemes that had captivated the nation? Or had it been the three great romances, and the continuing machinations of secret agent Mike Daly and mysterious Baroness Czorva? Either way, the cast were back at the Scala Theatre, this time listening to music by the BBC Show Band with the Stargazers, Bill McGuffie, Harold Smart, and the Show Band Singers. Gwen Berryman, fearful of again wearing an identical outfit to that worn by Lady Jacob, bought herself a long white dress, and Arthur Askey told her she looked ready for her coffin.

The thousandth episode was marked by a party attended by the Director-General, Sir Ian Jacob, who presented each member of the cast with an engraved silver cigarette box.

It was a time of self-congratulation, a mood in which Godfrey Baseley did not join. He had been listening to *The Archers* very frequently lately, he told members of the production team, and he felt that the quality of the programme was not up to standard. Denis Morris, who was still regional programme head, agreed. He found the phoney stage Irish 'nauseating'. In a scene between a phoney Irishman and a phoney Italian his patience, he said, had been practically exhausted.

These murmurings were not shared by the actors, nor, it seemed, by the listeners. In *Radio Times* Tony Shryane wrote: 'An old Persian saying has it that a man may count his wealth by the number of his friends. If that is still true today, the Archers are multi-millionaires, for never has any ordinary British family had so many loyal friends, both at home and overseas.'

8

'Dead Girls Tell No Tales'

IT WAS ALL SET to be a year of romance. Carol Grey and John Tregorran – Christine and dashing horse-owner Paul Johnson (he took her to Scowell Braddon to watch his filly Christina race; she rode a fiery mare belonging to his chum Reggie Trentham and broke her collar-bone) – the wedding between Philip and Grace.

'Please, please let nothing stop your wedding to Grace at Easter, as my husband who is in Central America on business for three months . . . is dashing home to listen.'

'Gran has taken such a liking to Anne Trentham and insists that we write and ask you to have her, and break off your engagement with Grace, whom, by the way, we all think is a spoiled brat . . .'

The letters poured in. Kenneth Connor (not yet a *Carry On* star but busy acting in a radio series about the lives of the saints) described some of the love scenes between Phil and Grace as 'amongst the most alive and absorbing moments in radio'. A listener sent the engaged couple a newspaper small ad. for a three-tier wedding-cake, that was now unwanted, and going cheap. There was controversy over the date of the wedding, when Phil discovered that he would save £90 if he married before the end of the financial year. Grace met the suggestion with an icy refusal. 'Much as I dislike Grace Fairbrother,' wrote an enraged listener, 'I would not stand by and see her bought as a chattel in a market for £90 . . . as a lover you make an efficient farm manager.'

The scriptwriters would have postponed the marriage had they been able to do so. They did not want Grace and Phil to wed. Lovers, they knew full well, make interesting drama; married couples (in art, as in life) do not.

The passions of the young couple, however, left them with no choice but to tie the knot. 'We shared all their desires, their temptations,' Godfrey Baseley wrote later, 'and were very much with them in spirit through situations when they were on the verge of submission to a pre-marital sexual relationship.'

Submission to a pre-marital sexual relationship? In 1955? The hot-blooded young couple were rushed to the altar.

The scene was recorded at Hanbury Church in Worcestershire. The date and time had been leaked to the press and huge crowds surrounded the village. PHILIP ARCHER 'WEDS' GRACE IN CHURCH: MILE OF CARS said a newspaper headline. Five hundred wellwishers crammed themselves into the church itself, members of the cast were unable to get through the crush, and for some time a policeman refused Walter Gabriel admittance. The OB vehicle was stuck behind traffic, and the real-life rector of Hanbury had to announce a long list of car registration numbers and ask that they be moved. Pressmen caused a scandal by clambering over the altar. The rector led the congregation in a short prayer, then handed over to the fictional vicar of Ambridge. The organist played the bridal chorus. The vicar said: 'Philip Walter, do you take . . .' and there were murmurs of excitement, we are told, as the congregation discovered that rascally old Walter Gabriel was Philip's godfather.

After the broadcast Philip and Grace were sent a Midland Bank gift cheque for ten shillings signed by A.L.L. ENGLAND. The money was given to Hanbury church funds. Norman Painting noted that the gifts sent to Grace and Philip all began with the letter 'C' – cards, cartoons, contraceptives and cakes.

In July Philip and Grace were invited to open the Shanklin Carnival. Everywhere they found posters: 'Shanklin welcomes the Archers.' They progressed through the town on a float and people stood four or five deep waving flags. A band played. They entered the County Ground to a roar of welcome from thousands of holidaymakers.

They were the most popular young couple in England. They belonged to everyone. They were loved. That other favourite, the beautiful Princess Margaret Rose, would cause sorrow and controversy when she gave up her true love, the divorced Group Captain Townsend – 'Mindful of the Church's teaching that Christian marriage is indissoluble and conscious of my duty to the Commonwealth' – but no Church or Commonwealth, it was thought, could ever spoil the fairytale love story of Phil and Grace.

Only Godfrey Baseley could do that. He was not present at Shanklin. He was in Birmingham, brooding over his toy farm, moving his little cows and sheep about, and plotting a terrible crime.

He was going to kill Grace, the nation's sweetheart.

He was going to make all those thousands of happy cheering holidaymakers at Shanklin cry. And to make it more effective, more terrible, and because Grace was occasionally shrewish and to be honest wasn't exactly a sweetheart to everybody, he was going to spend several months making her nicer and more lovable.

Grace had told Phil that she did not want to start a family – a shocking thing to say to family-oriented Britain in the Fifties. Now, Baseley decided, she would change her mind. She would tell him she wanted children. She would become pregnant.

Only then would she die.

After their fairytale wedding, Phil and Grace were welcomed by thousands of holidaymakers when they opened the 1955 Shanklin Carnival on the Isle of Wight. In Birmingham, the meanwhile, *Archers* creator Godfrey Baseley plotted a terrible event . . .

But why must she die? Why did this most cruel, most heinous of broadcast fictional deaths, have to take place? For more than forty years the BBC has been accused of killing Grace in order to steal the headlines on the opening night of commercial television. Time after time the BBC stoutly denied it, as did Godfrey Baseley at first, although in an interview in the *Sun* in 1972 he said: 'It went out the night commercial TV started. We did it on purpose.'

The death of Grace, in fact, had nothing to do with the opening of ITV.

In June 1955, at the quarterly script meeting, Baseley, as usual, had met the two writers Geoffrey Webb and Edward J. Mason and outlined to them the stories he had planned for the next thirteen weeks. These quarterly meetings were already established in a set pattern. Godfrey Baseley and the writers would spend the morning discussing storylines. Then Tony Shryane would be brought in and briefed. 'It was important for him to know what was going to happen,' said Baseley, who had a novel view of a producer's role, 'so that he could arrange to cast new characters and plan any location recording.' After that there would be lunch with what Baseley called the 'hierarchy'.

At the June meeting the 'hierarchy' were Denis Morris, the Head of Midland Region programmes, and H. Rooney Pelletier, Controller of the Light Programme. When they had eaten, Baseley announced that Grace was to be killed. There are conflicting accounts of what was said in reply. Some reports say that other victims were considered such as Christine Archer or Carol Grey. If this was so, Godfrey Baseley was just letting the meeting amuse itself: there was only one victim he had in mind, and that was Grace. Her death was presented to the meeting as a dramatic necessity. Nightly and weekly cliffhangers needed the spice of danger that could only come from listeners fearing a real tragedy. It was also important to plan a major autumn story to woo back listeners who would, inevitably, be lost during the warm summer evenings.

The death of Grace would open up a vast storyline for Phil. The young widower, the grief, the sympathy – in due time – of other young women. The eventual romance with another girl . . . a second marriage (but not for a long time yet).

The real reason why Grace must die was not mentioned.

The 'hierarchy' agreed to the death. There was a discussion of how, in practical terms, Grace should shuffle off this mortal coil. Baseley and the writers had first thought to kill her following a miscarriage – but had abandoned this idea because it would upset every expectant mother in the kingdom. They had decided, during their morning discussions, that she should be killed rescuing her horse Midnight from a fire.

The only change requested by the 'hierarchy' was that Grace should not die in the fire itself, which would be too gruesome, but in an ambulance, in Phil's arms, on the way to hospital.

It was to be a great secret and Valerie Hodgetts, the secretary, was told not to distribute minutes of the meeting. Webb and Mason went back about their business, writing the scripts for July, August and early September.

In the following weeks listeners noted with approval that marriage was making Grace into a warmer, kindlier, more considerate person . . . that she and Phil were more and more in love. The summer of 1955, wrote Norman Painting wistfully in *Forever Ambridge*, brought Phil and Grace 'the days that are not long, the days of wine and roses'.

Elsewhere in Ambridge dramatic interest was switched to Christine. She was soon up and about after breaking her collar-bone; she passed her scooter test; she went around a lot with dashing Paul Johnson and his racing chums Reggie Trentham and Toby Stobeman. Dan reprimanded her for going round with racy types. Doris spent the summer laying a crazy-paving path round her garden and John Tregorran told Carol Grey – who was, listeners discovered, the orphaned, natural daughter of a young aristocrat and a beautiful young housemaid – that he would pursue her no more, but would divert his attention to a more responsive woman.

July passed into August and the corn was cut. Phil was offered a directorship by Fairbrother, and arranged a celebratory dinner at Grey Gables, with John Tregorran, Carol, and Reggie and Valerie Trentham as guests.

Unbeknown to listeners or actors, the terrible moment was approaching. The cast were suddenly told that for a week in September scripts would be written on a daily basis as an 'exercise in topicality', and would be recorded in London.

To London they went, to Broadcasting House, to the home of *Mrs Dale's Diary*. Each day they recorded an episode in the afternoon, and it was played out at 6.45pm. There were rumours of some kind of sensational story, but nobody knew what it was. Norman Painting had taken advantage of his week in London to receive treatment for an ulcer, and on Thursday, 22 September arrived at the studio with only minutes to spare.

Ysanne Churchman was waiting outside the studio door, clutching a script. Norman was to remember that she had a tight, transparent smile as she said, 'They're killing me. Today!'

He went to collect his own script and found the entire production team 'lined up like the Supreme Soviet'. Nobody outside the cast and production team knew what was about to happen.

The episode was recorded but the last line proved difficult. The writers had written: 'She – she died in my arms . . . on the way to hospital.' But this could not be made to work for the very good reason that the last five words were an anti-climax – it was the death that was important, not where or how she died. Norman Painting recognized this and suggested changing the line. Godfrey Baseley, very unusually, allowed him to do so.

The BBC publicity office in London had been told that *The Archers* that evening would be 'quite interesting' (cautious Midlanders, keeping their secrets close to their chests) and newspapers had been invited to send reporters along to Broadcasting House at 5pm. They dutifully turned up. They listened to the episode. They heard the party at Grey Gables Country Club, and they heard Grace go back to her car to look for a lost earring, and notice smoke rising from the stables. They heard her dash in to save her horse, Midnight. They heard Phil try to rescue her, and the beam crash down on her head. They heard Grace recover consciousness in the ambulance, and Phil say: 'It's all right, Grace. Nothing to worry about,' and Grace reply: 'Phil. I love you Phil.' They waited for the cliffhanger, for someone to say, 'She's going to die!' when everyone knew that she wasn't. They heard the scene shift to the kitchen at Brookfield Farm, and the slow footsteps approaching from outside. 'Didn't expect you back quite so soon,' said Dan, comfortably, then: 'Phil . . . Phil lad . . . What's gone wrong?'

They heard Phil say: 'In my arms . . . on the way to hospital . . . She's dead!'

There was no signature tune. After a moment, we are told, the press went wild. One young reporter grabbed a phone to call his newsroom, only to discover that it was a studio prop.

The death of Grace. It was the most cataclysmic event in British broadcast fiction: an event that had more impact on the national consciousness than anything that has been achieved on radio or television since.

'Listeners sob as Grace Archer dies', said the *Daily Sketch*. 'Why do this to Grace Archer?' demanded the *Daily Express*. The *Daily Mirror* reported that a man going by car from Ashford to Dover saw people in villages standing at their doors openly weeping. A Londoner said: 'I thought I was in for a lively party when I was invited next door for the first night of ITV. Instead, it was like a house of mourning.' A family in Romney collected flowers to make into wreaths and crosses and a doctor claimed the shock had damaged the nation's health. The matron of an old folks' home complained her charges were too upset to sleep and the manager of a West Bromwich factory claimed the 'death' had held up production. In Bolton an accountant reported that his mother had fainted when the episode ended.

Two days later the BBC had to put out an appeal, begging that 'no more flowers should be sent' – and for fear of causing more national woe, scripts were hastily rewritten, so that the funeral of Grace was not featured in the programme as planned. Newspapers as far away as Malaya carried the story on their front pages. A pair of coffin handles and a brass plate inscribed with Grace's name were delivered to the Birmingham studios (and were kept by Ysanne Churchman, who found them a good talking point at her parties). Only the *Manchester Guardian* was brutally insensitive to the desolation of the nation. It was moved to parody:

GRACE ARCHER
(*Dulce et decorum est pro BBC mori*)

She dwelt unseen, amid the Light,
Among the Archer clan,

And breathed her last the very night
The ITV began.

A maiden in a fantasy
All hidden from the eye –
A spoken word: the BBC
Decided she must die.

She was well-loved, and millions know
That Grace has ceased to be.
Now she is in her grave, but oh,
She's scooped the ITV.

The controversy raged on. The Salvation Army's newspaper, the *War Cry*, devoted its entire front page to the death, and said: 'That charming, exasperating personality, Philip Archer's lovely wife, is gone from us. The marriage that was so full of possibilities has ended.' *Archers* fans had taken Grace and Philip to their hearts, said the *War Cry*'s reporter, 'but on Thursday, September 22nd, they turned sadly away from their hopes and faced an empty and desolate future'. The *News Chronicle* called the death a 'silly, cheap, unworthy way of getting BBC publicity on the night ITV opened'. The *Daily Mail* demanded to know, 'Who are the guilty men?' and set its investigative reporters to find the answer. They soon came up with the names of those who attended the script conference in June.

The 'guilty men' were alarmed by the ferocity of the attack. 'I had to hide for two days to escape the wrath,' said Godfrey Baseley. The BBC called a press conference in Birmingham and officials denied any attempt to create a sensation on the opening night of ITV. The decision to kill Grace had been taken, it was explained, in order to reduce the number of characters and to 'exploit the news situation created by the death of a major character'. Then they said it was because Ysanne Churchman was 'an accomplished artiste' and the BBC wanted her to come back into the mainstream of broadcasting. This last excuse was weakened by the fact that every national newspaper was carrying a photograph of Ysanne Churchman, and quoting her saying: 'It was no wish of mine. I enjoyed taking part.'

The *News Chronicle* was not satisfied with the explanations of the 'guilty men'. 'Surely it would have been more in keeping with the best traditions,' it said in an editorial, 'if Sir Ian Jacob, as Director-General of the BBC, had come forward and said: "The responsibility is mine. I alone must take the blame."'

By now the belief that the entire incident was a tasteless stunt to scupper ITV had taken firm hold. BBC denials were ignored. 'Of course we were accused of choosing this particular date to stage our event,' Godfrey Baseley would later write, 'but I must leave you to judge for yourselves because you know now that

The Salvation Army's *War Cry* reflected the nation's shock at the death of its favourite radio heroine. The *War Cry* was a lone voice in its approval of the storyline, saying how important it was to face death even in the prime of life.
The Salvation Army International Heritage Centre

our plans were made more than three months ahead . . .' – but he later contra-
dicted this, and anyway he was nursing his secret reason, his real reason for
killing Grace.

It may well be that the actual date of the death was changed, during the
scriptwriting stage, to coincide with the start of ITV, but even this presupposes
that the BBC realized the impact that the 'death' would have – and all the evidence is that the BBC was totally taken by surprise.

In the days that followed letters of condolence poured in for Phil, just as letters
of congratulation had poured in for his marriage. 'May I on behalf of my husband and my two neighbours say how sorry we are to hear of the death of your
dear wife and with such tragic suddenness too . . .' wrote one listener, and another was, like the *Manchester Guardian*, moved to verse:

> A cruel death, it would not be denied,
> That cut the bonds of love so lately tied.
> I did not think the call would come so soon,
> I found it night ere I thought it noon.

In Ambridge, the golden summer was over. Dan's sugarbeet suffered badly
from lack of rain. Doris moved into Coombe Farm to comfort Phil. Things got
even worse in January 1956, when foot and mouth disease was confirmed at
Brookfield, and all cloven-hoofed animals – cattle, sheep, and pigs – had to be
slaughtered. Godfrey Baseley was a good strategist. As in real life, there was to be
sunshine and sorrow. The Archer family was in trouble: there were no fairytale
solutions, just as there were none in the real lives of listeners.

Christmas at Brookfield was sad and reflective. Walter sang a song about a
turnip; Dan and Doris sang their old favourite, 'Down the Vale'. Perhaps the
anguish of Phil was taken too far. A letter from Swansea read: 'For the sake of
our sanity, please oh please give the sorrowing widower a break. Grace should
have died last March . . . when the stable caught fire, you should have sent Mrs
Dale in after her and locked the door on the both of them, men have had a
George Medal for less.'

Grace was dead and the destiny of Philip Archer was changed. To help him
overcome his grief, Fairbrother gave him a cine camera, and asked him to start a
cine club in Ambridge. In due course Phil would use the camera to film Christine's marriage to Paul Johnson – Doris wearing an empire line dress of purple
silk, and Christine a white lace dress with paper taffeta petticoats – and then to
film an attractive girl with blonde, urchin-cut hair, wearing a yellow dress, at the
Ambridge village fête. A few weeks after that he would propose to the girl at
New Street Station, Birmingham. Then he and Jill Patterson would marry; and
Shula, Kenton, David and Elizabeth would be born; and in the Nineties would
come the next generation . . . Philippa Rose, then Daniel . . .

All of which would have been completely different, if Grace had not dashed into those stables to rescue Midnight.

At the end of 1955 Godfrey Baseley could reflect on a year of extraordinary success. His programme had achieved a listening figure during September of twenty million, the highest that had ever been – or ever would be – recorded for a radio drama.

And he had got rid of Grace Archer.

In truth, it wasn't the character he was concerned about, or the problem of finding romantic storylines for Philip, the teenage girls' heart-throb, if Philip was a married man.

It was the actress, Ysanne Churchman. She was a splendid actress, an actress of distinction, but . . . 'She was trying to get the actors to join a trade union,' he told the author of this book, in 1995, 'so I killed her off. Very few of the original actors were professionals. I'd taken them on because they were countrymen with natural country voices. But she was stirring them up and trying to get them to join the actors' union, and saying we should only employ union actors, which would have been fatal.

'Eventually, of course, they had to join a union,' he added. 'But at least killing her off delayed it.'

Also in 1995, the author of this book asked Ysanne Churchman if she had ever known – or suspected – the real reason why Grace had been killed. Was it even true that she had encouraged actors to join Equity? She declined to comment. Surely, she was asked, she could reveal her true feelings after forty years? 'Dead girls tell no tales,' she said darkly – repeating a reply she had given to a newspaper at the time of Grace's demise.

9

Britain's
Secret Weapon

IN 1956 BRITAIN'S MANUFACTURING INDUSTRY was the second largest in the world, but it was faltering. Unless something was done, said the gloom-mongers, Germany would one day have an economy, if not a currency, as strong as that of England. How could British manufacturing be revitalized? How could trade unions be brought to their senses? How could small companies be persuaded to buy new machinery, to invest now for future profits?

Conscious of the new German threat, the BBC started to plan an industrial drama serial for the Light Programme. It would be based on the *Archers* formula – entertainment, but with a positive message. It would 'not antagonise the trade unions', said a memo, but would show factory workers the follies of demarcation and extended tea-breaks. It would show bosses the need to export or die.

The Director-General, Sir Ian Jacob, was doubtful. He was not convinced that the men who made *Mrs Dale's Diary* were qualified to rescue the British economy. He wondered if *The Archers* could not be changed, amended in some way – if Godfrey Baseley, as well as saving British agriculture, couldn't also save England from the menace of German bubble cars and Italian scooters.

He wrote, creatively, that a way of bringing in an industrial element would be for Fairbrother to open a factory in Ambridge. He added that he saw the industrial strand as less important than the country strand, although it might occasionally dominate the story.

Godfrey Baseley turned down the proposal flat. By so doing he opened the way for the rise of the Deutschmark and the sale of Rover to BMW. At this time, however, he had other burdens to bear. He had started a story about Dan Archer wanting to sell his British shorthorn cows and buy Friesians to get a higher milk yield. The British Shorthorn Society was so horrified that it had appealed to the Director-General. If Brookfield Farm abandoned the shorthorn, they said, their proud old English cattle would be condemned to extinction. Another organization was also demanding that *The Archers* should reflect the world they would like to see, rather than the world as it was. 'For several nights past,' the League Against Cruel Sports wrote, 'this feature has gone out of its way to favour foxhunting and eulogize it as a country sport instead of revealing it as despicable cruelty.'

The League called on the Director-General to take action against the scriptwriters. 'It may interest you to know that the British Union Against Vivisection, the League Against Cruel Sports and the RSPCA have all received numerous complaints about this disgusting programme,' said another writer.

Baseley agreed to reprieve the Brookfield shorthorns, for a few more years at least, but he did not bow to pressure from the anti-hunting lobby. He was a countryman. Hunting was, and had always been, part of the country scene. 'Hunting runs through country life like the wick through a candle,' agricultural editor Tony Parkin would say when he joined the programme, at a time when similar letters were still coming in.

Sex reared its head. When passion had threatened to overcome Phil and Grace, a year ago, Godfrey Baseley and his writers had rushed them to the altar: but they couldn't marry everybody off. 'The Archers used to be for family listening but recently it has become disgusting,' wrote a listener after a scene between naughty Rita Flynn and a village lad. Another wrote directly to the Director-General: 'I think it is disgraceful that the BBC should permit an episode in The Archers with implied immorality between Toby Stobeman and Carol Grey . . . it has debased the Archer programmes which, so far as I have heard them, have always been good, wholesome and helpful to country people.'

A memo about the offending scene was sent to Godfrey Baseley. The memo said that the scene had been faded out after so much passionate heavy breathing and 'what you will', that it could only lead listeners to suppose that Miss Grey had neglected her mother's sound advice. This was a caddish remark, considering that Miss Grey's mother had been a pretty young housemaid, made pregnant by the squire's son – but perhaps the London executive was unaware of Carol's unfortunate background.

Another executive wrote that he was getting many complaints himself about the 'sexiness' of The Archers. Even his own son in the Regular Army in Germany, was now eagerly listening in the Mess to see in what shape sex would rear its head each night.

Godfrey Baseley admitted that the episodes complained of had been 'on the whole a little cheap'. He and his writers hastily scrapped a plan for a story about illegitimacy. They were ahead of their time.

If the BBC in London was anxious about Archers stories, the wider world was not. South Africa wanted to buy the scripts and translate them into Afrikaans. They would change the setting and characters so that it became a saga of the veldt: Daniel van der Archer and his herd of wildebeest, perhaps, with Doris rescuing her chickens from deadly snakes.

The London Fashion Show of 1954. Gwen Berryman – very much a fashion statement herself
as she models London's answer to the styles of Milan and Paris – watches keenly as Diana Dors
shows the crease-resistant property of British-made material by stuffing a dress into
Jimmy Edwards' euphonium.

Hulton Deutsch

On this occasion it was the Controller, Overseas Service, Hugh Carleton
Greene, who knocked the idea on the head. He could not imagine, he wrote with
some asperity, how it would be possible to make in South Africa a programme
which was so close a reflection of English village life.

The Department of Agriculture in Washington wanted to know the secret of
The Archers' success. They were not satisfied with Godfrey Baseley's various
explanations, and asked to see scripts. For some reason the BBC was unwilling
to let them see any. Then an executive wrote a memo. Surely, he said, the
Americans could easily get what they needed just by listening. Shouldn't the
BBC give, with a good grace, that which could so easily be taken from them
against their will? After all, Britain got a good deal from America in various
ways.

Scripts were sent to Washington for Agriculture Department analysis; a
trade-off, perhaps, for US nuclear know-how that was flowing the other way
across the Atlantic.

The secret of *The Archers* success was not hard to divine. It was, as ever, the confusing but compelling mix of fact and fiction, and Godfrey Baseley was still going to extraordinary lengths to convince listeners that Ambridge was a real village inhabited by real people. In 1957 Christine was given a horse called Red Link, which would be ridden – listeners were told – by jockey Alan Oliver. When they opened their newspapers they read that Red Link, ridden by Alan Oliver, was entered at Badminton in April. Then they read that it was at the Richmond Horse Show in June and later had qualified for the Foxhunter Competition by coming second at Dagenham.

When they turned back to their wireless sets at 6.45, they heard Christine being congratulated on the result at Dagenham, and being happy about her horse's success.

Real people came to Ambridge to open the church fête – Gilbert Harding, Humphrey Lyttelton, and Richard Todd. Gilbert Harding had had a shadowy but persistent connection with the programme since it began – indeed, since before it began. In the war he had worked with Godfrey Baseley as an agricultural reporter. On one occasion he had had a terrible row with Mrs Baseley, when he objected to her pouring milk into the cups before she poured the tea. He had been at the Scala Theatre with the *Archers* cast at the 1953 Radio Awards, and on the panel of *What's My Line* when Dan and Doris finally appeared before him as celebrity guests.

Now he himself made a visit to Ambridge, to walk the village green and eat one of Mrs P's scones, and drink tea into which, presumably, the milk had been added in the proper manner.

It was little wonder that listeners were confused. 'I am sending this care of the BBC as I have no idea where else to send it,' wrote one, and a holidaymaker asked for details of camping on Dan Archer's farm. The leader of a Girl Guide troop tried to book Walter Gabriel's minibus to take twenty of her girls to a jamboree in Windsor Park. A woman with a chest complaint was advised by her doctor to take a holiday in the country, and wrote a most pathetic letter to Doris, asking if she could stay at Brookfield – a letter that so touched the heart of someone in the production office (Valerie Hodgetts, one suspects) that a kindly farmer was contacted and the sick woman was given a month's free holiday in Worcestershire. When Walter Gabriel complained of moth holes in his longjohns, a woman sent him a pair 'that belonged to my late husband'. At Christmas 1957, more than a hundred orders for turkeys were received by the BBC in Birmingham. 'Britain has always been a nation of hoaxers,' said the BBC Midland press officer, clinging to sanity, but then had to reveal that more than half the orders had been accompanied by money or postal orders. When Dan advertised in the *Borchester Echo* for a new farmhand, over a hundred applications were received – and the BBC had to return dozens of original testimonials. When actor Bob Arnold went shopping in Gloucester (his character, Tom Forrest, was in the city's prison on a manslaughter charge), an old lady shouted: 'What are you doing here? I thought you were in prison. How did you get out?'

Bob's wife Dorothy was with him at the time. She later recounted how impressed she had been by her husband's reply. 'That prison's terribly cold,' said Bob to the woman. 'They've run out of fuel for the heating. So the Governor said to me, "Tom, take half an hour off and trot round the town to get warm."'

The woman, Dorothy Arnold remembered, was quite satisfied and believed every word.

It was not to be the last time Bob Arnold would show his quick wit and skill as an actor. Many years later, in the mid-Eighties, when Liz Rigbey had been appointed editor but had not taken up her job, Bob was sitting outside Studio 3 at Pebble Mill waiting to record a scene. A woman in her early twenties came in. It was Yo Yo, the Blackpool pop musician and singer, who was to record the music for an Elizabeth Archer party at Brookfield. She had bleached white hair streaked with fluorescent green and magenta dye, a ghastly white face slashed with dark maroon lipstick, and a tight-fitting see-through dress that revealed her underwear. The member of the *Archers* production team who was showing her round was struck by a mischievous thought. 'Bob,' he said, 'I'd like you to meet Liz Rigbey, the new editor.'

He expected, and certainly hoped, that Bob's jaw would drop and his eyes bulge in horror. What happened was far more impressive. Without a second's delay Bob bounded to his feet, shook Yo Yo's hand warmly, beamed a great smile, and with absolute conviction said, 'I'm very pleased to meet you, I'm sure you'll do very well.'

In 1957 a new character was needed to replace farmhand Simon Cooper. The actor who played Simon, Eddie Robinson, had died and it was decided not to re-cast. A new worker would be introduced at Brookfield, and Godfrey Baseley knew just the man to play the part.

His name was Bill Payne, and he was from Ebrington, a village in the north Cotswolds known to locals as Yibberton. Yibberton folk – they'll tell you in nearby Shipston-on-Stour – are not clever. They once put manure round the church tower to make it grow. It was a Yibberton man, reeling home drunk, who fell into a newly-dug grave and cried, 'I'm cold, I'm cold' – and another Yibberton drunk who heard him and shouted out, 'I'm not surprised you'm cold, you'm thrown all't earth off.' Bill Payne was a Yibberton man, and a teller of such stories. He was not a professional actor, but a village plumber and farmworker who had somehow come to the notice of the BBC as a 'character' – a genuine rustic not afraid of the microphone. Godfrey Baseley wanted him for the part of the new Brookfield farmworker. 'There was, however,' Godfrey said later, 'one very big problem.'

It was that, just as the BBC regarded Bill as a bit of a character, Bill regarded the BBC as a bit of a laugh. He liked to spend his time in the studio playing practical jokes. He had a flexible, rubbery face, and used it, while standing at the microphone, to imitate, in mime, the emotions of the person standing opposite.

'I wrote to Bill,' said Baseley, 'and told him that the job was his . . . but he would have to assure me that there would be no nonsense in the studio. He assured me that there would be no tricks and, except for an occasional lapse, all was well. He carried my letter to him in his pocket for years.'

Bill Payne joined the programme to play Ned Larkin, father of Jethro, grandad of Clarrie, and great-grandad of young William and Edward. Ned quickly became one of the programme's best-loved characters, and indeed the Larkins would always be held in warm regard by listeners. They were hard workers, hard done by, honest as the day is long and tragically linked in later years to the terrible Grundys.

10

The End of the Fifties

THE UK DAILY AUDIENCE for *The Archers* had dropped by a million in 1957. Nobody blamed the programme itself – soaring television audiences were held responsible – but by 1958 there was a growing number of complaints about the quality of the scripts and the production. A London executive wrote on one occasion that he found the cricket match desperately unconvincing, with applause that was far too slick and unlike any applause he had ever heard at a village cricket match in his life. A lot of the remarks, he said, 'creaked'.

The truth was that the writers and the production team were tired. Geoffrey Webb and Ted Mason had been writing *Archers* scripts for eight years. They had written more than two thousand episodes, and before that they had written *Dick Barton*. Since 1951 Tony Shryane had directed *The Archers* in the studio without a break – five episodes, a special edition for the General Overseas Service, and an edited Omnibus for the UK every week. Godfrey Baseley was still running the country's most popular programme as a part-time job. 'I was doing market reports every day and dozens of other programmes. On Sundays, in the summer, I had three programmes going out – a market round-up in the morning, a gardening programme at lunchtime, and an outdoor programme in the afternoon.'

He had taken his eye off *The Archers*. Now he turned it back again. He sent a letter to the writers saying that recent scripts had been depressing and sordid and sounded tired, with the same characters saying the same things in the same dreary way. Ted Mason wrote back to him saying that the 'dreadful sameness' of every episode was caused by the small number of characters allowed – 'so, whatever the story, it is the same old voices telling it'.

Baseley asked Tony Shryane if the writers could be given more characters. Shryane, in all his years, had never gone over budget (and never would, in the years ahead). He wrote back saying he agreed with Ted Mason, that it was difficult to get much variety into the programme when writers were only allowed three extra characters per episode. But, he added, if more characters were used it would mean an over-spending of his 'present allowance'.

An answer suggested itself. For small parts they would use members of the BBC Repertory Company. The only cost to *The Archers* would be their expenses. London programme accountants reluctantly agreed. It was better to let

Birmingham use the Rep than increase a regional budget. Despite the success of *The Archers*, they were loth to let more money trickle out to the provinces than they could possibly help.

Baseley next moved to sharpen up the acting. Each member of the cast received a long, closely-typed letter about their character and the way they played it. One actor was told that Godfrey wanted a much bigger note of confidence in the way he was playing the part. The letter went on to say that the two authors would write his material quite differently which would help him to achieve this new characterization.

It was decided to maintain strong stories during the summer when the audience traditionally fell away. Listeners to *The Archers* in 1958, desperate to get on with their gardens and allotments, found themselves glued to their wireless sets as the big guns of soap opera – money, marriage, birth, and death – thundered. Dan and Doris were almost forced to leave Brookfield when they lost hundreds of pounds from potato blight and a fire in the Dutch barn. Tom Forrest – enlivened by his manslaughter trial at Borchester Assizes – proposed to Pru Harris and married her after a lightning romance (lightning for Tom, at any rate – they were at the altar in time for the 2,000th episode). Lettie Lawson-Hope died, and for her funeral Dan tracked down old Boxer, his faithful shire horse, and brought him back to partner Blossom in pulling the haywagon that carried the coffin to the church. The will was read. Lettie had left Glebe Cottage to Doris for her lifetime.

In August Jill gave birth to twins, and Dan was surprised – the nation was surprised – to find he had grandchildren called Kenton and Shula.

The magic of Geoffrey Webb and Ted Mason was still there. They still had a sure touch. They even made Doris have all her teeth taken out.

In September 1958, to mark the 2,000th episode, the first *Borchester Echo* was published – interviews with the cast, an account of how the programme was made, a résumé of the 'story so far' with pictures of the cast in character in Ambridge. It sold hugely – over a million copies at 6*d*. each – and was to be repeated several times in later years.

For the first edition Godfrey Baseley – still determinedly viewing Philip Archer as a young heart-throb, speeding along on his motorbike with his scarf flying behind him in the wind – insisted that Norman Painting be photographed in the role.

Norman, however, could not ride a motorbike. Tony Shryane gave him lessons in a field in Worcestershire. On a grey, misty Sunday morning Norman mounted the machine and sped past the waiting photographer.

'I grinned at the camera,' he recalled, 'and, scarf trailing in the wind behind me, shot on towards a stone wall . . .'

He ended up in a bed of brambles. The photograph was a disappointment and was not used.

Walter Gabriel (Chris Gittins) arrives in his minibus at the Dorchester Hotel, London, to publicize the release of an *Archers* record – Dan and Doris singing 'Down the Vale' and other favourites. The following year, 1959, Chris Gittins suffered a heart attack through overwork.
Hulton Deutsch

The *Daily Sketch* jumped on the bandwagon and produced the first of a series of inserts called the *Borchester Sketch*. 'Dan Archer is poised today on the brink of a gigantic gamble,' reported one edition, commenting on a proposed £3,000 bank overdraft, 'a gamble that may save him from ruin – or send him plunging into it.' Another edition carried the astonishing story – from a *Borchester Sketch* special correspondent – that Mike Daly, MI6 agent, summoned away from Ambridge four years ago by Baroness Czorva, had been found 'stabbed in a back alley in the Middle East town of Feren el Kebir'. Another headline screamed: WHO ARE THE KILLERS? and went on: 'Suspicion seethes in Ambridge today over the Mystery of the Secret Slayer. Who is the silent poisoner of Ambridge? Is he a sadistic madman – or some fanatic with a secret purpose?' The actual story, in the programme, was of a mystery illness that had overcome four of Charles Grenville's foxhounds.

Adverts in the *Borchester Sketch* broke every guideline in the BBC charter: 'Jack Archer's regulars agree Smiths Crisps improve the taste of every drink,' said one. A bulb collection was recommended by 'Harry Oakes of *The Archers*'. Elsewhere at this time, members of the cast were seen in adverts happily recommending cattle feedstuff bags and shoes. 'The "Archer" family all find shoes to suit them in the Spire and White Queen range,' readers of one newspaper discovered.

The first novels involving *The Archers* had come out: *The Archers of Ambridge*, *The Archers Intervene*, *Ambridge Summer*, *Springtime in Ambridge*, and a record was issued – villagers having a sing-song on one side, Dan and Doris wandering down memory lane on the other. Pye Records did an expensive launch at the Dorchester Hotel, with the cast arriving in Walter Gabriel's minibus. 'I found them in the bright lights of the Dorchester, drinking champagne and eating scampi,' wrote a gossip columnist, as confused as anyone else by the mix of fact and fiction. 'In a cosy corner I spotted Beverly Nichols chatting with Carol Grey.'

The 2,000th-episode party, on 26 September 1958, was a Harvest Home evening at the Warwickshire farm of the chairman of the BBC's agricultural advisory committee. Everybody was there, including cast past and present. Phil was photographed enjoying a glass of wine with his dead wife Grace and his living wife Jill.

It was, seemingly, only the writers, Geoffrey Webb and Ted Mason, who were uneasy about the future. On the day of the Harvest Home they met to ponder on the dangers that lay ahead. They told Baseley that they felt the need to attract teenagers – 'to reflect in the programme the real problem of the teenager of today'.

They weren't sure what teenagers were. Teenagers had only been invented during the Fifties. By the end of the decade there were believed to be five million of them, sitting in coffee bars drinking frothy coffee out of glass cups. They did not have a good image. Geoffrey Webb and Ted Mason made a list, on that afternoon before the high celebrations in Warwickshire, of what comprised a teenager. On their list was: 'Peacock-like attitude towards clothes . . . perpetual fight against adults . . . a desire to show independence . . . complete aimlessness and lack of ambition.'

If they had a teenager like this in *The Archers*, they believed, it would help relate the programme to younger listeners. Perhaps it could be a teenager who played skiffle and wanted to be a pop star.

Godfrey Baseley was not enthusiastic. He did not think the *Archers* listener tuned in to hear about rock 'n' roll and skiffle groups making records. If these 'teenagers' wanted a record they should be encouraged to buy the *Archers* record (NEP 24096 on the Nixa label) and hear Dan and Doris singing 'When We Are Married'.

In the end, however, the writers were given the go-ahead. They could intro-
duce their singing teenager 'as long as the treatment was woven into the pattern,'
said Baseley, 'and the impression was not given that this was typical of the whole
generation of teenagers.'

The final year of the decade saw the story mixture as rich as ever – a comedy
romance involving Walter Gabriel, Mrs Perkins, and a second Mr Perkins; a
mystery romance involving Carol Grey and Charles Grenville (who had bought
the Fairbrother Estate) that caused John Tregorran terrible jealousy; the
astounding revelation that Grenville's housekeeper, the strange Madame
Garonne, was actually a diamond smuggler. Then came a new story element, the
fruits of that script meeting in September 1958: Jimmy Grange, Brookfield's
apprentice farmhand, suddenly started to spend time in Borchester, where he
formed a skiffle group and started getting into bad company. BOY HE'S HOT
screamed a headline in the *Daily Sketch* next to a picture of Jimmy Grange with
his guitar. 'He's just Jimmy Grange – the boy from Brookfield Farm,' said the
Sketch. 'Certainly he likes to strum a guitar. Certainly he likes fun. But that
doesn't make him a rock-crazy degenerate.'
  On the air, Dan and Doris were heard trying to be modern, with-it, and
understanding. They went to one of Jimmy's skiffle concerts, and Doris said that
young people must be encouraged to do their best.

At the end of the decade *The Archers* still claimed around eleven million regular
listeners (seven million each weekday, four million on Sundays). It was bigger by
far than anything on television. Its only rival on radio was the Palm Court
Orchestra's weekly concert from the Grand Hotel, Eastbourne. *The Archers* had
started when Mr Attlee was Prime Minister, food rationing was a fact of daily
life, motorcars were only for the rich, and the most popular entertainment was
the *Adventures of PC49* and Wilfred Pickles on the wireless. It was still there, still
a huge success, when Harold Macmillan was in Downing Street, the British
Motor Corporation had launched the Mini, and Cliff Richard was being promoted as the 'British Elvis Presley' on television pop shows like *Six Five Special*.
  The Fifties had been the decade of *The Archers*; no other entertainment programme had come close to equalling its success. Now, however, the cast, like the
writers and production team, were tired. They complained that they were being
exploited. The relentless demand for publicity material meant repeated photo-
calls, which often had to take place on Sundays and were without fee. But it was
not the money they complained about, it was the pressure of work, the loss of
precious free time. Gwen Berryman genuinely tried to leave the programme –
she actively looked for other work – only to discover that she was the victim of
something else that had been invented in the Fifties: she was typecast.
  In the summer of 1959 Chris Gittins was admitted to hospital in Truro with a
minor heart attack. He was put into a private ward to protect him from the

curiosity of other patients, but to no avail. He awoke in the middle of the night to see two old ladies from the ward below, sitting at the end of his bed, watching him intently. 'The number of places in the world where we could find peace was relentlessly diminishing,' wrote Norman Painting, looking back in *Forever Ambridge*. In October 1959 Harry Oakes collapsed with nervous exhaustion. He was unable to work for several weeks so, in the programme, Dan was also sent to hospital, suffering from a broken leg. In November, Oakes was allowed out of hospital to make a recording of Dan coming home for Christmas at Brookfield Farm – said by those who heard it to have been one of the most emotional scenes ever done on the programme.

The Fifties ended on a high note. It was announced that Canada, Australia, and New Zealand had bought *The Archers*, and would broadcast it on a nightly basis, quite separate from the Omnibus edition that was being broadcast on the BBC's General Overseas Service. The programme's audience worldwide, at the start of the Sixties, would be bigger than it had ever been before.

But, as with earthly empires, the seeds of decline had been sown.

11

Television, Pigs
and Percy Thrower

Towards the end of the fifties, an imaginative journalist made an attempt to discover *Archers* storylines. Believing that cast members of *The Archers* knew what the future held for their characters, he took trusting Gwen Berryman to a clairvoyant and put her under the influence. 'I've got news for you, Gwen,' said the clairvoyant. 'Your programme will soon be on our television screens.'

Fear of television now haunted radio chiefs. They had once believed it to be a gimmick, an irritant. In 1950, when *The Archers* started, more radio licences had been issued than ever before. In 1953 Godfrey Baseley had been so confident of radio's supremacy that he had allowed Walter Gabriel to try and build a TV set so that Mrs P could watch the Coronation. But by 1957 television was devastating the Light Programme. In one year alone its evening audience, including that for *The Archers*, dropped by almost a quarter. It desperately introduced hourly news bulletins to try to bring its listeners back. In 1959 the *Daily Sketch* wrote: 'When *The Archers* ends at 7.00 to-night millions of Ambridge fans will turn to TV for the rest of the evening' but the *Sketch* was living in the past. Where both licences were being bought, households were watching television at 6.45pm, not sitting round the old wireless. A Sunday newspaper condemned what it called 'the box' as being a 'siren luring people to its mindlessness' and said *The Archers* was 'one of the ships most likely to run aground'.

'Humbly we pay tribute to our friends who, after all these years and in spite of small-screen counter attractions, still loyally tune in to the Light Programme at six forty-five every evening from Monday to Friday,' said Edward J. Mason and Geoffrey Webb in a rather sad interview.

By the end of the Fifties colour adverts for Ferguson stopped saying RADIO AND TELEVISION and started to say TELEVISION AND RADIO. Broadcasting critics were already writing almost exclusively about television. *Punch*'s column 'On the Air' was one of the few places left where radio was still reviewed – but even here entire columns were now devoted to television alone. 'I can still find nothing on ITV to challenge the BBC between 6.45 and 7.30pm, not even *Find the Singer* which features what is advertised as the Mink Tone music of the Lou Preager Orchestra,' wrote Bernard Hollowood commenting on the success of the BBC's *Tonight* programme.

The buzz in the entertainment world was not about a new rival for *The Navy Lark* or the Radio Personality of the Year – it was about *Emergency Ward Ten*, *The Army Game* and *Take Your Pick*. In 1959 even *Hancock's Half Hour* made the journey from the Light Programme to the little flickering screen. No wonder the clairvoyant tried to please Gwen Berryman by predicting the same road ahead for *The Archers*.

When the first *Borchester Echo* was produced many of the cast were dismayed by what seemed an act of great treachery. The editorial, by John Dunkerley, went out of its way to promote television from the Midlands: 'From the window of "The Archers" office one looks across a narrow intervening yard to another building, recently erected. That is the home of another kind of farming enterprise – the BBC television programme "Farming", televisioned each Sunday afternoon – and well worth watching if you want to know more about the problems Dan Archer is contending with.'

Could Godfrey Baseley not have stopped television being promoted even in *The Archers'* own newspaper? Baseley had a different battle to fight. The BBC in London wanted Dan Archer to buy a television, and thus set an example to the nation. Baseley refused on the grounds that every viewer gained by TV was a listener lost to the wireless. He was right, but it was a hopeless battle: Dan Archer bought his television set in the end.

Even as the *Archers* cast had been celebrating their 2,000th episode, back in September 1958, a young man called Tony Warren had been busy hawking an idea for a serial round television studios in Manchester. *Our Street* was its title when he approached the BBC; *Florizel Street* was its title when it got to Granada; *Coronation Street* was the title that came up on the screen in 1960. Soon the popular papers were raving over yet another provincial, low-budget programme that was a runaway success – but this time the provincial programme was on the telly, where actors had luxurious dressing rooms and were treated like stars, while the poor old *Archers* artistes were still climbing two flights of dreary stairs (how Gwen did hate them, particularly when her arthritis took hold) to reach the cramped and dismal Broad Street radio studios in Birmingham.

If audiences were falling and newspaper columnists proving fickle, the programme was only just starting to broadcast in Canada, Australia and Rhodesia. In Rhodesia, curiously, the signature tune 'Barwick Green' was already being used by an agricultural advice programme, and had been so used since the mid-Forties, long before *The Archers* was started. The Rhodesians, with commendable grace, found a new signature tune for their own programme.

Godfrey Baseley went on Canadian radio to tell the colonials what it was all about. Dan Archer, he said, was a man who 'had a good voice and who could

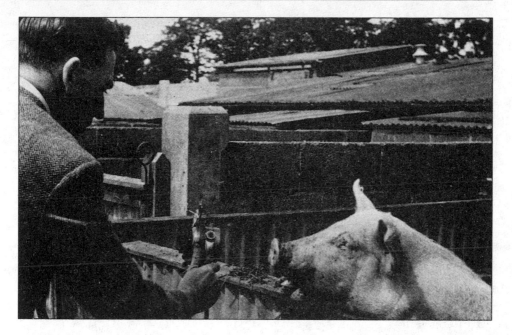

Tony Shryane goes out and about to record perfect pig noises – which Godfrey Baseley later
played in an instructive programme on Canadian radio. On another occasion Percy Thrower was
employed to blow pipe smoke into a pig's face to make it cough.
Birmingham Post & Mail

sing, took part in village concerts and took his place in the choir at Church' and
Doris was a woman whose 'main feature was to be domestic, on good relations
with her husband, but plenty of leg-pull and occasional bristles'.

He went on to describe the varying degrees of importance attached to the
people running the programme. 'Firstly there must be a creator, editor, call him
what you like,' said Baseley (the cast called him many things). 'The Editor I con-
sider as the first unit in the development of this successful programme. The
second unit I would describe as the writers.'

The third unit, according to Baseley, was the producer, whose main function
was to control the actors. 'After a while,' he explained, 'the job of the actor
becomes so simple that they become stale or they can take advantage and not
give of their best.'

The fourth unit, right at the end, comprised the actors themselves. 'There is
no need for them to have any knowledge of agriculture,' said Baseley. 'Their main
purpose is to interpret what the editor and writers have set out on paper. Their
most important job is to be able to maintain their character week by week and to
be quick workers.'

To explain the importance of sound effects he played the sound of a hungry
pig. 'Now,' he said, putting on another effects disc, 'the pig after feeding.' Listeners heard the sound of a contented pig. 'It would be useless for us to develop a

scene where two farmers were looking over the pig-sty wall saying, for instance, how well they were getting on and how comfortable and happy they looked, if we had a background like this . . .' Again he played the sound of hungry pigs. 'But how right it would be and how conducive it would be to good dialogue if this comfortable happy sound was going on behind.' Up came the sound of happy pigs.

What the Canadian grain farmers and lumberjacks and Eskimos made of it all, is not known. In fact, one of the programme's pig noises may not even have been made by a pig at all, but by Percy Thrower the TV gardener. Sound effects engineer John Wallis had been ordered to record a coughing pig, and had gone to a pig farm with his 'giant size tape recorder set up in a motor van'. When he failed to persuade a pig to cough, it was suggested that smoke be puffed into a pig's face. 'Percy Thrower was with us – and he was smoking his pipe,' remembered Wallis. 'So Percy went into the sty and puffed smoke . . . and went on puffing and blowing until . . .'

Either a pig or a Percy coughed. Wallis was never sure which.

At the beginning of 1961 the tenth birthday of *The Archers* was marked with a party and – a sign of the times – they borrowed the BBC's television studio in Birmingham to hold it. The actors were despondent. Harry Oakes was ill, and unable to attend; there were rumours that the programme was to be killed off. Denis Morris, the man who had fought to get the programme started in 1950, and who was now Controller of the Light Programme, was reported to have said enigmatically: 'It will go on as long as it remains true to itself.' What on earth, thought the nervous, troubled actors, was that supposed to mean?

The party was dutifully attended by the Director-General, following the tradition of previous years, but this Director-General (Hugh Carleton Greene) was seemingly cool about being dragged up to Birmingham. He did not make a fuss, the way Sir Ian Jacob had made a fuss, or present them all with silver cigarette boxes. 'The evening seemed to have got off on the wrong foot: the tone was not only different from that on previous celebrations, it was wrong,' recalled Norman Painting in *Forever Ambridge*.

The actors, nevertheless, had two things to cheer them. *The Times* had marked the event with a leader. Like everybody else, it puzzled over the inexplicable success of the programme during the previous decade. 'Whether it is because of wide-spread loneliness, whether it is the satisfaction of becoming absorbed in a continuing simple human drama as an escape from a world in which so much is disjointed, complicated and inhuman, whether it is that the call of the land is heard by all, "The Archers" formula has never had to be varied. The clever and smart may be superior about it; it deals with enduring things. And they do endure.'

The other thing to cheer the cast was that the clever and smart people of television had come to Birmingham to pay tribute to them. The *Tonight* team with

Derek Hart was in Birmingham en-masse. *Archers* actors, asked to take part, were excited and nervous. With the limitless money that television commanded, a mock-up of the Bull had been built and the cast were to be interviewed in character, and then asked questions. At first it seemed to go smoothly enough. Only gradually did it dawn on the actors that the *Tonight* programme was not actually paying tribute at all. It was actually sneering and poking fun. Gwen Berryman, nervous about being written out of the programme, upset by the long illness of Harry Oakes, suddenly realized that the questions she was being asked were tongue-in-cheek and the young men from London were trying to make her look silly. 'Whether or not they succeeded I don't know,' she wrote later, 'but they made me feel very cross. I think it was the last straw and I can't honestly say I saw too much to celebrate then, but being an actress, I just about managed to maintain some semblance of cheerfulness until I got home and cried.'

Norman Painting was equally dismayed. 'We old radio folk had seemed to be in collusion with bright young telly people in order to help them to knock us,' he wrote, and the *Observer* commented the following Sunday: 'Ambridge, the village that is more real than reality to eleven million listeners, was put on trial on its tenth birthday by the bright young men of *Tonight*.'

It was a mere six years since *The Archers* had been a bright young programme itself, daring to kill one of its major characters, holding twenty million listeners in thrall. But nobody, it was now realized in the Broad Street sound studios, would ever call *The Archers* 'bright' or 'young' again – no matter how many stories of teenage angst Ted Mason and Geoffrey Webb introduced, no matter how many other perhaps warmer and more valuable compliments were paid to the programme.

The cast thought it was all up; that everything would soon all be over. 'We've had a wonderful run,' Norman Painting told a meeting (worrying, as ever, over work conditions and pay, and security), 'but we must be realistic. With television becoming so popular we must gradually fade away . . .'

Some actors – the most prominent being Gwen Berryman – would have liked to leave straight away. They knew that one of *Coronation Street*'s favourite characters, Albert Tatlock, was played by an actor who had jumped ship from *Mrs Dale's Diary*, where he had been Mr Maggs for over ten years. If Mr Maggs could turn into Albert Tatlock, perhaps Doris could turn into an Ena Sharples?

But, sadly, no offers came from Manchester. (The only connection between *The Archers* and *Coronation Street* came in the late Eighties, when a recording of a bell was needed for Martha's shop in Ambridge, and a tape of the shop bell in *Coronation Street* was obligingly provided by Granada.)

In the end only one member of the *Archers* team was lured away to television. That was Godfrey Baseley.

He had never been fully committed to *The Archers*. In the late Fifties he had quietly secured the part-time job as country correspondent of *Television Newsreel*

– out and about in the Midlands each week, smiling into the camera, filing stories to London. Now he was off to London himself – with the job title, far more impressive than anything he had enjoyed in Birmingham, of Rural Programme Organizer, Television.

He did not give up his job as editor of *The Archers*, however. He would do both jobs. His secretary, Norma, was sent to London to 'learn the ropes' of television and he followed her in due course, having settled *Archers* storylines for the next six months. The impact of this move was most drastically felt by Tony Shryane, who at last got an office of his own to work from. When *The Archers* had started he had been given a small desk in Godfrey's office, where he had sat, quietly trying not to get in the way. In due course Valerie Hodgetts, the programme's shy young continuity girl, had also fitted into the office with Godfrey, Tony, and Norma. 'It was a bit of a squash with four of us,' Godfrey admitted later. What Tony Shryane thought is unrecorded, for he was always a quiet, uncomplaining chap.

Now the cats were away. Tony and Valerie started a romance, and eventually, though not until some years later, were married: a love story to equal anything in the programme, and with as happy an ending as anyone could wish for.

Godfrey Baseley was gone and Tony Shryane, the producer of the nation's most popular radio programme (recognized as such by his Sovereign – he was given the MBE in the 1961 Birthday Honours), no longer had to work from the corner of somebody else's office.

12

Round the Twist

BASELEY TOOK THE TRAIN SOUTH, to the base camp which Norma had set up in tellyworld. He was, he admitted later, 'lost among a lot of strangers and in trying to understand all the complexities of television'. During his time in London he set up a gardening programme. As with *The Archers*, he did not produce it himself, but cast around for a London version of Tony Shryane – in this case an up-and-coming chap called David Attenborough. With considerable energy young Attenborough built a garden on the roof of Lime Grove studios. Baseley did much of the interviewing and Percy Thrower, a gardener who had worked with him in the Midlands, and was keen to get on the telly, did most of the demonstrating.

Baseley was in London for two years. He would claim that the job itself came to a natural end, but the truth was that television, London and Godfrey did not get on well. His roots, like those of his famous character creations, were firmly planted in the soil. 'In many ways those years were difficult and frustrating,' he wrote in his book, *The Archers – A Slice of My Life*, 'in trying to convince people whose life was mixed up in a world surrounded with bricks and mortar, whose major interests were closely bound to economics, politics, science, music, poetry and all the rest of the arts, that there was another world outside. A world where the pace was steadier, where one could observe all the wonders of nature . . .' In summing it all up he said: 'Perhaps a younger generation was better equipped to bear the growing pains of this new medium in our lives.'

He resigned. He was not only out of London, he was out of the BBC. After almost twenty years he was no longer a member of staff. His pension contributions were paid back to him. He was given a freelance contract so that he could continue to edit *The Archers*. His responsibility, it said, 'shall include your personal supervision and checking of all scripts before the programmes are recorded and your advice on agriculture and all other matters (whether topical or otherwise)'. He moved back to the Midlands, to his family in Worcestershire. He had never, in spirit, been away.

In 1961 Harry Oakes died. In a newspaper interview he had listed, with rare bitterness, the illnesses that he believed had resulted from overwork: 'A heart attack, bronchitis, a nervous breakdown, a severe chill, stomach trouble, bronchitis (again), a throat-and-mouth infection and a third attack of bronchitis.' The newspaper called it: 'The astonishing burden of the nation's farmer-figure.'

Gwen Berryman thought the programme would fall apart. She had relied on Harry – 'He would not have allowed a television team to give us a rough ride on what was supposed to be a happy occasion' – and when he died she wrote: 'When I cried for Harry I cried for much more besides.'

She cried, according to her own account, because she had started to believe that she really was Doris Archer.

Some members of the public, of course, had always believed the characters were real. They sent flowers to funerals and pleaded for bits of wedding cake or tried to buy their Christmas turkeys from Brookfield Farm. At some point in the late Fifties Gwen Berryman herself had started to slip over the edge. 'In the studio and on the air I feel, act and think exactly like Mrs Archer, but once outside the BBC I'm Gwen Berryman and as unlike Doris as it's possible to be,' she confidently told a women's magazine in 1959 but, in fact, she was already confusing fiction with reality. People called her Doris, and she responded, automatically, in her Doris Archer voice. She started to feel jealous of Harry Oakes' wife, Dorothy, when Dorothy was called Doris by confused fans. 'For reasons I find it hard to explain, I became very fond of my husband and children,' she confessed later to the ghost-writer of her autobiography *The Life and Death of Doris Archer*. She stopped calling members of the cast by their real names. 'The fact that she called me by my character name made me feel straight away that I had really become a citizen of Ambridge,' said actress Ann Kindred, trying to be understanding, but Gwen was going against the etiquette of the theatre, and other members of the cast found it disturbing. Fellow actors were also surprised to find that her private notepaper had *From Mrs Doris Archer, Brookfield Farm, Ambridge, Near Borchester* printed on the top. One seasoned actor, who like Gwen had been in the programme from the beginning, saw what was happening to her, and took particular care to develop a life of his own, away from the studio, under his real name.

Gwen's mental confusion first showed itself in December 1959 when Harry Oakes was taken to hospital suffering from exhaustion and, in the programme, Dan was also sent to hospital. Gwen, playing Doris, visited Dan in Borchester General and found him hale and hearty, recovering from a broken leg. Gwen as Gwen visited Harry Oakes in hospital and found him ill and depressed. She was angry and upset. She was even more confused when a fit Dan returned home to Brookfield but Harry Oakes did not do the same. 'For a short time she simply could not understand what was happening,' said Jock Gallagher, the man who helped her with her autobiography. Gwen had convinced herself that Harry Oakes, like Dan, had a simple broken leg. She had believed it, she later said, because it was 'more comfortable' than the truth.

For Gwen the confusion between reality (an elderly spinster living with her brother in Wolverhampton) and fiction (a farmer's wife with a warm, closely-knit family) lessened after the death of Harry Oakes. He was her first Dan – the man who had been her 'husband' at all those fêtes in the mid-Fifties, who had practised duets with her in the car on the way back to the studio, who had invented limericks to amuse her. He had, it was true, been a husband she had had to share – 'The three of us travelled all over the country and had some marvellous times together with Harry, a great practical joker and natural comic, always proudly showing off his two wives' – but he had been the only husband she had known. In her own life, as a young actress in the Twenties, she had been engaged to marry a young, newly qualified doctor, but he had died of tuberculosis just weeks before the wedding.

The confusion lessened, but it was not resolved. When, in the late Sixties, the name 'Doris Archer' was printed on packs of Ambridge fudge (an early commercial venture) she demanded to be paid a royalty for the use of her name, and was puzzled and suspicious when the BBC told her she was not actually Doris Archer at all.

Harry Oakes was successfully re-cast. Monte Crick became the second Dan – he had understudied the part during Harry Oakes' final illness – and Gwen settled down again. She was allowed a holiday in South Africa and while she was there she went to look at a rhinoceros. An American woman spoke loudly which upset the animal and the warden panicked and told them all to run for their lives. Gwen tried to run but collapsed as the rhino thundered down on her. It could well have been a cliffhanger ending for the aborted Afrikaner version of *The Archers*. There was a happy ending in that the animal did not trample her to death, but an X-ray showed that she suffered from rheumatoid arthritis.

Back in England she tried to carry on without revealing the extent of the pain. She wanted to leave *The Archers*, but was terrified of being sacked: 'I decided that, whatever the consequences, I would carry on as long as possible.'

She collapsed, and was in hospital for five weeks. Tony Shryane, who had no intention at all of writing her out, recorded scenes at her bedside.

It was the start of the Sixties, the swinging decade, but nobody could foresee the full horrors that lay ahead. *Archers* stories were full of confidence. Jimmy Grange and his skiffle group were showing the programme to be relevant to the teenage generation. Walter Gabriel was busy running a school bus and breeding pigs with Ned Larkin. The Ministry of Agriculture was keen to show small farmers that they must amalgamate to increase efficiency (they pointed to the success of the British Motor Corporation, compared to individual firms like Austin and Wolseley and Morris) so Dan formed a milking co-operative with Fred Barratt and Jess Allard, and built a new milking parlour. (Fortunately it was easier to dismantle co-operatives like Ambridge Farmers Ltd than it was to dismantle BMC, or we would all have starved to death.)

There was plenty of scandal and intrigue, too. Christine's husband had turned out to be a bit of a bad 'un – off to Paris with Phil, and getting mixed up with a girl called Marianne. The romance between Carol Grey and John Tregorran was embarking on one of its major phases. She had married Charles Grenville, but it was still John who was privy to her innermost feelings. He had an antique shop in Borchester, and one day Carol had a terrible shock when she saw a painting and recognized the room that it portrayed – but could not say where it was. John Tregorran discovered that the picture had been painted by an artist called Beatrice, who had had a love affair with another artist, and they had had a baby girl – and yes, that baby girl was Carol. (What Godfrey Baseley made of this revelation is unclear. He was still stoutly maintaining, ten years later, that Carol Grey was the result of a moment of passion between a lovely young housemaid and an aristocrat.)

The writers were intent on warning the teenage generation of life's pitfalls. Sixteen-year-old Jennifer had an affair with a glamorous foreign ski instructor called Max (she was pretending to be eighteen), but when Max turned up at the Bull he was revealed to be really Max Bailey from Wolverhampton. Lilian, on the other hand, was shown as a good teenager. She spent the summer doing odd jobs to buy hay for her pony during the winter. Bad teenagers came to bad ends. When three of them on motorbikes started a barn fire and kicked Walter Gabriel's head in, Grenville arrived and broke one of the teenagers' arms with a judo blow. This was linked to a call by Grenville, in the *Borchester Echo*, for the return of capital punishment.

Ted Mason and Geoffrey Webb knew their listeners, and how to please them. In January 1962, for the fifth year in succession, the *Daily Telegraph*'s Gallup Poll voted *The Archers* the nation's favourite radio programme. July brought another *Archers* anniversary – the 3,000th episode – and a fulsome article in the *Daily Worker*. 'Television screens scowled black and neglected,' said the official Communist Party's daily organ quite untruthfully, 'while the 3,000th anniversary episode played.' The article continued: 'Its faults are plain to anyone who is socially conscious, and its virtues are clear to anyone with a taste for the little dramas of everyday life. Indeed, it is stage-craft applied to life, with an extra dab of make-up for the rough spots. It is near enough to reality to be believable – but not too close to be uncomfortable.'

The interest of the *Daily Worker* could be explained. Its readers were likely to be old-fashioned types, still sticking to steam radio, too poor to buy television sets, scornful of the BBC's glitzy *Compact* or ITV with its brash advertising jingles and materialist quiz shows.

In October 1962 the *Sunday Citizen* investigated a variety of the nation's favourite programmes and condemned the 'artificial mateyness' of Ambridge life, which, they claimed, 'makes you feel sick'. But the cast and production team were comforted to find that they were still a 'top programme' – up there with television shows like *Emergency Ward 10* and *The Rag Trade*.

Dan Archer and brother-in-law Tom Forrest on the look-out for poachers. Harry Oakes,
the first and most famous Dan Archer, died in 1961. Monte Crick took over the part
and made it very much his own.
Hulton Deutsch: Bert Hardy

The central characters were changing, and with them the actors who met each week in the scruffy little green room in Broad Street. More than ten years had passed since that first episode had been recorded. Grace Fairbrother was gone, and with her both Monica Grey who first played the part, and the supposedly-militant Ysanne Churchman. Leslie Bowmar, who played Fairbrother, and Pamela Mant, the first and very successful Christine, had gone. Eddie Robinson had died. Robert Mawdesley had died. Denis Folwell was still playing Jack, but was having to spend much time in hospital, suffering from tuberculosis. In 1961 Harry Oakes had died.

Several members of the cast were invited to appear on television. Godfrey Baseley was either unable to stop it happening, or was too distracted by other things. The *Archers* actors – whom Baseley had once insisted should not be seen as celebrity guests on *What's My Line* because it would rob them of dignity – were now put in front of the television cameras to see if they could 'do the Twist' better than the lads from *Z Cars*. They gyrated away, wriggling their hips to 'Ya Ya Twist', but to no avail. *Z Cars* won.

13

Another Death

APART FROM *Mrs Dale's Diary*, *The Archers* had not had a rival. A Lancashire woman, Margaret Halliwell, wrote about her Fifties childhood when her father, a cotton spinner, would arrive home just before six o'clock, have his tea, and then switch on the wireless to hear what Walter Gabriel had been up to. 'We all talked about *The Archers* at my secondary modern school,' she wrote, 'everybody listened to it in those days.'

The Archers was lively, popular, and in touch with the people. Even at the turn of the decade it was in tune with television programmes like *Life with the Lyons* and *Dixon of Dock Green* – 'Evening All,' said PC Dixon, touching his helmet on Saturday-night telly. 'G'd evenin' all,' said Tom Forrest, unseen but definitely doffing his cap on Saturday-night radio.

But by the early Sixties cotton spinners in Bolton were watching *Tonight* on BBC TV before switching to *Coronation Street* on Granada. In 1962 the BBC entered the battle of the television soaps with a glamorous designer-product called *Compact* which was set in the offices of a women's magazine. 'Now that *Compact* is with it, *Coronation Street* begins to look increasingly drab and dusty,' said *Punch* – itself trying desperately to keep up to date. The article added that *Compact* was 'smart, sophisticated, the very stuff that the adman's dreams are made on'.

If *Coronation Street* was already drab and dusty, what chance did *The Archers* have, chuntering away every night on the wireless? Ted Mason and Geoffrey Webb were both exhausted. Godfrey Baseley was busy trying to set himself up as a Birmingham public relations executive. The production office was in chaos. On one occasion, in 1961, ten scripts had still not reached the studio by the Friday before recording on the Monday. A frantic phone call revealed that Ted Mason believed that Geoffrey Webb was writing them. Another frantic call revealed that Webb thought they were being written by Mason.

Webb was brought into the studio and worked through the weekend, writing ten scripts, and finishing them in time for recording on the Monday morning. Officially this was seen as a triumph: 'The quality of the writing was every bit as good as it had always been . . . the only ill-effect on Geoff was a rash he developed from an old blanket he had found and used to keep himself warm as he dozed off between typing sessions . . .'

Script editors who have worked on material produced in that fashion, by a writer tired out and under intense pressure, will have their doubts about the quality. So will actors who have had to make those scripts work in the studio. And why had nobody from the production office chased up the scripts before the Friday afternoon?

The system of writing the programme had been established when the programme started. One writer wrote for a month, twenty scripts, then handed over to the other writer. Scripts were sent in batches of ten to Valerie Hodgetts or, after she married and left the programme, to Sylvia Cartner, who checked for continuity problems and filled in the index cards.

The cards dated back to May 1951. They were started after a serious continuity error: one writer announced a forthcoming wedding, and the second writer ignored the event. Listeners, then as now, like a wedding. They switched on expecting wedding bells, and found the supposed bridegroom suffering from total wedding amnesia, swilling out the pig pens. They complained bitterly. Valerie Hodgetts started her filing system, although she already had a most awesome reputation for being able to remember everything – birthdays, wedding anniversaries, events – without having to look anything up. 'One quizzical look in Valerie's direction and out would come the answer – chapter and verse,' said Godfrey Baseley. (Gwen Berryman expressed the secret belief of the cast that Valerie actually ran everything.)

The index cards were the Bible, the law. In an early episode Phil casually expressed a dislike of Gorgonzola cheese: in forty-five years thereafter he has never been allowed to eat Gorgonzola. In the Seventies, drama director Anthony Cornish, standing in for Tony Shryane and rehearsing a scene involving John Tregorran, pressed the talkback and said: 'I'm sick of Tregorran always having a dry sherry, for God's sake let him have a gin and tonic' – and the frivolous, irresponsible change was made, and the scene was recorded, all before the horrified continuity assistant could get to a phone to ask Godfrey Baseley, the Director-General, or the Prime Minister to stop it from happening.

Scripts in the Fifties and Sixties were delivered only a week before recording. When they were late there was no time for re-writes – and in any case, alone in the gallery of famous BBC drama producers, Tony Shryane never showed a powerlust to change the material given to him. Handed a script in which Dan turned vegetarian, Phil formed a rock band, and Doris took to gin, Shryane would simply have assumed that *The Archers* was moving with the times. He had enough to do actually making the programmes; scripts and stories were Godfrey Baseley's province.

Baseley, however, was no longer editing scripts on a daily basis. Very often only Valerie Hodgetts – a continuity assistant – stood between a writer and more than seven million listeners, a situation that today would give BBC libel lawyers screaming nightmares.

In 1962 Geoffrey Webb was taken ill. He went into hospital in London 'for observation'. It was not clear what was the matter with him. The hospital arranged a course with a psychiatrist, a Middle-European lady whom he mocked. Eventually he underwent an operation, and was sent back home to the country. He was killed, shortly afterwards, in a car accident. Webb was one of the three men who had created *The Archers*. He, Ted Mason and Godfrey Baseley had been there right from the start.

For several weeks Ted Mason – himself showing grave signs of nervous stress – wrote every script. Then David Turner – the Midland writer who was to achieve great success with television plays like *The Train Set* and a noted stage play of the Sixties, *Semi-Detached* – joined the team. It was an uneasy experience. Writers who have striking individual talents often find it difficult to fit into serial writing. They accept the work because they need the money, but they often feel the need to justify what they are doing in artistic terms. David Turner claimed it was an opportunity to experiment 'just as old Bill Shakespeare did with a character called "Walter Gabriel Falstaff"'. But soap operas do not pay good money and risk the enjoyment of listeners so that gifted writers can experiment. When David Turner joined *The Archers* the cast found their characters suddenly expressing new and surprising views. Further confusion followed when a third writer joined the programme: a writer of thrillers, and a specialist in the macabre, John Kier Cross. If David Turner's scripts seemed to some people to turn faithful old Tory characters like Dan into mouthpieces for radical Sixties politics, they at least had one redeeming feature when compared with those of John Kier Cross: they were not written in Scottish dialect.

Kier Cross's scripts were full of 'quirky life'. The dialogue had much to recommend it, but was possessed, the actors discovered, of an unmistakable Scottish flavour. In the studio the cast worked through David Turner scripts in which their characters sounded like angry young men, and then struggled through John Kier Cross scripts containing dialogue natural only to the inhabitants of Tannochbrae.

It was the Scottish scripts that they had most difficulty in coping with, but it was David Turner who decided to leave the programme. 'There are occasions in the life of any long-running serial like *The Archers* when, for no obvious reason, an atmosphere of dissension occurs right through the whole organization,' said Godfrey Baseley later, smoothly gliding over months of tension and fretful nerves, 'and this discord in its turn brings fears and doubts into the minds of everyone concerned. Such a period emerged while David was a member of the team and as a consequence he resigned.'

Much later, speaking to the author of this book, Baseley said: 'He had to go. He was taking no notice of the notes I sent. Writers are writers, they should do as they're told.'

Baseley was right about the fears and doubts. The actors were infected and did something quite extraordinary. They wrote a memo to the Head of Programmes in Birmingham asking for a meeting 'to represent the feelings of at least half a dozen of the cast; that they should in fact put forward suggestions, based on their own experiences and contacts outside, for the writers to use, and also that they should be informed ahead of the story-line development.'

Actors suggest stories? Artistes be told what was happening? Where did they think they were, Bolshevik Russia?

Godfrey Baseley wrote crisply that he would not dream of doing either thing. He was, he said, quite capable of providing the right kind of stories for the programme and if they were any good as actors they should be capable of interpreting what was written down on paper for them.

Baseley went on to say that Tony Shryane was told about future story developments, and could therefore direct them in the studio so that their acting was consistent with what was to come. They, the actors, would certainly not be told what the future held in store for their characters. They would discover that in due course.

The actors were not in Bolshevik Russia. They retreated in dismay, and worried about their contracts.

Fears and doubts. A programme sounding tired. When John Kier Cross attended his first script meeting in Birmingham he was told: 'What we need is more humour, more sex, more drama . . .' but there were soon complaints from London 'on the subject of smoking, alcohol and lavatory humour'. With David Turner gone and Kier Cross still finding his feet, Ted Mason battled wearily to give the programme new life and pull it into the Sixties – which was already showing itself as a decade of rapid and remarkable change.

Reggie and Valerie Trentham left the village – old rake Reggie, a Fifties cad if ever there was one, and Valerie his secret-service agent wife. They were replaced by Jack Woolley, a self-made Brummie businessman who planned to turn Grey Gables into an exclusive holiday centre for tired businessmen. Jimmy Grange went – what good was a Fifties skiffler when *She Loves You* by The Beatles was number one in the charts?

The audience continued to fall. *That Was The Week That Was* was on television, the Profumo scandal had broken, and Labour's new leader, Harold Wilson, was promising a 'Britain that is going to be forged in the white heat of this scientific revolution'. In Ambridge Dan was signing a sugarbeet contract at the Kidderminster factory and planning to buy a precision drill and down-the-row thinner. It was storylined that Ambridge should win the Best Kept Village competition, and that Dan and Doris would go on holiday to Guernsey.

These were solid background stories, the very stuff of what the programme would become, so successfully, in the Eighties – but they were not in tune with the early Sixties, not enough to fight off *Compact* and *Coronation Street* in the popular soap opera stakes. A new storyline was devised: a 'Cellar Club' would be opened at the Bull, a place for the village youngsters, the 'teenagers'. But in the real world, teenagers had already stopped listening to Ambridge affairs. They were all watching The Beatles on *Ready Steady Go*.

Another sensational death was planned. As with the more famous death, eight years previously, the situation was carefully set up. John Tregorran finally got married – to an attractive, sympathetic nurse, Janet Sheldon. The great romance of Carol Grey and John Tregorran was, it seemed, over – the flame finally extinguished. Carol herself had long been married to Grenville, the businessman.

In October 1963 Janet was killed in a car crash. In the same accident Grenville was badly injured and had to have his leg amputated. It was a re-run of 1955. Actress Judy Parfitt, who played Janet Tregorran, arrived at the studio having not received her script through the post. She sat down to read it quickly, gave a smothered scream and said, 'My God! They've killed me!'

Once again, just like in the good old Fifties, the letters poured in: 'You've done it again. First it was Grace Archer and now Janet Tregorran. There's only one word for it – murder.'

Brookfield Farm in the Fifties looked grimly realistic, with no hot running water, and washing-up done in an enamelled bowl in the scullery. Attempts to make the young actress Pauline Seville look like a granny by putting her in a strange hat were less successful.
Hulton Deutsch: Bert Hardy

'Tony Shryane, I hate you, I hate you, oh I hate you! I didn't mind when Grace bought it. Her voice always did drive me up the wall, but that nice nurse . . .'

'I wasn't listening too deeply last evening, but by Jove the shock of realizing what had happened made me sit bolt upright, and now I can't wait for the programme to continue . . .'

The programme, it seemed, was back on form. Between December 1963 and January 1964 – at a time when Mary Quant was opening her first boutique, *Steptoe and Son* was top of the TV ratings, and the Fab Four were singing *I want to hold your hand* – the *News of the World* ran a series of huge features: the 'never-before-told story of The Archers of Ambridge'.

There was tension among the cast when the *News of the World* reporter was doing his research in Birmingham, because the actors were nurturing a great secret. Two of them – Monte Crick, playing Dan, and Anne Cullen who played Carol – were in love, and planned to marry once a divorce was out of the way.

The secret was kept. The articles were adulatory, just like in the old days, and showed the cast that despite the terrible listening figures they were still up there, with *Coronation Street* and *Compact*.

14

A Challenge
from the Motel

BY 1964 THE GREAT THEMES of the Fifties were playing themselves out. Major characters that would move the story into the future – characters like Polly Mead and Brummie Sid Perks – were thin and insubstantial. Grenville disposed of his majority interest in Octopus Ltd and went, alone, to America – scriptwriters desperate to know what to do with a character. Jack and Peggy bought a moped for Jennifer to get home from college (Jennifer was perhaps the only genuine Sixties character in the programme: a college girl thrown out of her digs after rowdy parties, she insisted on keeping up her relationship with boyfriend 'Max') and worried over how to find the money for a new pub dining room. Paul Johnson tried to raise finance to buy his agricultural machinery firm. Many stories relied on this sort of mechanically-plotted trivia – someone needs some money to buy something, and asks six different people to lend it, thus giving the writer six scenes, if not six episodes.

Walter Gabriel developed his entrepreneurial instincts, and the writers did not restrain themselves. He bred maggots in a shed next to Mrs Turvey's garden, and bought a hot-air balloon from a Mr Snout of Hollerton. He sold his Granny's chamberpot to John Tregorran for £15 and purchased a stuffed gorilla called George from a man in Felpersham.

But Walter Gabriel's antics could not sustain an entire programme. *The Archers* sounded tired, a senior London executive complained. Action was taken. The weekly recording session, it was announced, would be extended by half a day. The cast rebelled and threatened to go on strike.

It was partly about money (the BBC had not offered any increase in fees) but also about working conditions. The green room in the Broad Street studios was cramped and windowless. They called it the Black Hole of Calcutta. The BBC – frightened by the thought of higher fees – said they could sit in an alternative room, a room with a window, provided it was not being used for something else. The cast – frightened by a spatter of amused press stories about their revolt – backed down. They told newspapers that they had never threatened to strike at all. They told Godfrey Baseley that it was a storm in a teacup, that they had no real complaints.

Then an announcement was made that convinced the cowed actors, sitting in their tiny, cramped green room, that the end was finally approaching.

The weekend *Archers* Omnibus edition, said a BBC spokesman, was being moved from the Light Programme to the Home Service, together with *Down Your Way*, *Chapel in the Valley*, and *Listen With Mother*. In future the speech content of the Light Programme would be drastically reduced. Fifteen hours a day would be devoted entirely to 'gay and cheerful music', said the BBC spokesman; and this music would include 'current popular numbers'.

The Beatles, the Rolling Stones – these were the weapons being brought into play to stop the terrible haemorrhage of listeners to television. Religious organ music had failed and must make way for Gerry and the Pacemakers. Dan and Doris must move aside and give Billy J. Kramer a chance. The change was made. Telephone helplines were set up. 'The BBC's output in radio is being extended', parroted the girls on the switchboard. '*The Archers* Omnibus will, from now on, be on the Home Service . . . all you have to do is switch to the Home Service and you will get it.'

Officially, the cast were never told the true audience figures after the switch. It was a closely-guarded secret. In fact, the *Archers* Omnibus, in the space of seven days, lost half its audience. Two million listeners decided they could live without Paul Johnson's financial problems over Octopus Ltd, Jack Archer's financial problems over his new dining room for the Bull, Dan's financial problems buying-out his partners in Ambridge Farmers Ltd, and even Walter Gabriel's financial problems selling maggots and buying elephants. They would stay with cheery tunes on the Light, rather than twiddle their wireless dial in search of the Home.

BBC's audience research was commissioned to do an urgent survey. It revealed that *The Archers* listenership was predominantly working class and two-thirds female. Listeners said they enjoyed hearing facts about the countryside, human interest stories, farming matters, comedy, and Walter Gabriel. They were asked if they thought the programme accurately represented various issues, such as religion, blood-sports, and youth. A depressing 80 per cent thought the stories about young people sounded phoney.

If the programme was failing to hold its audience it could well have been because Godfrey Baseley and Tony Shryane were busy with other work (Baseley was running his own PR company; Shryane was producing *Guilty Party* and *My Word*), because the writers were exhausted, and because society was changing and *The Archers* still – after six years worrying over the problem – had no idea how to reflect the Younger Generation.

The dialogue was in the wrong idiom for the young people of the Sixties, said a memo from London. The writer added that if they must resort to slang they ought to use 'contemporary' slang.

Press coverage was now very different. When Grace Archer had died the *Daily Mail* was reflecting genuine shock and indignation when it demanded to know 'Who Are The Guilty Men?' The death of Janet Tregorran produced mockery from the *Evening Standard*:

'Who, I asked the BBC today, killed the pretty blue-eyed Janet Tregorran? . . .' I eventually tracked down the real criminals to a private meeting in a large Victorian mansion on the outskirts of Birmingham . . . Mr Baseley, seething with blood lust, demanded a death soon. He had already been responsible for the ritual burning of Grace Archer in 1955, and the accidental slaying of a poacher a few years later. But he was not satisfied. Only one of the other men, described as scriptwriters, disagreed. He was tortured with cunningly designed cynicism and ridicule until he came round to the majority viewpoint . . .'

Cynicism and ridicule – a sort of kindly contempt, even – was manifest for *The Archers* itself. Several of the longest-serving members of cast found that they were becoming uneasy about giving press interviews. Only too often they were sneered at or treated unkindly. When Ellis Powell was removed from her part as Mrs Dale, the *Daily Express* brutally asked Gwen Berryman: 'How does the uncrowned queen of Ambridge feel, now that Mrs Dale has been toppled from her throne?'

Gwen felt terrified. 'If it hadn't been for the pain from my arthritis,' she said later, 'I think I might have suffered a bit from knocking knees.'

She cheered up when she was invited to meet the Queen Mother and present a cheque for thirty pounds, raised by the *Archers* cast, towards Freedom From Hunger in the Developing Countries. When she queued to hand the money over she found herself behind the new Mrs Dale, Jessie Matthews, who had been raising money among the cast of *Mrs Dale's Diary*. 'Jessie Matthews went forward with her cheque,' recalled Gwen, 'and I could not help having a quiet chuckle to myself when the Queen Mother's aide introduced her as Lady Attlee.'

Then Gwen was introduced, and tried to curtsey, but her arthritic joints locked and the Queen Mother had to haul her upwards, at which point 'the stubbornly-locked joints melted under her regal charm' said Gwen. She went back to Birmingham to report to the cast that the Queen Mother was a regular listener.

In the autumn of 1964, a new television soap started; and this one was made in their own home territory of Birmingham. Within weeks the nation's schoolchildren – who only a few short years ago had been keen *Archers* listeners – were rushing home from school in time for the 4.30pm transmission. 'Crossroads Motel, can I help you?' asked pretty Jane Rossington, on that opening November night, wearing a tightish jersey that showed her figure. (Jane was not the first person actually to be seen on *Crossroads* – the first person seen on the screen was

Noele Gordon's mother, who ought not to have been seen at all, as she had only come to watch the recording – *Crossroads* bravely setting out the way it intended to continue.)

Ted Mason turned down an offer to write for the new soap. 'You cannot serve two masters at the same time,' he told the *Guardian*. 'Apart from disloyalty it would drive one round the bend.' Ted renewed his efforts to enable *The Archers* to meet the challenge of the mid-Sixties. His only fellow writer was now John Kier Cross – whose main characteristics, according to Godfrey Baseley, were a passionate dislike of change, and a fascination with the past.

Stories in 1965 were a throw-back to the good old days of mysterious strangers, spies, crime, and glamorous foreigners. Aunt Laura's chauffeur, a young darkly-handsome young man called Patillo, turned out to be an imposter. His real name was Roger Travers-Macy and his family, listeners were told, had money and breeding, but were cold and indifferent to him, which was why he went about under an assumed name. Laura was taken aback, but grateful when he gave her a good tip for the Stock Exchange.

Elsewhere cattle were rustled and Brookfield was burgled. Walter Gabriel's antics got wilder and wilder. When he played Long John Silver in the vicar's production of *Treasure Island* at Christmas 1964 he had a real parrot. Then he gave his parrot to a certain Mrs Twelvetrees of Felpersham, bought himself an elephant called Rosie, who had a baby called Tiny Tim, and at the church fête Rosie and Tiny Tim were a huge success. Charles Grenville, now with only one leg and living mysteriously in America, was struck down and killed by a bug he had picked up in the East. Actor Michael Shaw had spent several months out of work when his character was sent to America, and in desperation had taken another job. *The Archers* writers, who had been planning to bring him back, thought he had behaved with great disloyalty and killed his character off.

In the summer of 1965 Dan and Doris were sent on holiday to Ireland, and the actors were actually taken there to record the scenes. Tony Shryane went, and so did Godfrey Baseley, and two scriptwriters – all off on a two-week jaunt. Officially, the editor and scriptwriters were there to 'accurately reflect the differences between farming methods in Ireland and England'. In fact, the entire venture – travel, hotels, hospitality – was paid for by the Irish Tourist Board. It was perhaps not entirely in line with the BBC charter, but it was hugely successful. The Irish had not yet caught on to television. Gwen Berryman and Monte Crick were treated like Hollywood stars: at a reception in Dublin Gwen wore an amazing hat made out of white goosefeathers, and all the newspapers wrote about it. The chairman of Guinness, Lord Elmdon, showed them round the Dublin brewery. In Killarney they drank Gaelic coffee (nobody told Gwen it contained alcohol) and in the Portaferry bar, in Northern Ireland, an old man with a wooden leg sang *The Mountains of Mourne* so soulfully that John Kier Cross was reduced to floods of tears.

Two writers – Geoffrey Webb and Ted Mason – were responsible for all *Archers* scripts until the death of Geoffrey Webb in 1962. In his youth, Geoffrey Webb had been destined to become a sanitary inspector, but his family finances would not run to the training so he became a journalist. Ted Mason worked in Cadbury's chocolate factory in Birmingham until writing a successful sketch for Stanley Holloway. Here the original production team are out on one of their regular farm visits. From left: Geoffrey Webb, Tony Shryane, Ted Mason, Dr W. Blunt (agricultural advisor) and Godfrey Baseley.

Hulton Deutsch

The Irish Tourist Board was pleased as well. At the end of the year it reported that holiday enquiries from the UK had increased from 76,000 to 95,000, and credited *The Archers* with the upsurge in interest.

Parliament was less tolerant of the Ambridge influence when, after the 1965 budget, Dan was heard complaining about the extra penny on his pint of beer. Labour MPs demanded that the Postmaster-General, Anthony Wedgwood Benn, should direct the BBC 'under section 14 (4) of its Licence and Agreement, to drop views on public policy which have no foundation in fact'.

15

1966:
The Swinging Year

Ted Mason wrote a memo to Godfrey Baseley. *The Archers*, he said, should reflect the world as it was – a world 'that does include vulgarity, that does include sex, that does include strong language and that does include violence . . . a world in which values are constantly changing, in which the youth culture is dominating and in which cosiness plays little part.'

For how long, he demanded, was '*The Archers* to be preserved in aspic'?

Neither Godfrey Baseley nor the BBC hierarchy knew how to respond. In radio terms *The Archers* was still a hugely important programme. Listening figures were declining, but were still around six million. It was the year of Carnaby Street and Twiggy, of Swinging London and the Pill, of *Aftermath* by the Rolling Stones and *Day Tripper* by The Beatles, but not everyone in England wanted to swing: Ken Dodd and The Bachelors were still doing good business.

Where was the place of *The Archers* in all this? Ought Dan and Doris to cling to the old, singing 'Down The Vale' round the Brookfield piano, or cleave to the new and release a single with Cilla?

This time BBC Radio asked the Birmingham information officer, Kenneth Bird (who had devised and edited the *Borchester Echo*, and during the mid-Sixties had become a key member of the team), to present an in-depth report on *The Archers* – on its strengths, its weaknesses, its future.

Bird wrote that *The Archers* was written by middle-aged men trying too hard to be with it. He gave an example. The writers had tried to write a 'with it' scene in which Polly Perks and Lilian fantasized about a sexual encounter with Sean Connery. They had been eager to write the words, but somehow their nerve had failed them. Polly and Lilian were heard talking not about sex with Sean Connery, but, coyly, about what it would be like to 'go away' with him. This 'mincing language,' wrote Bird, risked upsetting the elderly and making younger people scornful.

Bird criticized the laboured dialogue – John Tregorran referring to the smell of coffee as 'the golden good spirits of the old returned master' – and the awful servility of Tom Forrest with his 'sirs' and Ned Larkin with his 'Master Philip'.

(This criticism was fortunately ignored, leaving the way open for Ned's son Jethro to call Phil Archer 'Master Phil' to his dying day, a source of endless amusement to Elizabeth Archer in the Eighties.)

Bird's report was critical but ended on a surprisingly passionate note: Ambridge, he said, was a 'gentle relic' of Old England. It was nostalgic. It was munificent. It was incorruptible and it was intrepid.

Nostalgic, generous, incorruptible and valiant? Maybe, but Ted Mason wanted the programme to be contemporary. He wanted it to be relevant. Again he made trouble at a quarterly meeting attended by the Controller, Light Programme, demanding that *The Archers* be given some of the 'unlimited licence' granted to television.

The Controller dismissed television out of hand. The television service, he said, 'could not be taken as a reflection of the general opinion in the BBC'.

In May 1966 came the 4,000th episode, and for a while it seemed that Ted Mason was wrong – that the programme was still successfully holding a place for itself. 'If you want to start worrying about your identity or wondering if the boundary between reality and fantasy really exists,' said the *Guardian*, 'do not go to the modern playwrights, poets and painters. Go to the village of Ambridge. If you get there, you will know that for you the thin line has broken – but not more than for millions of others.'

It was a year of weddings. Sid and Polly were married. Jack Woolley and Valerie Trentham were married. Tony Shryane and Valerie Hodgetts were married. In this last, real-life wedding, Ted Mason was best man and Norman Painting presented the happy pair with a silver salver from the cast.

Gwen Berryman took three months off with ill health, which meant that Doris could not be heard, so Brookfield stories faded into the background. A fourth *Borchester Echo* was produced. It had two pages of colour and featured Sid and Polly's wedding (with bridesmaids Jennifer and Lilian in amazing blue brocade dresses). The head of Radio Saigon visited the studios and discussed a Vietnamese *Archers*, and Ted Mason said: 'I can't quite imagine old Dan discussing warble fly in the paddyfields.'

The year progressed. In the real world the Moors murderers were tried and sentenced; England beat Germany to win the World Cup; *Paperback Writer* for The Beatles was followed by hits for The Who and The Kinks. Warren Mitchell was voted best TV actor for his portrayal of Alf Garnett in *Till Death Us Do Part*.

Ted Mason had campaigned for a big story – a modern story, a story that would establish *The Archers* as a programme of the Sixties. Instead, 1966 saw a long, long saga of arsonists (a second-time-round story, the first time it had been 'teenagers' out for kicks, this time it was Polly Mead's dad). Nelson opened a casino in Borchester and Jack Archer developed a taste for gambling. Another long story involved two Irish newcomers: Paddy Redmond, and a new barmaid at the Bull, Nora McCauley. John Tregorran opened a bookshop in Borchester and gave Roger Travers-Macy a job. Walter Gabriel found forty-two gold sovereigns hidden in his chimney. It was desperately dreary stuff. Then a story was started that prompted an article in the *Sunday Telegraph* that frightened everyone to bits.

The story was done at the insistence of Godfrey Baseley. He had come back to live in Gloucestershire after his sojourn in London, and noticed that people with urban backgrounds were moving into villages and immediately taking an active part in community affairs. His own village was virtually becoming a part of the nearby market town. 'Life in Ambridge was not quite in step with reality,' he wrote later. 'We had somehow lost a couple of years.'

He set out to put things right. Jack Woolley was heard announcing plans to turn Ambridge into an urban overspill area. John Woodford of the *Sunday Telegraph* heard the story and detected a sinister BBC plot. 'There have been signs lately,' he wrote, 'that *The Archers* is winding itself up for the final curtain.'

His theory was that BBC bosses wanted to kill the programme, but did not want screams of outrage from loyal old listeners. The programme therefore would be killed from within. Ambridge would cease to exist. It would commit a fictional suicide. Everybody would hear the bulldozers and concrete mixers rattle and roar through the Borsetshire lanes, tearing up the pastures, spreading concrete over the old village green. There would be no point in continuing with the 'everyday story of countryfolk' when Ambridge had become a vast suburb.

Woodford's article was complimentary about the programme: 'A joke to the occasional listener, mannered and contrived with its farming hints, *The Archers* yet wields a remarkable holding power for almost anyone who tries following the story.' He appealed to listeners to stop the BBC's cunning plot. 'I suspect that the BBC wants to test the strength of listeners' concern, and that if enough letters arrive saying, "Don't let this happen," it won't.'

The production team did not wait for listeners' letters. The overspill story was thrown into rapid reverse. But the damage was done as far as the cast were concerned. Always nervous, always fearful that somebody was out to get them, Woodford's article was proof that the end was nigh. 'We all knew it was only a matter of time before the gravy train ground to a halt,' said Gwen Berryman. 'Even a BBC denial that any consideration had been given to taking *The Archers* off the air, did not much help our nervousness.'

Gwen was slumped in depression. 'I could see a sad and lonely old-age pensioner knitting her life away between bouts of pain,' she said later. 'I had no illusions about finding other work . . . I could not even envisage going back into business again because I could not hope to survive being on my feet around a shop most of the day.'

Morale declined further when it was announced that the evening episode was to follow the Omnibus, from the Light Programme to the Home Service. Everyone knew that moving programmes about was a traditional BBC way of softening them up for the chop.

Behind the bar in the Bull with Peggy (Thelma Rodgers) and Jack (Denis Folwell).
In 1966 Jack and Peggy were blissfully unaware that daughter Jennifer was about to shock
both of them, the village, and the nation.
Hulton Deutsch: Bert Hardy

The changeover took place, and at the same time the Light Programme and
Home Service gave way themselves to the Swinging Sixties, and became Radio 2
and Radio 4. The Third Programme brought itself massively up to date by calling itself Radio 3.

As with the Omnibus, it was fortunate that the cast was not privy to the ini-
tial audience response. There was a big romantic theme running – an old theme,
one of the great themes – the love story between Carol and John. These two
lovers from the Fifties – cruelly kept apart for so long by Mason and Webb –
were finally to be brought together. The listeners on Radio 4 (always to be a
carping, crabby lot, so unlike the generous and uncritical listeners to the Light
Programme) were not impressed. They didn't, quite frankly, care about Carol and

John. They complained that the 'lovey-dovey talk' between the romantic couple made them sound more like 'a couple of love-sick teenagers' than two mature and sensible people.

There was irony here. Ever since the word teenager had been first voiced at a script conference in 1958, the writers had striven in vain to write 'with it' teenage dialogue. Only now, with a couple of middle-aged, middle-class lovers, had they succeeded.

John Kier Cross was taken ill and had to go into hospital. Once again Ted Mason was responsible for all of the scripts. It was an impossible burden. Another writer would have to be found, and urgently. 'There was an actor in *The Archers* who had played a leading role right from the start . . .' Godfrey Baseley would write later. 'We had always known him as a writer as well as an actor but had never connected the kind of work he did with the style required for *The Archers* . . .'

Well, no. Norman Painting did not write Shavian dialogue and did not write Scottish dialect, but his fellow members of the cast would not reproach him for that. He had researched Anglo-Saxon poetry at Christ Church, Oxford, and built a reputation for his adaptations of classic novels on the radio, as well as for original radio dramas and children's programmes. Now Godfrey Baseley phoned him at his flat in London. He was to write nine scripts, the first three plotted and cast by Ted Mason. Later that evening Tony Shryane and Valerie called at his flat – they were in London recording *My Word* – and gave him a folder containing background notes on the characters, and summaries of recent script meetings.

He was suddenly on the inside. He was no longer an actor sitting in the stuffy Broad Street green room, worrying about his character being written out. Now he was looking down on Ambridge from the vantage point of the Gods.

He opened the folder and peered into the future: his own future, and the future of others.

His eyes hit on an item marked 'Jennifer's Pregnancy'.

Ted Mason's gritty, contemporary story, long in maturing, was about to unfold.

16

Jennifer's Baby

JOHN KIER CROSS DIED in January 1967, and Norman Painting was immediately brought in to join Ted Mason as a permanent member of the writing
team. Going to Kier Cross's funeral in the West Country, Painting had arranged
to meet Ted Mason beforehand. He was startled and confused when they met
and Mason's first words were: 'Of course, you know who the father is, don't you?'

Jennifer's baby . . .

It would be the last of the big *Archers* stories, the last time the old guard of
Godfrey Baseley and Ted Mason would display their formidable storytelling
skills. It would be the last time *The Archers* would hold a mass populist audience
– the audience of *Coronation Street* and *Crossroads* – before retreating into its
new, middle-class, Radio 4 domain.

The story of Jennifer's baby had started just before Christmas. Jill was pregnant (with Elizabeth, who would be born in April 1967, shortly before a little boy
called Nigel would celebrate his eighth birthday in Lower Loxley.) After a general family chat about there being another little Archer on the way, and what it
would be called, Jennifer tearfully confided to sister Lilian that she, too, was
expecting a baby.

What would Peggy say? What would weak Jack say? What, oh what, would
Dan and Doris say?

It was a secret between the sisters until January when Jennifer told the vicar.
She asked him to tell her parents, but he said she must have the courage to tell
them herself. After a few episodes she almost did so, and after another few
episodes – these scriptwriters were experts – she came clean.

What she did not divulge, of course, was the identity of the baby's father.
Listeners were glued to their wireless sets night after night as Godfrey Baseley
and Ted Mason – and now Norman Painting – spun the story out.

Jennifer had still not revealed the name of the father by June when the baby –
christened Adam – was born. The finger of suspicion pointed in many directions,
but it pointed most accusingly at Nelson Gabriel who had been secretly going
out with Jennifer. Walter was convinced that his son was the rascal. He was even
more convinced when Nancy Tarrant from Penny Hassett turned up on the
doorstep and said that Nelson had made her pregnant as well. (Walter told her to

move out of the district, promising to send her money, and the incident was forgotten for twenty years, until an attractive young girl walked into Nelson's wine bar in West Street, Borchester, and said, 'Hello Dad!')

For the first time in a decade the audience figures were rising. It was an Indian Summer for Ambridge. It was the Fifties revisited. And as the story of Jennifer's pregnancy unfolded there flowered a host of other Fifties favourites – skulduggery, violence, melodrama, and, of course, false identity. Sid Perks discovered that the pig farmer he was working for at Paunton Farm, a Mr Brown, wasn't a pig farmer at all: he was a professional gambler hiding from gangsters who were demanding protection money. There were strange goings-on at the 'disused airfield at the edge of the village' he told Polly. (Whatever happened to the airfield? Is it still there?)

Then Nelson Gabriel was reported killed when a light plane crashed into the sea. And when the police raided Paunton Farm it transpired that Mr Brown was only pretending to be a professional gambler pretending to be a pig farmer – his true identity was that of a mail-van robber – but not the chief mail-van robber, because the chief mail-van robber was Nelson Gabriel, who was only pretending to be dead (his fingerprints were discovered on an empty whisky bottle at Paunton Farm) and who was the brains behind the mail-van job, flying himself in and out of Ambridge at dead of night, and known in the criminal world as 'the Boss'.

Tracked down by Interpol Nelson was brought home under arrest and languished in gaol for months before being acquitted. The stress on Walter was so great that villagers had to club together to buy him a tank of tropical fish.

And nobody dared miss an episode, because if they did they might never know who the father of Jennifer's baby was. (For those still in the dark it was Paddy Redmond, Phil Archer's quarrelsome red-haired dairyman – Aunt Laura sniffed him out.)

Through the summer of 1967 yet another story was afoot, involving people with false identities. Valerie Woolley, who had so long ago been revealed as an MI6 agent, was suspected of having an affair with young Roger Patillo, who had revealed himself to be Roger Travers-Macy. It only needed Doris to reveal her true identity to be Squire Lawson-Hope's natural daughter for the entire village to collapse with shock – but, in the event, the shock Doris caused all Ambridge, and six million listeners, was to be coshed and left unconscious by a burglar who broke into Brookfield Farm.

Godfrey Baseley, speaking on Canadian radio back in 1960, had revealed many of the tricks of writing a successful soap opera. 'Always run three stories,' he had said, 'one of a week's duration, one of a month's duration, and one for a longer period, say up to three months. It is through these longer stories that you are able to maintain the attention of your audience and make it necessary for them to continue to listen the following night.' And he had revealed other cunning methods to keep listeners away from the pub, the allotment, and the flickering TV

Recording *The Archers* in London during the mid-Sixties, Gwen Berryman was greeted at Broadcasting House by Jessie Matthews who played Mrs Dale. The two leading ladies did not get on. Jessie Matthews told the press that she greatly enjoyed *The Archers* but Gwen said bluntly that she did not listen to *The Dales*.

Hulton Deutsch

screen. 'Never satisfy them,' he advised the Canadians. 'And even if one of your stories must come to an end, make it end in the middle of an episode and start on a new one immediately.' End every scene, said Godfrey, with a question, or with a situation that needs further explanation. End every night on an 'upward questioning inflection'.

Skilful plotting, stories woven in and out, mystery, suspense, and the workings of a vivid imagination – it might almost have been Geoffrey Webb back writing again, and perhaps it was, because Norman Painting, who had been thrust suddenly into the job of writing half the scripts, believed that the spirit of Geoffrey Webb was guiding his pen.

He was sitting at his typewriter one day when he was aware of Geoffrey Webb in the room with him, and heard him laugh. 'Fanciful? Self-deception? Wishful thinking?' he would write later in *Forever Ambridge*. 'Up to this time I had written fairly slowly. Now, suddenly, I wrote very fast, at white-hot speed . . .'

Painting believed that Geoffrey Webb was guiding his hand from beyond the grave, 'from another level of existence'. It was a confession, he said, that he did not expect anyone to believe. We do not need to believe it literally. Norman Painting had acted Geoffrey's lines week in, week out, for seventeen years. He was mentally in tune with Geoffrey's style, the way he thought, the way he developed scenes. They had become friends during that final illness, when Geoffrey had given him help with his writing. 'His loss to the programme was incalculable,' Painting wrote when he died.

At last Ted Mason had a fellow writer who understood the programme and its characters, who was not a Scottish romantic or a radical Sixties playwright. Norman Painting – whether influenced from beyond the grave or not – was a writer who would hold the programme together during its most difficult years, and who would keep it true to its origins.

Jennifer's baby brought publicity on a scale not seen since Grace's death. The story had 'spoiled the whole character' of the serial according to one listener, while another called illegitimate babies 'a drastic innovation' and yet another said: 'What with gambling dens, take-over bids, adultery and unmarried mums, Ambridge is not improving.' The *Daily Mail* headline said: 'Miss Archer Expecting (BY KIND PERMISSION OF SIR HUGH GREEN)' and reported: 'Jennifer's baby was conceived over a cup of coffee in the BBC canteen by Godfrey Baseley and Ted Mason.' It went on to report that because the baby had been born out of wedlock, the storyline had been referred to the Director-General 'and his advisers' for approval. It quoted twenty-six-year-old actress Angela Piper as being embarrassed by the reaction of her neighbours in Roydon, Essex: 'They're shocked. They seem to think it is really me . . . they're not sure whether they ought to speak to me.'

There were letters, too, from people who believed that it was all actually happening. A listener wrote to Peggy: 'Just a few lines, did you know that your Jennifer is expecting a baby in six months time . . . Theres only three people who know about it. The doctor, the vicar, and your daughter Lillian.' Two sisters in Hove wrote: 'We sincerely sympathise with you for the terrible heartbreaking news you will receive from your daughter Jennifer sooner or later,' and went on: 'Your parents the Archers will rally round you, and Jack your husband you will find hidden depths of love and kindness in him . . .' But they had little sympathy for the girl who had become pregnant without a wedding ring on her finger: 'If one is not ashamed of that there is nothing else worth being ashamed of! Find the father and make him marry her.'

To add to the public confusion, Angela Piper was herself pregnant. The *Sun* printed a photograph of her with her two-day-old son Benjamin, and she received a letter from a London couple, offering her a roof over her head if Jack and Peggy turned her out. They'd redecorated the best bedroom, they said, and they even told her which train to catch.

The mystery over the father's identity became a national obsession. A television documentary producer, filming in the directors' dining room of a major industrial company, claimed to have been quizzed solidly for two hours by the men he was supposed to be interviewing. June Spencer discovered that her little girl had been called away from her ballet lessons by the school's proprietress, Dame Marie Rambert, and questioned in depth.

A BBC audience survey showed that for once *The Archers* had caught the national mood: 'The scenes concerning Jennifer were beautifully handled by the scriptwriters and the conversation between her and the vicar was especially warmly praised.' In the House of Lords, Baroness Serota declared that Doris Archer's acceptance of the illegitimate child (Doris had declared, tearfully but stoutly, that 'A baby is a baby and that is all that matters') had represented a 'sensitive and courageous step' by the BBC.

In the summer Gwen Berryman and Monte Crick went jaunting off round Scotland. The Scottish Tourist Board had complained bitterly about their Irish trip so, after the birth of baby Adam in June, Godfrey Baseley and Tony Shryane took Dan and Doris holidaying north of the border. It was a happy time for Gwen. Fears that the programme might be axed had receded – indeed, it seemed more successful than ever. She and Monte were a hit at the Braemar Gathering. In Aberdeen she was given a butter dish by an old-age pensioner, who told Gwen it was the only thing of value she possessed, and pleaded that it be used in the kitchen at Brookfield. 'I cried and the tears rolled down my face,' said Gwen, 'as I tried to tell her how much the gift meant to me . . .'

There was tragedy among the cast. Bill Payne, the plumber from Ebrington in Gloucestershire, died, and so Ned Larkin died with him. Since 1956 Ned had been one of the programme's best-loved characters, renowned for his famous stories about the mythical Coppy Treadwell.

Godfrey Baseley was still keeping Equity at bay, pursuing his policy of employing genuine countrymen with genuine country accents whenever he could. After Bill Payne's death he brought in George Hart to play Ned's son, Jethro. George was born, bred, and still lived at Chipping Campden, only a couple of miles from Ebrington. He had a broad Gloucestershire accent and looked for all the world like a village rustic. In future years he would sit quietly waiting to record his episodes, deep in the thoughts of a countryman, musing perhaps (young actors up from London on the Intercity 125 would surmise) on seedtime and harvest. When not recording in Birmingham he was often to be found in the back bar of the Red Lion in Chipping Campden still pondering deeply.

Appearances, however, were deceptive. George was a former captain in the Eighth Army and a Freeman of the City of London. During the war he had hauled a German piano from North Africa to Italy, then through France, Belgium and into Germany itself – terrorizing Hitler's armies with the sound of his concert parties.

Another genuine country character was brought into the programme. Mollie Harris was cast to play Martha Lily, widow of Herbert Lily, postman of Penny Hassett. Mollie was an Oxfordshire girl who had worked on farms in the early Fifties, singling sugarbeet and sorting potatoes for two shillings an hour. She had become popular on Midland Region radio as a cookery writer and giver of country 'talks' and was to write a highly-praised autobiography of her childhood called *A Kind of Magic*.

Casting people who had drifted accidentally into acting – through village concerts like Bob Arnold, or amateur dramatics like George Hart, or through wireless 'talks' like Mollie – would soon be a thing of the past. 'Eventually they had to join the union,' said Godfrey Baseley, sadly, and indeed no other actors would be taken on in this manner. Soon they would all be professional, all of them the product of drama schools, all of them members of Equity. But George Hart's 'My eye! Master Phil,' was as authentic and true as the Cotswold Hills themselves, and gave the programme a reality that no stage-school actor could equal.

17

End of the Sixties

FOR A TIME THE PROGRAMME was back in fashion – a programme to be listened to, not to be laughed at; a programme with its finger on the pulse of English life. Audience figures were healthy at five million – a million down on 1965, but nobody blamed the storytellers of Broad Street. 'Tastes have changed ... television has extended its grip,' said a London BBC document, resigned, finally, to the loss of radio's pre-eminence. At least the overseas market for *The Archers* was still expanding: in 1968 Botswana joined the list of countries listening in to Ambridge life. There was justified pride when members of the Writers' Guild awarded a 'scroll of merit' to Ted Mason and Bruno Milna to mark the quality of their scripts in 1967. Bruno Milna was the pen name used by Norman Painting. He had thought of calling himself George Farmer, or possibly N.P. Kay (N, P and K representing the plant nutrients nitrogen, potassium and phosphorus) but had settled finally on Bruno Milna. 'Oh Bruno, Bruno!' a young, over-ample Italian girl in a swimsuit had once called out to him, mistaking him for her boyfriend. Milna, he had worked out, was a name capable of being pronounced without alteration in almost every European language.

For the first time, *The Archers* showed signs of becoming a cult. Bradford University had a fan club, as did the University of East Anglia (members wrote to say they particularly liked 'the high moral tone'). A fan club started in Wales, and two in the Home Counties. Before the end of the year a national Ambridge Appreciation Society was formed.

How different it all was from the fortunes of *Mrs Dale's Diary*. Despite the best efforts of London drama department – based in Broadcasting House, just north of Oxford Circus and only a Rolling Stone's throw from Carnaby Street – Mrs Dale and Jim had never learned to swing. Perhaps *Mrs Dale's Diary* was too close to its enemies. Perhaps the London radio producers were too busy swinging themselves to care about the gentle saga of a middle-aged middle-class doctor and his wife. Perhaps they found a better use for the programme budget. Who knows? The skeletons still lie dark in the Broadcasting House cupboards. In 1968 *The Dales*, as it was called in its last attempt to get 'with it', was chopped.

The *Archers* cast were not malicious or unfeeling, but they felt safer. The thunderbolt had come down, as they had feared it would, but it had not come

Godfrey Baseley pictured in his study at home. In 1968 he was writing gardening features for the *Birmingham Mail*, writing *Archers* storylines, editing *Archers* scripts, and playing the part of Brigadier Winstanley in the programme.

Farmers Weekly

down on them. They noted the flood of protest letters to the BBC and to *Radio Times*, the brief surge of press interest, the obituaries – then the fall into oblivion.

It was 1968, and the world could not stand still – not when The Beatles were opening their Apple boutique, and the rock musical *Hair* was showing full-frontal nudity; when students were rioting in Paris, and Bobby Kennedy was being fatally wounded in Los Angeles; and when Martin Luther King was being gunned down in Memphis, and Russian tanks were rolling into Prague.

It was not a world for Mrs Dale and Jim. They were better off out of it.

Was it a world for Godfrey Baseley? In the early Sixties, in London, he had been disillusioned by metropolitan life and the bright young men of television. He had yearned for a world where the pace was steadier; a world free from the 'turmoil and complexities of life'.

Returning to the Midlands, and his freelance contract on *The Archers*, he had tried his hand as a public relations adviser. According to his own account he enjoyed 'considerable success' – only giving it up, he said, because *The Archers* was too demanding of his time. Those who know Godfrey might surmise that he lacked the oily charms and glossy ways of the PR man. Forty years of reading PR handouts and chucking them in the bin did not necessarily equip a man to write the things.

In 1968 he was gardening correspondent to the *Birmingham Mail* and writing features on the changing face of agriculture. He was sixty-four years old. When his contract as 'story consultant' on *The Archers* was renewed there was a significant change in his role – at least, as perceived by the BBC. Tony Shryane – who had been working on temporary contracts ever since leaving the Engineering Department in the early Fifties – was given a staff post. The status of a staff producer in the BBC was immeasurably higher than that of the freelance. A BBC booklet about *The Archers* in 1968 answered the question 'Who runs *The Archers*?' in the following way:

'In charge and responsible to the programme Head of BBC Midlands (David Porter) is Tony Shryane, the producer. The script-writers are Edward J. Mason and Brian Hayles (both resident in Birmingham) and Bruno Milna (who lives near Warwick). The editor is Godfrey Baseley . . .' This was low billing for the man still called 'God' by the actors; the man who still ruled over the stories, the cast, and the writers.

Within the programme Baseley had long ago invented a part for himself. He was Brigadier Winstanley, landowner and foxhunter, a role that allowed him to ride the actual pastures of Ambridge and keep an eye on things from the inside. What the actors felt when they met Godfrey's ferocious gaze across the microphone was never publically revealed.

Brigadier Winstanley was an important character in the late Sixties. It must have seemed to Baseley – as he mentally donned jodhpurs and pink coat for a day with South Borset Hunt, or a ride round Ambridge bossing his tenant Greg Salt about – that he was still firmly in charge of events, both inside and outside the story.

But his grip was not as firm as it had been. In 1968, when Tony Shryane was made a staff producer, there commenced the story of Brigadier Winstanley's downfall.

In 1969 it was announced that Canada and Australia no longer wanted to take *The Archers*. (In the programme, Brigadier Winstanley was brought crashing to the ground by hunt saboteurs, cracking his ribs and injuring his knee.) It was a loss for which Botswana could not compensate. New Zealand remained faithful, as did the British Forces Network, but the cast suffered an immediate drop in income of one-third. There was no talk of strikes or walk-outs. They were all as quiet as mice. Two-thirds, they said to each other, was a lot better than no thirds.

Monte Crick – who was ill, seemingly with acute laryngitis – told them they were lucky even to be working, in a profession so famously insecure, and doubly lucky to be working on a programme they all enjoyed. He would not be with the programme himself for much longer. He and Anne Cullen had married five years previously, and it was now Anne who told Tony Shryane that her husband's throat complaint was far more serious than anyone had suspected.

Monte Crick had cancer of the throat. Doctors had told Anne that he had only a few months to live. She asked that nothing be done in the programme to make him suspect the truth, and – it being, perhaps, a gentler age, or perhaps *The Archers* itself having a team loyalty that was beyond the normal – both the cast and production team conspired to put an optimistic face on events, to pretend that everything was all right. When he could no longer climb the two flights of stairs to the Broad Street studio – those stairs that had finally been too much for Harry Oakes, and up which Gwen Berryman toiled even now, despite her arthritis, fearful of being written out – a small studio was made available for him on the ground floor, where he recorded separately from the rest of the cast.

Anne Cullen brought him to the studio each week. She also played her part as Carol Tregorran. In the scripts for this period she had to act the role of a happy woman, newly-married to the man she had always loved, and looking forward to having a baby (Anna Louise born in September 1969).

Monte Crick died on Easter Monday. 'Their days together had been all too short,' wrote Norman Painting, 'their delight in each other and in the programme was disarmingly obvious.'

Another Dan Archer was cast: Edgar Harrison, a Bristol actor whose voice closely matched that of Monte Crick. He was given a medical examination before being confirmed in the part. Gwen Berryman had to get used to yet another fictional husband, and at first she was cold and unfriendly towards him. She did not confuse fact with fiction, as she had when Harry Oakes died, but she resented acquiring a new husband without having any say in the matter. 'It was not something I could talk to the man himself about,' she said in *The Life and Death of Doris Archer*, 'because he would have thought I was dotty to get so worked up about a simple change of casting.'

She thought Edgar Harrison looked too old. She herself had aged alongside Monte without noticing. Now she was playing opposite a man who was clearly not in the prime of youth, or the prime, even, of middle age. It was even worse when she discovered that Edgar Harrison was a year younger than she was herself.

She eventually settled down, comforted, perhaps, by the knowledge that if her husbands were disappearing without her being consulted, at least they were being promptly replaced.

In Ambridge, as the Sixties drew to a close, Jennifer married Roger Travers-Macy and they took a flat in Borchester. Lilian married a Canadian Air Force pilot called Lester Nicholson – a pointless story, this, designed to suck-up to the Canadians, but they dropped the programme all the same, and it was another year before the scriptwriters felt they could decently kill him off.

Reflecting the perceived new tenor of rural life, Polly Perks and Walter Gabriel were attacked in the post office by a thug and Polly suffered a miscarriage. At the Bull, Jack opened a 'Playbar' with fruit machines and espresso coffee. It was a year of minor stories: Irish barmaid Nora McCauley married tenant farmer Greg Salt; Dan, Phil, Jack Woolley and Brigadier Winstanley joined together in a shooting syndicate; Jill stood for the Rural District Council; Paul Johnson sold his garage business to Ralph Bellamy – a succession of the sort of 'so-what?' stories that scriptwriters come up with when they can't think of anything better; fodder to keep the story machine turning over, stories that one writer starts and other writers avoid because they can't remember all the boring details.

In the last months of 1969, though, Godfrey Baseley and his writers buckled down to plot another major story: a story they believed would seize the headlines, grip the nation, and divert attention from the new threat of colour television; a story to make Canada and Australia regret their decision to drop the programme.

After Jennifer's Baby would come the story of What Happened to Jennifer's Baby.

18

Kidnapped!

THE STORY BROKE ON THE AIR in January 1970. Jennifer and Roger Travers-Macy – who were living in Borchester – received a threat that Adam, now two and a half, would be kidnapped unless a large sum of money was paid over. Jennifer, instead of telling the police, promptly sent Adam to stay with Jack and Peggy at the Bull in Ambridge – at which point the kidnappers descended, snatched Adam in broad daylight, and carried him off.

Godfrey Baseley and the writers expected the story to have as big an impact as that of Adam's conception and birth. In truth, it was a melodrama too far. Listeners were incredulous and there was a surge in letters of complaint. Godfrey's 'hierarchy' in London reacted sharply. 'That we are in trouble is now becoming very obvious to our most loyal and keen listeners,' wrote the Controller of Radio 4, 'particularly those who have always appreciated the accuracy and authenticity of the programme.'

So what was wrong with the story of Adam's kidnapping? *The Archers* had carried stories almost, if not quite, as fantastic in the past. There was a faint shadow of justification – Roger Travers-Macy's father was a very rich man – though why kidnappers should believe he would stump up for the illegitimate child of his son's wife by another man was not explained.

Unlike the original story of Adam, the kidnap story was not rooted in character or in probability. In the mid-Sixties Jennifer had been the most genuinely modern character in Ambridge – a teenager wearing lipstick and stiletto shoes at fifteen; going off to teacher training college and getting thrown out of her flat for riotous behaviour; having a relationship – its precise nature left ambiguous, as so many parents of the time were forced to leave their daughters' relationships – with a man her parents did not trust; riding a scooter and writing a novel (this storyline only taking flight from reality when the novel was supposedly published). When Jennifer became pregnant it was an event true to her character. Everybody could hold an opinion. The story reflected the national debate about the Younger Generation, Flower-Power, declining moral standards, and the dangers of trusting – or failing to trust – the contraceptive pill.

The kidnapping story did none of this. It did not even conform to the basic precepts of soap opera – those precepts that Ted Mason and Godfrey had during the past twenty years actually created, precepts that were being learned and followed by the writers of *Coronation Street* and *Crossroads*. It was not a story that could be kept going over weeks and months, with new twists and developments. It was impossible, in fact, to have a tragedy of such proportions in the heart of the programme and still continue with other stories. Jack and Peggy could not be heard arguing about the fate of the Playbar when their grandson was being held prisoner; Dan and Doris could not ponder over their holiday plans, Walter Gabriel could not indulge in comic antics, when little Adam had still not been found. The story did not involve any clash of moralities. There was no opportunity for opposing points-of-view: nobody in the saloon bars of England would speak up in the kidnappers' interest.

After only the briefest attempt to string the story along (suspicion fell on young Sid Perks, Brummie tearaway trying to make good), the kidnappers were discovered in Birmingham. They were called Henry Smith and Chloe Tempest and were total strangers – yet another sign that the writers had lost their way, an elementary rule of crime detection being that listeners, or readers, feel cheated when the villain turns out to be somebody that no one has ever heard of.

It was all over within a week. Adam was brought back home. The writers hurried to extricate themselves from a story that neither they nor anybody else believed in. Dan and Doris started talking about nothing but their impending move to Glebe Cottage and Lilian and Nick's plan to go to Canada so that Nick could have specialist treatment for his eye complaint. A collective amnesia fell over Ambridge, an amnesia that unfortunately did not extend to the Radio 4 bosses in London.

There was a hard and critical look at current storylines. They were judged to be dire. Controller Radio 4 said that if the situation was allowed to go on for much longer he would find it difficult to justify the programme as being what it advertised itself to be: a 'reflection of the social and economic life of the countryside'.

Brigadier Winstanley, as he rode to hounds on those cold bright February days of 1970, might well have twitched uneasily.

The *Archers* cast knew the programme was doing badly. It was the year of *Broadcasting in the Seventies*, the year when radio networks were reorganized. Radio 4 was re-styled. The old regional services were axed and many programmes were chopped with them. When the 5,000th episode came round, the cast did not wait for the BBC to throw a party – they threw one themselves. They invited everybody of importance they could think of, and were relieved when not only the Director-General, Charles Curran, but the new Managing Director of Radio, Ian Trethowan, and the new Controller of Radio 4, Tony Whitby, came up to Birmingham to partake of the feast they had dug so deeply into their pockets to provide.

Gwen Berryman was in two minds about attending the party. She was upset that Dan and Doris were going into retirement at Glebe Cottage – a move that underlined her own increasing age. She wondered if she ought to give it all up, and retire to a little Glebe Cottage of her own somewhere. Her health had taken a turn for the worse: on top of her arthritis she had developed Bell's palsy, which caused her facial muscles to distort, and she had recurring scalp trouble from psoriasis.

In the end she bought a new evening dress, went to the party and enjoyed herself. Indeed, all the cast enjoyed themselves. There was a nice editorial in *The Times* for them to pass around – they had a 'vast listenership' and brought 'a whiff of unpolluted air to people who don't know a pig from a potato and for whom Spring is three daffodils in a window box'. Charles Curran cut the cake (made in the shape of a reel of recording tape), and said, 'The longer I stay the longer the series stays. I have been involved with *The Archers* almost since its beginning.' The cast listened to Godfrey Baseley announce: 'Farming and the countryside are entering a very exciting decade with intensive methods of farming and increasing use of the country for leisure purposes,' and he told them that they would be part of the exciting decade themselves, helping to interpret and explain these changes to their listeners. It was 'one of the best celebrations of an *Archer* anniversary in a long series,' said Norman Painting, and next day the *Daily Telegraph* agreed and said the programme was set to run for another ten years.

It was only the *Morning Star*, always fascinated by *The Archers*, that saw something different. As the organ of the Communist Party of Great Britain it was well used to sniffing out conspiracies and plots. It had no direct knowledge, we can assume, of behind-the-scenes threats to *The Archers*, no mole in the privy councils of BBC Radio, but its correspondent was there at the feast. He spotted the falsity behind the smiles of Ian Trethowan and Tony Whitby. He recognized that it was 'more like a night of the long scythes than a convivial occasion', and that the actors were 'more concerned with contracts than compost and combine harvesters'. Godfrey Baseley's speech, he said, was liberally laced with hope that the programme would continue, while the Director-General's reply 'gave no indication that Mr Baseley's hope for the future was founded in fact'.

In the short term nothing was done to change the programme. It was a turbulent summer for the BBC. Reorganization meant that Midland Region was now designated a Network Production Centre and would have a new boss. A job that had never existed before was advertised in the press: Network Editor, Radio. The man appointed (all the decision-making jobs were held by men in those days) would be directly in charge of all network radio from the Midlands.

Godfrey Baseley sat down with Tony Shryane and attempted to pre-empt criticism. They wrote a paper (at least, Baseley wrote a paper) called '*The Archers* as Radio Entertainment in the 1970s' which posed the question 'Is there a future for a programme that explains changes in agriculture and the countryside?' so that they could answer 'Yes.'

Baseley wrote that it was no longer possible to think in terms of roses round the door and quaint old village pubs and 'gaffers' sat on the bench outside. But

Asked in 1995 if he had a favourite character and actor in *The Archers*, Godfrey Baseley replied:
'Tom Forrest was my favourite – and Bob Arnold played him very well.' Bob Arnold started
working life as a butcher's boy in Burford, then progressed to painting white lines on the road for
Oxfordshire County Council. He was a pub singer (Bob Arnold – the Farmer's Boy!) when the
BBC used him in a rural programme in 1937.
Camera Press: Tom Blau

human problems still existed, he said, relating to age, health, youth, social life and administration.

The document said that the programme should concentrate more on the Archer family, and that Phil should take over the role of father figure in the place of Dan.

It indulged in the traditional obsession with percentages: was the balance of 60 per cent entertainment, 30 per cent information, and 10 per cent education the best? It concluded that the percentages were just about right, although perhaps there should be a documentary flavour, that would 'explore a range of issues from the social and political to economic and administrative – but without reducing the programme's entertainment value.'

It was a document designed to placate the *Broadcasting in the Seventies* men, the new rulers of Birmingham's Network Production Centre. In the event the new men had their own ideas, and Godfrey would have been better employed on improving the quality of *Archers* scripts.

The programme was drifting, sorting out loose ends, repeating stories from the past. Lilian and husband Lester Nicholson flew off to Canada, so that the writers could kill off Nicholson quietly out of sight – there was no point to making a song and dance in Ambridge with such a doomed character. Walter Gabriel found £500 in used banknotes down the back of a sofa, and the police thought it was part of Nelson Gabriel's ill-gotten gains (Nelson told them, smooth as ever, that he had hidden the money in the chair as a surprise present for his father). At Brookfield Farm, Jill reflected the modern age by getting a French au pair. Tony talked about emigrating to Australia. Dan arranged for the erection of a sun lounge extension at Glebe Cottage for Doris's birthday (amnesia fell over the sun lounge: built, greeted with joy, almost immediately forgotten about).

In October 1970 there was another edition of the *Borchester Echo* – and moving with the times it wasn't actually the *Echo* newspaper that went on sale to the public, but a 'Colour Supplement'. It had a picture of Phil and Jill standing looking at Brookfield Farm, and the caption 'The Fourth Generation Takes Over'. It tried to relate Ambridge to the outside world – Jennifer Travers-Macy saying: 'I did try living it up, attempting to convince myself that Borchester was "Swinging London" but it didn't work out,' and Lilian saying: 'I do feel the lure of the bright lights from time to time. Trouble is, when I'm there, I suddenly remember my ponies . . .'

Lilian was played by Liz Marlowe, an actress whose voice greatly excited male listeners. Many of them wrote to her. 'There are more invitations to illicit weekends than proposals of marriage,' she told *Farmers Weekly*, whose reporter visited Birmingham to write an article on the forthcoming twentieth anniversary of the programme, and found her in the Green Room knitting jumpers and reading stories to her small daughter.

The reporter also interviewed other members of the cast. 'I hear the Tregorrans are heading for disaster,' he said chattily to Philip Morant, who played John

Tregorran. 'It's the first I've heard of it,' Philip replied, startled. 'Jennifer's going through a pretty difficult time,' he said to Angela Piper, and Angie replied robustly: 'Oh, she always is. I haven't much sympathy for her really.' Colin Skipp, playing nineteen-year-old Tony Archer, was revealed to be actually thirty. 'I try to sound younger and more enthusiastic,' he said, and stoutly defended his non-agricultural background: 'Last October I spent two days at Shropshire Farm Institute'.

By the autumn of 1970 the new posts at BBC Birmingham had been filled. Godfrey Baseley, Tony Shryane, and the writers were invited to meet the new head of Production Centre, Alan Rees. At the meeting was a young journalist called Jock Gallagher. They all knew him slightly – he had been a reporter on a paper in Sutton Coldfield, and had worked for a short time in the BBC Midland regional newsroom in Broad Street – one of those shadowy news people who did not always have the respect they might have had for *Archers* artistes, and occasionally whistled 'Barwick Green' when older members of the cast were puffing their way up those two terrible flights of stairs.

Jock Gallagher, they now learned, had been appointed to run all network radio programmes from the Midlands. At the meeting he joked that he had always resented *The Archers* because it had killed off his boyhood hero, Dick Barton.

The story got back to the cast, reached Gwen's ears, and worried her terribly.

Godfrey Baseley's views on the future were ignored ('I wrote a long memorandum to nine top BBC executives and got no reply,' he later raged), but this was perhaps as well: in other places, at this time, he was predicting that most of South West England, Wales and north Derbyshire would have to be designated as 'leisure parks' where animals could be used as mowing machines in the spring and summer and then dispatched to intensive housing or the abattoir. Milk supplies would soon all be canned or dried, he believed, and all potatoes canned, dried or frozen. As far as Ambridge was concerned, he saw it as 'one farm linked direct to the processors'.

Gallagher, the new boss, was concerned with the present. He was horrified by the hostility he found to *The Archers* in London. Listening to the programme he was deeply depressed. 'When the stories weren't insipid they were incredible,' he said later. 'One minute the cast was drooping over the teacups, the next Jennifer's son was being kidnapped. People were switching off in droves.'

He told Tony Shryane: '*The Archers* needs to be less cosy, and it needs to reflect current behaviour in society' – an echo of what Ted Mason had been saying for years. He told Shryane to avoid propaganda, however worthy the cause. There was no longer a need to 'educate' small farmers or, if there was, it should be done elsewhere. The job of *The Archers* was to entertain.

Tony Shryane carried the message back to Baseley and the writers. 'Not all of us agreed,' said Norman Painting, which was a considerable understatement, and Baseley declared himself totally opposed to the views of the new radio head, the 'young townie' who was trying to subvert his programme. There was to be no re-thinking *The Archers*, not while he was in charge.

Jock Gallagher said later: 'I wrote privately to Tony Whitby, Controller Radio 4. I said that *The Archers* was a valuable BBC property. It was especially important at that moment that it should maintain its hold on the radio audience as the schedule patterns changed. If, in order to ensure this, we had to make radical changes . . . then we should not fear to do so.'

The axe was poised over Brigadier Winstanley. By the end of 1970 only political caution, the caution that successful BBC executives drink in with their mothers' milk, was stopping it from slicing down.

There was no party to celebrate the twentieth anniversary of the programme. Norman Painting's book *Forever Ambridge* records that 'Jock Gallagher dropped into the Green Room during rehearsals one Monday morning . . . we were told that the twentieth anniversary was being played quietly so that we could really go to town for the twenty-first the following year.' (In private, Norman Painting said that the story of the visit to the Green Room was all nonsense – it had been inserted by the BBC when they vetted his book before publication.)

In January 1971, the *Sunday Times* marked the anniversary by publishing a letter accusing *The Archers* of ham acting, superficial relationships and 'facile analysis'. The actors, said the critic, should all have been given the OBE and an Equity pension, 'in recognition of the dreadful experiences they have undergone merely in order to make a living'.

There was a flood of indignant replies from loyal listeners, but also many letters of support for the *Sunday Times*.

In February Ted Mason died in a Birmingham nursing home. He was writing *Archers* scripts to the end – a hundred of them in his last year. He, more than anyone, had kept the programme going during the Sixties – that most difficult decade which saw *Mrs Dale's Diary* go under. He more than anyone had sought that elusive 'teenager', had struggled to keep *Archers* characters believable and its stories relevant. Had he not been ill, the Adam kidnap story would have been done very differently, or not done at all – in twenty years he and Geoffrey Webb had never bungled a story in such a way.

His last script was recorded the day before he died. 'With the passing of Ted, the last link with the origin of *The Archers* was severed,' wrote Godfrey Baseley. 'There is no one left in the Corporation who has any personal knowledge of that time when the idea was conceived . . . Somehow it brought to me a feeling of great loneliness, like being a stranger at a party where everyone was speaking in a foreign tongue.'

Norman Painting was now the only regular writer. After Ted Mason's death he was required to write fifty episodes in eighty days.

19

The Fall of Brigadier Winstanley

DENIS FOLWELL, THE ACTOR who had played Jack Archer since the first trial episodes in 1950, died in the summer of 1971. An actor of the old school, he had not been to RADA but had started his working life as a salesman, selling zip fasteners for ICI. He had somehow drifted into theatre management in London, and then into professional acting (he was the original radio Worzel Gummidge and played Larry the Lamb in *Toytown*) and had returned to his home city of Leicester after the war. He was a member of the BBC's Midland Repertory Company when Godfrey Baseley chose him to play Jack Archer: intuitive casting, for there was said to be much of Jack Archer's wayward spirit in the actor who played him.

Denis Folwell had not looked after himself. He had first developed tuberculosis as long ago as 1952, but had, he said, 'stopped taking the tablets because they interfered with my social life'. Illness had forced him to take repeated periods away from the programme – absences accounted for, in Ambridge, by Jack's little stays at the county hospital for mental disorders. 'I had seen him burn the candle at both ends,' said Gwen.

There were now only four members of the original cast left. Gwen Berryman, Norman Painting, June Spencer – who had returned to play her original role as Peggy – and Bob Arnold: and poor Bob was never acknowledged by the others as being an original, because he didn't join the cast until February 1951, when the programme was four weeks old.

Godfrey Baseley and Norman Painting met with Brian Hayles, the replacement for Ted Mason. They decided against trying to re-cast Jack Archer: Denis Folwell had played him for twenty years; it was impossible that any other actor should have the part. Within the programme it would make a dramatic and satisfying development for poor Jack – the restless, feckless serviceman returned from the wars to the village where he could no longer settle happily to the common round – to be released from his rack of alcoholism and failure. He would fall asleep in his chair, worn out with worry over the failure of the 'Playbar' in the Bull, over daughter Lilian's widowhood, over daughter Jennifer's acid tongue and illegitimate baby, and over teenage Tony's strange desire to emigrate to Australia. (What can actor Colin Skipp have done to have deserved the punishment of such a threat? No one who went to Australia ever came back, as Meg in *Crossroads* found out).

Jack would fall asleep, Godfrey Baseley decided, and Peggy would find him, and only slowly would she realize that he was dead.

The storyline was written and copied to Jock Gallagher, who promptly vetoed it.

Gallagher knew what Godfrey Baseley did not: that *The Archers* was in deadly danger of being axed. On his appointment as Network Editor, Radio, he had been invited to a private, informal lunch with Ian Trethowan, the new Managing Director, Radio, who had told him he had six months to turn *The Archers* round, or it would be taken off.

Trethowan had spelt out the job losses that would follow in Birmingham if the money and the slot were clawed back to London. He had made it clear that the money would not be allowed to stay in the Midlands and that a large part of Gallagher's empire was at risk. Gallagher, utterly shocked, had promised 'radical changes'.

The six months was gone. He feared every day that the next phone call he took from Trethowan or from the Controller, Radio 4, would open with the words: 'I've got some bad news about *The Archers*.' He was determined not to give London an excuse to make that call. However dodgy, however uncertain it had become, *The Archers* was one of the BBC's most famous properties, and it was in his care. Jack Archer must not be allowed to die, not until the storm clouds had dispersed and the 'radical changes' he had promised could somehow be put into operation. He insisted that the storyline should be rewritten.

Listeners heard Jack suddenly develop an illness – similar to Denis Folwell's own – and be sent to a sanatorium in Scotland, a bizarre geographic twist that somehow gave it all an air of reality and conviction: nobody would make something like that up, would they?

In fact, he was sent to Scotland because it messed up storylines when characters had to keep visiting him in Borchester General Hospital. Switzerland would have been better, but was presumably thought of as too esoteric; Wales was too close, and Scotland was the next nearest place with mountains.

Occasionally Peggy journeyed north to visit him, and tell him about events in Ambridge in this summer of 1971: about the campaign to keep Ambridge village school open, about John Tregorran's friend Hugo Barnaby who was opening a rural arts centre at Nightingale Farm; how young Tony was going out with a girl called Roberta from the stables, and how Doris was having trouble with decimal coinage. He was not, presumably, told how Nelson Gabriel, rolling in money, had 'forced his attentions' on Lilian one night at Hollowtree Flats but he was told all about Lilian's wedding to landowner Ralph Bellamy, where Tony had to take his Dad's place and give the bride away. At the reception they all thought of Jack, the bride's father, up there in Scotland, lying all alone in his hospital room looking out over the heather.

Why the script team ran such a story, which was bound to point up the oddness of Jack's illness, nobody now can say. By October, maintaining the storyline with any sort of credibility was becoming impossible. It was a dramatic necessity, Godfrey Baseley insisted, that Jack should either die or should be heard on the air. As he could not be heard he must be killed off. Tony Shryane was caught in the middle. Godfrey was telling him what to do, then Jock was telling him to do the opposite. In the end, Baseley went to see Jock Gallagher himself. Gallagher was implacable. Jack must be kept alive until after the twenty-first anniversary celebrations. If Jack must be heard, he said, they must get somebody to imitate Denis Folwell's voice.

The actor chosen was Edgar Harrison, the third Dan, who had already so successfully imitated the voice of Monte Crick. The scene was recorded one day after the cast had broken for lunch. Jack was heard on the telephone from his Scottish sanatorium – phoning home on his birthday, which was also his mother and father's golden wedding anniversary.

The next day Tony Shryane played the recording to the cast in the studio. When the voice of Jack Archer was heard saying 'Hello Peg!' the impersonation was so accurate that several members of the cast were visibly upset, and one of them, an old friend of Denis's, burst into tears. They were not just actors with the superficial friendship that actors cultivate when they know they will soon move to another company. The *Archers* 'family' had become very real. They had travelled the road together for over twenty years and many of them had become deeply involved in the characters they were playing. 'There have been times when I have cried at home after reading over a script that was particularly harrowing,' June Spencer had told the *Derby Evening Telegraph* in January 1971. 'One occasion which brought tears to my eyes was when Lilian lost her husband who was away working in Canada . . .' Here was an actress, weeping over made-up tragedy in the life of her fictional daughter.

June Spencer found it difficult to fully accept the death of Denis Folwell. She was troubled, as Gwen had been troubled all those years ago when Harry Oakes died but Dan did not. 'I simply didn't believe Denis was dead because we were still talking about Jack in the script,' she told *Woman* magazine. 'It was only when Jack died that it hit me. After that recording I went away and cried for both of them.'

Jack was not allowed to die until the beginning of 1972.

The BBC's new Network Production Centre at Pebble Mill was opened. *The Archers* left Broad Street, the tatty old studio over the car salesroom, and the little canteen the cast had shared for so long with vulgar news reporters. (In 1970 a hack from *Midlands Today* famously threw a plate of cottage pie at another reporter, and hit several members of the *Archers* cast instead.) Ambridge's corporeal existence went with them – the kitchen door at Brookfield Farm, the gate to Glebe Cottage, the recorded discs of pig noises and cows milking and pheasants rising on a winter's morning, all so carefully compiled by BBC Midland sound engineers over the years.

Pebble Mill was a new building in a leafy suburb. Gwen no longer had to toil up those two flights of stairs into the cramped confines of Studio 2. Now the fields and farms of Ambridge spread themselves luxuriously in Studio 3, Pebble Mill – 'the Rolls-Royce of radio!' – where the sound suite had thick carpets and comfy green chairs for the cast to sit on.

The centre was opened by Princess Anne. It was stage managed so that she would arrive at Studio 3 just as the villagers of Ambridge were clapping a concert in Ambridge village hall, thus enabling them – they were royalist to the core – to clap for her as well. It all went off nicely. She called Shula Archer 'that ghastly child' which at least showed that she listened. Gwen Berryman presented her with a solid gold medallion that had been struck to commemorate the twenty-first anniversary of the programme, and the Princess was privately reported by one member of cast to have said (believe it if you will) that she was 'right chuffed'.

A great number of copies of the medal were struck in shiny gold alloy for sale to the public: so many, in fact, that four years later they were being given away as 'entry tickets' for the twenty-fifth anniversary party.

A book appeared called *Doris Archer's Diary*, written by Jock Gallagher. The cast carped and criticized, partly over the faint Scottishness that infected Doris's words (calling girls 'lass') and partly because nobody had ever heard Doris mention a diary in all her years of married life. But there had already been a Doris Archer cookery book, and Doris's diary enjoyed similar success.

Behind the scenes Gallagher and Godfrey Baseley were still locked in battle. Audience research was devastatingly critical. In 1968, after the story of Jennifer's baby, almost 80 per cent of listeners believed the programme to be true to life. By 1971 only 60 per cent believed this to be the case. Godfrey Baseley was still insisting on his magic formula – 60 per cent entertainment, 30 per cent information, 10 per cent education – that had for so long transmuted base words into gold. Jock Gallagher was determined that it should be changed.

The time had come to act.

The Controller Radio 4, Tony Whitby – who was far from being an enemy of the programme – made a final attempt to influence Godfrey Baseley. He wrote a tactful memo pointing out the vast number of facts being provided to a Radio 4 listener during the course of a single day. He wanted *The Archers*, he said, to provide 'an island in this sea of information'.

Godfrey Baseley was unmoved.

A meeting was called, and in the face of Baseley's bitter opposition it was formally decreed that *The Archers*' mission to educate and inform should be jettisoned. From now on, farming facts and agricultural information should be included only when they formed part of the plot.

A great number of shiny alloy medallions of Dan and Doris were minted
to mark the twenty-first anniversary. They did not become collectors' items.
Bristol United Press

And so, at some point in the autumn of 1971, the last 'Min. of Ag.' handout
was heard on the airwaves. It was an event more significant in the history of *The
Archers* than any anniversary. Never again would farmers be told about the early
detection of warble fly ('I just happened to have my hand on her back when I was
washing her down from milking this morning') or the proper identification of
pig diseases ('Just because one of them might be troubled with scour it doesn't
necessarily mean she's got swine fever'). Farmers might listen eagerly, but they
would listen in vain. Twenty years later, people visiting the studio would still
smile knowingly and say how they listened out for the 'Min. of Ag. bits' – but
they were deluded. There have been none since 1971.

When Godfrey Baseley continued to voice his opposition he was told the
results of the latest audience research survey. For every listener who thought the
programme had improved in recent months, five thought it had deteriorated.

The writers set out to obey their new masters. Changes in the programme were
soon noted by Sean Day-Lewis in the *Daily Telegraph*. He said the programme
had become 'uniformly insipid' and Ambridge had become a village in which
those who were successful 'sound and think like a grey variety of Birmingham

business people, the more humble are goody-goody, and many of the bit parts are frankly embarrassing in both their writing and their acting.'

Norman Painting was upset by the criticism. He was writing to order, trying to provide the entertainment demanded, but his heart was with Godfrey Baseley and he agreed wholeheartedly with Sean Day-Lewis's final comment: 'Only if *The Archers* return to the land, its wonders, and its problems, will a 22nd birthday be justified.'

Shortly before Christmas Godfrey Baseley demanded that his name be taken off a week of programmes. He was talked out of it, but nothing was resolved. He was sixty-seven – long past the official age for retirement – and was only surviving because Jock Gallagher hesitated to wield the axe during a time of celebration.

In the New Year, the programme's twenty-first birthday party was held in the boardroom at Pebble Mill. The Controller of Radio 4, Tony Whitby, made a speech and Tony Shryane replied. There were no cheers for Godfrey Baseley, the true founder of the feast, because he was not there. He had sent a telegram of good wishes, but had refused to attend.

The bitterness was now out in the open. From the point of view of BBC management there was no longer any reason for delay. Gallagher said later, 'I wrote to London saying that Godfrey was a forceful character. For eighteen months I tried to make him see our point of view. Eighteen months was enough.'

Gallagher was ready with his 'radical changes.'

In March 1972, in his home near Tewkesbury, called 'Ambridge', Baseley received a letter saying that his contract was not being renewed. The letter said that a leading dramatist was being brought in to head the writing team.

He instantly told *The Times* that he had been dismissed without warning or consultation.

'The final decision was, to my mind, mutual,' said Jock Gallagher.

Godfrey told the *Daily Telegraph* that he had been sacked.

Jock Gallagher said: 'Godfrey and I had several long discussions over the preceding eighteen months about the way the programme should go. He, understandably, was adamant that things had gone extremely well for more than twenty years and that there was therefore no need for change. Tony Whitby and I thought differently.'

In Ambridge, Brigadier Winstanley had already gone. First he had withdrawn into seclusion, refusing to give advice on running his Ambridge estate, even when assured that his opinions were valued.

Then he had fallen while out hunting, and had died from his injuries.

20

The New Men

THE OLD ORDER HAD CHANGED. There were new men prowling the corridors and Godfrey Baseley, the brilliant storyteller who had single-handedly created the BBC's most successful radio drama, was vanquished. Brigadier Winstanley had been snuffed out.

They were lost and adrift, sluggishly bobbing along on Radio 4's airwave, trying to amuse Radio 4's acid, complaining listeners – so different from the old, amiable Light Programme crowd, those cheerful fans who were now, in their millions, watching *Crossroads* and quiz shows on ITV. *The Archers* had always been a people's programme. It had never been highbrow. It had captivated its audience with spies and skulduggery, with romances and the caperings of rascally Walter Gabriel. Now many of the old Radio 2 fans had forgotten they even existed ('*The Archers*? It isn't still going is it?' a member of the public marvelled to one of the cast in the early Seventies).

It was still going, just – sailing unknown seas with 'God' no longer at the helm, and all their futures were in the palm of a young Scotsman, a journalist. There were rumours of mass sackings and character write-outs. 'Neither *The Archers* as a programme nor the cast will be killed off,' Jock Gallagher told them firmly – but added, mysteriously, 'There might be some new voices – possibly younger ones, but this will depend on the new man.'

They didn't want a new man. Gwen Berryman said: 'I like the Archers as they are. Things are changing but I hope Ambridge doesn't become too trendy.' Anne Cullen was more practical: 'With seventy-five per cent of our profession out of work, I'm just too jolly pleased to read what they give me.'

Godfrey Baseley had not gone quietly. 'The BBC have too many "townies" at the top, they've lost touch with the country,' he thundered in the *Sunday People* in March 1972. Then he sold his story to the *Sun*. They ran it over several days, under the heading 'Spilling the Beans on *The Archers*'. WHY THEY KICKED ME OUT OF AMBRIDGE said the first headline. 'The BBC want a soppy soap opera, all cosy, and without any information or topicality . . .' said Baseley, adding that he had been paid only £3,000 a year to edit the programme, and had had to pay all his own research and secretarial expenses. He had been lucky, he said, to make £20 a week.

Gallagher edited the scripts himself while he searched for 'the new man'. It was a considerable burden – he was not just responsible for *The Archers*, he had the whole of the Midlands' network radio output under his wing: agriculture, the Midland Light Orchestra, talks and documentaries – so he asked Anthony Parkin, the producer of *On Your Farm*, to keep an eye on the agricultural side until the new editor was appointed. Parkin agreed – rather cautiously, because he had kept his distance from *The Archers* during his time as an agricultural programmes producer.

Everybody wondered who the new editor would be and when the name was announced, it came as a huge shock. Gwen Berryman said she was 'horrified'. It wasn't the name of the new editor that caused the upset – it was where he came from. Gallagher had pulled off a publicity coup. He had pinched Malcolm Lynch, the script editor from *Coronation Street*. (The only person shrewd enough to have foreseen his appointment had been Godfrey Baseley himself – 'They want to turn *The Archers* into a radio-style *Coronation Street*,' he had told the *Sunday People* sneeringly.)

Lynch abandoned the Rover's Return, the tales of Ena Sharples and Albert Tatlock, the romances of glamorous young Elsie Tanner. He swapped ageing juvenile-lead Ken Barlow for ageing juvenile-lead Phil Archer, and Minnie Caldwell for Mrs P and took the road south from Wetherby, Lancs, to Ambridge, Borsetshire.

He was immediately shown an audience survey – 'Many former listeners have stopped listening because they find the programme dull and the characters and the storyline unreal' – and Jock Gallagher said to him: 'I want you to examine every aspect of the scripts, from scene length and dialogue to characterization and content. I want you to take the programme apart.'

Gallagher had promised Ian Trethowan 'radical changes'. At last, he intended to deliver.

Malcolm Lynch sat at his desk in the *Archers* office. It was a thickly-carpeted, pleasant room on the fourth floor at Pebble Mill, overlooking the leafy quadrangle, one wall completely filled with *Archers* scripts bound in red and green, another wall bearing a painted map of Ambridge. It was a bit like a library, with production secretary Lynne Grainger quietly preparing for the studio, Polly Brain typing her scripts, and the programme assistant, Valerie Fidler, forever busy checking through those famous continuity cards.

He took out his pen and started to think up stories.

'The winds of change positively blasted through Ambridge as drama and realism became the order of the day,' wrote Gallagher later, with considerable satisfaction. Malcolm Lynch had been ordered to liven the programme up. He had done so. That Jack Woolley should be attacked by burglars was par for the course – Ambridge had suffered more violent robberies in twenty years than downtown

Chicago – but in late 1972 gossip in the village shop could hardly keep up with the news. In one week alone, as the *Observer* marvelled, there was 'a plane crash, a train crash, a quasi-rape and the church bells fell down' (actually Dan and Tom were checking the bells when a beam crashed down on top of Dan's head). Jill had a nervous breakdown. She walked out on Phil and the children, and disappeared to London, which would have provided enough gossip for a month had not Tony Archer been involved in a particularly violent punch-up with Joe Grundy and his sons (Alf and young Eddie) after Joe had spread rumours about Tony enjoying three-in-a-bed sex with two girls at Rickyard Cottage. Then Tom Forrest had a hoax phone call saying that Pru was in hospital seriously injured –

Breakfast at Brookfield, in the heyday of the programme. (Centre: Len Thomas, the shepherd, played by Arnold Peters.) In 1971 the new regime promised radical changes, and in one week alone there was a plane crash, a train crash, a quasi-rape, and a beam in the church fell on Dan's head. Godfrey Baseley would claim: 'The BBC has too many "townies" at the top. They've lost touch with the country.'
Hulton Deutsch: Bert Hardy

only to discover, after dashing into Borchester, that wicked poachers had stolen his pheasants.

Tony Parkin was sitting in his office one day when Malcolm Lynch appeared and demanded to know the name of a sheep disease. Parkin ran through a list of ailments and came to orf. 'Orf!' Malcolm cried out, 'Orf! That sounds good. How do you spell it?' He then hurried off, Tony would often recall, to kill half a flock from an ailment that had never before proved fatal.

Horrified, fascinated, amazed – dozens of listeners finally reached for their pens when the scriptwriters plumbed the very depths and Doris was heard slurring her words, inebriated after a cheese and wine evening.

'The BBC bosses described all this as "a breath of fresh air",' Gwen Berryman later wrote, 'but for those of us standing in the draught it felt more like a howling gale.' June Spencer commented that she was going not through her change of life, but through her change of script editor.

'Any proposed breath of change . . . is inevitably accompanied by melodrama of monumental proportions,' Gallagher had noted wisely, in the days when he first took over *The Archers*. As he had sown, so now he reaped. Letters of complaint poured in – not only to the *Archers* office in Birmingham, but to the Controller Radio 4 and the Director-General in London, to the newspapers and to *Radio Times*. Tony Whitby had declared that listeners wanted an 'island in this sea of information' and in this grim and gloomy year they were overwhelmed with information – hearing on *The World at One* about Direct Rule in Ulster, Americans dropping napalm bombs on Vietnamese children, Black September terrorists slaughtering Jews at the Munich Olympics, and the British embassy in Dublin being burned to the ground. On *The Archers* they wanted the reassurance of hearing, even if it was for the twentieth time, the story of the life cycle of the warble fly. They wanted to hear Phil come into the Brookfield kitchen on a bright, frosty morning with Jill saying 'There you are, Phil. One egg or two?' They did not want to hear that she had run off to London after a nervous breakdown, or that the new keeper on Woolley's estate was an alcoholic, or that Elizabeth was being rushed to hospital after eating mercury-dressed grain, or that Phil (amazingly the new leader of Ambridge Scout Troop with a bugle given to him by Jack Woolley) had crashed his car when suffering from overwork and stress.

Listeners to Radio 4 had enough overwork and stress in their own lives, thank you very much.

The cast were deeply despondent. 'During the most traumatic moments,' said one actor, 'the management maintained a tight-lipped silence, neither seeking our views nor offering their own.' At a script conference chaired by Jock Gallagher the flood of complaints was discussed at length. Malcolm Lynch conceded that 'the revolution had gone a bit too far'. It was agreed to tone down the aggravation and dramatic tension – but not too much, because it was also reported that, for the first time in several years, the audience figures had actually increased.

This may have been true. More than likely it was made up. Radio listening by the Seventies was so low and fragmented that accurate figures over a short space of time were – and are – virtually meaningless.

In the last twenty years there have been more lies told about *The Archers* listening figures than there are pebbles in the Am.

Gwen Berryman discovered (though she ought not to have done, for the information was confidential) that Doris Archer was no longer the most popular character in the programme. She was now only the sixth favourite. She blamed Malcolm Lynch and the new scriptwriters: 'As young men, they did not really understand the ways of an elderly lady. Nor did they seem inclined to try. Unlike Ted Mason and Geoffrey Webb, they did not come to talk to us very much.'

In the programme Doris had become very odd. She had become irritable and had taken to going out early in the morning without saying where she was going. When finally challenged by Dan, she said it was to teach him a lesson for going to Scotland with Jack Woolley and not returning when he said he would. No wonder Gwen felt she was falling in popularity. She tried to resign – to 'hand in my cards' as she put it. As usual Tony Shryane talked her round. In truth it had only been a demand for reassurance, rather like Doris's queer behaviour in the programme.

Another illness, but from a totally unexpected quarter, devastated not only the victim but Jock Gallagher's hopes and plans. After only a matter of months Malcolm Lynch became seriously ill. He took time off, tried to return to work, then said he would have to leave. 'The strain of his enormous efforts to change the direction of a great institution was too much and after less than a year in the job he was forced to give up and retire to the peace and quiet of the West Country,' wrote Jock Gallagher, who was finding *The Archers* something of a handful himself, and perhaps, in odd moments, yearned for a bit of peace and quiet as he again pushed his other duties to one side and became emergency script editor. *The Archers* might be the jewel in BBC Radio's Midland crown, but it was a demanding jewel, a jewel with a price.

When not working on scripts late into the night, Gallagher started looking round for a new editor. The writers, and the actors, and most certainly Anthony Parkin, fervently hoped for one with knowledge of the English countryside, a man steeped in farming as Godfrey had been. Some members of the cast, indeed, hoped that Godfrey might return. Perhaps, far away in his little village, Godfrey himself waited for the call. If he did, then he waited in vain.

It was time for reassurance. Time for things to settle down. It was time, at long long last, for the professionals to have a go. After more than twenty years, the BBC's radio drama department was to be allowed to peek inside the portals of the BBC's most famous radio drama. The new script editor was to be a London man, one of the BBC's most respected drama producers. His name was

Charles Lefeaux. He had, in his time, been a noted actor on the West End stage. He had flowing white hair and a goatee beard and had recently retired. He knew nothing whatsoever about farming, or the countryside, other than what he learned from his daily walk on Hampstead Heath. He personified what Godfrey most loathed and distrusted: he was as far away from Ambridge as it was possible to get.

He did have one quality, however, that qualified him to fit as comfortably as Brigadier Winstanley into Ambridge. Just like Mike Daly, special agent; Valerie Grayson, MI6; Roger Patillo, aristocrat-in-hiding; and Mr Brown, mail-van robber of Paunton Farm, Charles Lefeaux had a hidden identity. When not producing radio dramas at Broadcasting House he travelled the country, incognito, as an undercover inspector for *The Good Food Guide*.

Calm and reassuring and good humoured, Lefeaux put the chaotic writing schedule into order. There would be three writers on the team, and they would each write a week in turn. Writer number one would send carbon copies of his scripts to writer number two, and carbon copies of his synopses to writer number three. Thus continuity would be improved and the stories would flow smoothly. There would be script meetings once a month to discuss storylines. It was how they had done things on *Mrs Dale's Diary* and how they did them on *Waggoner's Walk* (the new challenger to *The Archers* for radio soap opera popularity) and it was how they would now do them on *The Archers*. Each script, as written, would be posted to Lefeaux's flat in Hampstead. Late scripts would result in irate phone calls because Charles liked to edit scripts after breakfast and post them off, each day, to the production office in Birmingham where the programme assistant Valerie Fidler was ready with her index file to check for continuity errors.

The office in Birmingham, scene of so much turmoil and stress, settled into a placid routine. One day Tony Parkin went to see Jock Gallagher. He had done his two or three months on the programme, he said – in fact he had done well over a year. When was a permanent agricultural adviser going to be appointed?

As there wasn't actually any money in the budget for an agricultural advisor, and as Tony Parkin was doing the job terribly well, suggesting many stories on his own initiative, Jock said, in the wily manner of the BBC manager: 'Do it for just a bit longer, and I'll sort something out.'

And Tony, a trusting sort of chap, agreed to stay on for just a few more months. And he devised and printed up *The Archers' Agricultural Calendar* which showed every scriptwriter at a glance what was happening on all the farms in Ambridge at any given time of the year, so ensuring the farming pattern became authentic, the same as that of the West Midlands. And he arranged regular visits to farms, and used his own budget to buy a nice hotel lunch for Tony Shryane and Charles Lefeaux, and the three writers and production assistant.

Godfrey Baseley's vigorous leadership was ended. His wild if likeable successor had done his manic worst and had departed to the seaside. Now the world had come to rights; the revolution had swept through the fields and woods, but Ambridge had survived. Farming was back in the programme – mainly because nobody other than Tony Parkin had any ideas – and farming matters were reassuring, like the familiar burbling of a brook. The pace of events slowed as the writers made an awful lot out of very small ideas.

A drowsy cosiness fell over the programme. In the short term it was no bad thing. In the long term it would prove very dangerous.

21

The Deep Snooze

'ʜTony Shryane and company . . . contented themselves with a quiet period, consolidating their position,' Jock Gallagher would later write in a BBC-sponsored publication. Privately he would confide that the mid-Seventies were 'the Dog Days'. Extracts from an audience research report in 1974 sum it up: 'Some of the characters are so unpleasant and so wrigglingly embarrassing that one listens with an awful fascination'; 'Although I'm hooked on it, I find the serial is often trivial and boring with unreal characters'; 'It isn't interesting and it isn't worth hearing.' And a most pertinent comment, recognizable to every soap opera script editor going through a bad patch: 'Almost everyone in Ambridge seems abnormally selfish or bitchy and guaranteed to misunderstand everyone else and yet, at the same time, they are evidently meant to be normal and reasonably likeable people . . .'

Writers with no story to tell but fifteen minutes to fill, desperately getting mileage out of artificial arguments, making supposedly-intelligent people misunderstand things and take offence without reason just so that they can have a long and tedious reconciliation, characters either eating humble pie or – in the *Archers* jargon of the times – giving people 'a slice of tongue pie' . . . there was an emptiness at the heart of the storyline.

Attempts to write dialogue for young people were as uneasy as they had always been: middle-aged male writers still trying to be trendy. 'Just get that guy, what a hunk!' 'Yea, he's a real hunk!' said two teenage girls in one script, provoking an acid exchange about toe-curling false slang at the next script conference. Many stories were silly and unbelievable: Joe Grundy opened a caravan site; Walter Gabriel sent some tinkers to stay on it; Joe sent the tinkers back to Walter's caravan site; everybody chuckled or was scandalized. Relationships were formed and un-formed in a mechanical sort of way. Jennifer and Roger Travers-Macy parted, and she started going bowling with Woolley's second keeper, Gordon Armstrong (played by Midland TV's newsreader Tom Coyne), but the writers didn't have the heart for a real Lady Chatterley story. Jack Woolley proposed to Peggy but she refused him, and had an unconvincing friendship with an unconvincing salesman called Dave Escott. Shula became friendly with an older man, improbably called Eric Selwyn, a hi-fi fiend she had met at Borchester Tech. John Tregorran went on a lecture tour of America after warning Hugo Barnaby to stay clear of Carol. Nora, the Irish barmaid who had been living in sin with drunken gamekeeper George Barford, moved back to the Bull, then discovered she was pregnant, then had a convenient miscarriage.

It was all a bit dreary, if not actually sordid. Unimaginative stories that could just as easily have been done on *Waggoner's Walk*, punctuated by old, bad Archers influences that could never, seemingly, be eradicated. The postbus was attacked by bandits and escaped by driving through fields. The only casualty was Aunt Laura, who cracked her false teeth. After two comic scenes about teeth the story flickered out, never to be mentioned again. At the next script meeting the story was heavily criticized – why had the credibility of the programme been jeopardized for the sake of a few filler scenes? But Charles Lefeaux defended the story. Writers had to write about something. Post offices were raided in the country, he presumed, as often as in the town.

In the *Daily Mail* Shaun Usher wrote critically about the quality of the scripts, and stirred up Godfrey Baseley in his Tewkesbury fastness. In a Letter to the Editor entitled 'An Everyday Story of Trendy Folk' Baseley said that he had been made a sacrificial goat and described the new men running his programme as 'gimmicky boys' – which might have been an understandable comment about Jock Gallagher, but was a bit tough on an upstanding and mature BBC figure like Charles Lefeaux.

If anyone saved the scripts during this time it was Norman Painting, writing as Bruno Milna, and Anthony Parkin the agricultural editor. Painting represented continuity with the past – the influence, whether paranormal or not, of Geoffrey Webb. Alone on the script team, Norman believed passionately in *The Archers*, and what it represented. He summed it up: 'Two men see a pile of horse droppings in the road. One says, "See – that is life, that pile of stinking worm-infested corruption," and the other man says: "What splendid manure for the roses."' The second man would be an *Archers* listener. It was all a matter of how you looked at things.

Parkin was putting through a long-term plan to reorganize the farms in Ambridge so that they would more accurately represent a typical Midland village. This meant dismembering the Bellamy Estate. Lilian and Ralph retired to the Channel Islands, much to the annoyance of actor Jack Holloway, who found he had to go to Hong Kong and become a media personality. Actress Elizabeth Marlowe was more fortunate: Lilian would return on and off to Ambridge for several years, a rich, lonely widow, too fond of the bottle, maintaining an intriguing friendship with Nelson Gabriel, the man who raped her (almost) that hot summer's night long ago at Hollowtree Flats.

With the Bellamy Estate gone, Parkin was able to create Willow Farm (a 100-acre holding suitable for a new young farmer starting out on the ladder);

Bridge Farm; and the 1,500-acre Home Farm, which it was thought could be bought by a chap with money from outside the village. This man would be marginally more county than country, and was described in storylines for several months in 1975 as 'Mr Jennifer'. Brian Aldridge, as he was eventually named, was played by Charles Collingwood who had also played Peggy's smoothie conman Dave Escott.

Tony Parkin was also supplying a string of short-term agricultural stories that 'educated and informed' but in a lively and dramatic manner. Young farm apprentice Neil Carter forgot to give the Hollowtree pigs their iron injections, and they developed anaemia. Dan cut the feed to his in-lamb ewes on Lakey Hill, and several of them developed twin-lambing disease. At Brookfield, Phil tried growing maize, and was delighted with the results. Mary Pound was a village stalwart, worrying about husband Ken's poorly foot which he stabbed through his wellie with a pitchfork. Mary was played by Ysanne Churchman, now back in the cast: lovely, passionate young Grace Archer reincarnated as the gruff-voiced, thick-thighed Borsetshire women's ploughing champion.

Parkin was to say that the days when Charles Lefeaux was in charge were the most agreeable he spent on the programme; working with a small group of interested and involved writers whom he could educate in farming practice. Under the next editor he would be less happy.

If Charles Lefeaux was not improving script quality as quickly as Jock Gallagher wanted – according to audience research he was not improving script quality at all – he was working gently to remove the programme's more obviously dated elements. Ambridge's roadman, Zebedee Tring, was discovered dead in his cottage at Christmas 1973 – thus allowing a useful public service warning about old folks at the festive season, and getting rid of a caricature character with a ludicrous name. In one storyline Lefeaux told the scriptwriters to stop writing Mrs Perkins as 'Mrs Buggins'. The Sixties 'Steak Bar' at the Bull was modernized into the Seventies 'Ploughman's Bar'. Farm apprentice Neil Carter went to a wild party in Borchester with a girl called Sandy and cannabis was slipped into his pockets: the simple country lad deceived, everybody in the village stood by him.

Robin Freeman, Hugo Barnaby – *Mrs Dale's Diary*-type characters with soap opera names – were easing their way off the stage. John Tregorran was again dispatched on a long (very long) lecture tour of America: nobody wanted to kill off so famous a character, but the writers despaired of finding a story for him. Carol, on her own, could run the WI and have a few horticultural problems at her market garden.

Moving centre stage came Sid and Polly Perks and Jack Woolley (having endless trouble with his adopted daughter Hazel). At Brookfield, Shula was being heard, though only as a minor character. Judy Bennett, who played the part, was also playing Elizabeth her own younger sister, and Kenton her twin brother.

A shadowy character, Joe Grundy, used as a foil for Walter Gabriel, was starting to be heard more often. Joe talked about Alf and Eddie, his two sons, while at Brookfield, Jethro Larkin occasionally talked about his daughter Clarrie.

Characters from the past were being eased out, more believable characters were being eased in. But it was happening too slowly. Falling listening figures and low audience appreciation meant that something would have to be done and, as always, Jock Gallagher's taste was for the dramatic.

He told a quarterly script meeting that there was to be a major change of focus. Brookfield would no longer be the central farm. Jill and Phil would not, after all, take over in the place of Dan and Doris. The most interesting statistic revealed by the latest audience research was that *The Archers* had a slightly lower age profile than the average for listeners on Radio 4. The future success of the programme, he said (how many times had it been said before?) lay with the young folk.

A generation would be skipped. The new leading character would be young Tony Archer (as planned, interestingly enough, by Godfrey Baseley four years previously) struggling with his small farm. The other leading character would be Tony's wife, who would be a farm-secretary called Mary.

Tony and Mary – the future of *The Archers* – the future Dan and Doris?

Well, no. Tony and Mary became engaged in January 1974 (they had a party in the new Ploughman's Bar in the Bull) but the actress who was cast as Mary Weston was suddenly found to be unwilling to commit herself to a main role. To the annoyance of the writers she was frequently unavailable and her character had to be written out for long periods, just when they wanted her most. By the summer the writers lost patience. They would find another girl to lead Tony to the altar. Pat Lewis, a girl from the Valleys, was rapidly spirited to Ambridge to look after her Uncle Haydn. She proposed to Tony – who was a bit confused, understandably, about losing his first fiancée – and they were married by the end of the year. Pat quickly and mysteriously lost her distinctive Welsh accent, and after a relatively short time as Tony's wife emerged as a radical feminist.

So it was not Tony and Mary – it was to be Tony and Pat.

The writers did their best. For Tony to be the new Dan he had to be a strong, sturdy, manly character. To capture all those (mythical) teenage girl listeners he had to be a bit of a heart-throb. The writers gave him a sports car just as Phil, in his youth, had been given a motorbike.

For some reason it all failed miserably. When Tony sold his sports car to buy a van, it did not indicate strength of character – it just made him sound like a wimp. When girls flitted in and out of his life, as they had flitted in and out of young Philip's, it did not show what a virile, desirable chap Tony was – it just made several listeners, and a newspaper reporter, speculate that he was a homosexual. (Why had that nice Mary Weston suddenly called off the engagement? What had she discovered?) BBC publicity pictures of actor Colin Skipp didn't help. Norman Painting might have had Billy Bunter spectacles, and crashed his motorbike when he tried to ride with his scarf flying in the wind, but at least he was not going bald.

Script meeting minutes from the mid-Seventies show Jock Gallagher insisting, time after time, that Tony and Pat be promoted as the central characters. Philip Archer was not charismatic enough to be the lead, said Gallagher (insensitive to the presence of Norman Painting, who was wearing his Bruno Milna hat). Come what may, Tony must be turned into a dashing young hero, and Willow Farm turned into the main location.

But he never was, and Willow Farm, in the end, disappeared. Characters in soap operas are moved by mysterious forces. They develop in ways that neither writers nor script editors can predict. Tony was his father's son, he was Jack Archer's lad, and however much Jock Gallagher might demand that he be made a hero, the scriptwriters could not overcome blood. Tony had an eye for the girls, but not the courage to do anything about it. Like his Dad, his grand ideas were betrayed by a taste for cans of lager and evenings in front of the television. The scriptwriters wanted him to marry a cheerful, English, farm-secretary. But he married, in the end, the sort of woman men like that do marry: a bossyboots feminist who nagged him.

Jock Gallagher's involvement in the storylines was spasmodic. Had he been editor he would have forced Tony Archer to the centre of the stage, if necessary by killing off Phil Archer (he found the character deeply boring), but he was too good a manager, and too busy elsewhere, to interfere often.

His efforts to publicize and promote the programme, on the other hand, were intense and unremitting. He had inherited *The Archers*, he said, with a sense of horror, but he was determined that it would not be axed whilst under his stewardship. He brought out another *Borchester Echo* in 1974, editing it himself. Many members of the cast – even those who looked on Jock, in these early days, with deep suspicion – regarded it as the best ever produced.

There was a triumphant public relations stunt. Within the programme Sid Perks organized a coach trip by the Ambridge football team to play a Dutch side; and at Pebble Mill Jock Gallagher organized a coach trip so that several members of the cast and virtually the entire production team, together with three reporters from the national press – *The Times*, *Daily Express* and *Sun* – could go overseas on a jolly promotional tour designed to show that Ambridge, like everywhere else in Britain, had now joined the Common Market.

They caught a ferry from Hull to the Hague, and Gwen Berryman had a terrible crossing. She couldn't get down the steps to her cabin, so they tucked her into a cot in the ship's hospital. The cot had high sides, and she could not get out in the night when she wanted to go to the lavatory. Otherwise, the trip was a great success. Scenes were recorded daily, and transmitted to the UK each evening from Dutch Radio at Hilversum. The actors discovered that *The Archers*

June Spencer and Chris Gittins, outside *The Archers'* new studio at Pebble Mill.
William Smethurst

had ten thousand regular listeners in Holland, a good many of whom turned out to ask for autographs. The English reporters did them proud – a front page story in *The Times* and a big photo-spread in the *Express*. The only worried man was Jock Gallagher whose modest BBC supply of guilders was vanishing at an alarming rate. Coffee for the cast in a hotel cost him £75 at a time when a cup of coffee in the UK was not more than two shillings (or, in the new decimal currency that Doris still found so confusing, 10p). On the final night he found that he could not afford to pay the bill at the Hotel Bel Air at the Hague.

He sent Tony Shryane round the cast to collect everybody's spare guilders and ask them not to eat any dinner. Would Doris and Dan and Phil be forced into the kitchens to wash up? We shall never know. The local tourist officer arrived to say that the entire bill was being paid for by the Dutch National Tourist Agency, who were astonished by the sudden surge in holiday enquiries coming from the UK.

In England, meanwhile, there was a lively row in some Sunday papers about the lack of coloured immigrants in *The Archers*, and a story in the *News of the World* – 'The Wife Swappers of Ambridge' – which exposed a scandal in Inkberrow, the Worcestershire village used occasionally for *Archers* publicity photographs. In *The Times* it was reported that the British Forces in Hong Kong were using *The Archers* to teach newly-recruited Gurkha soldiers how to speak colloquial English. The story speculated that Gurkhas on guard duty outside Buckingham Palace would be heard saying 'Arr, me old pal, me old beauty.'

Jock Gallagher wrote triumphantly to London: what other drama programme on the radio could command this sort of press attention? London could not reply. It was true. Nobody ever wrote in the papers about *Waggoner's Walk*.

By 1976 there was a general agreement that *The Archers* was getting better, that its success was reviving. 'People in London think *The Archers* is good because I keep telling them it's good,' said Gallagher, in a moment of candour. For the twenty-fifth anniversary Gallagher persuaded BBC2 to make a documentary – *Underneath the Archers* – and authorized paperback novels about the programme by Keith Miles and Brian Hayles, and a book, *Twenty Five Years of The Archers*, which he wrote himself. He was less happy about Norman Painting's memoir, *Forever Ambridge*, and at first tried to stop it, which upset Norman (who had cause to cheer in the end: *Forever Ambridge*, when it came out, was a best-seller). He fed out a series of exciting statistics to the national press: 'While the programme has been on the air, the cows at Brookfield have been milked 26,000 times and between them the villagers have drunk about 20,000 cups of tea.' These dubious statistics became the basis of figures produced for the thirtieth, and the thirty-fifth and fortieth anniversaries . . . worried production assistants with calculators trying to assess the latest tea count.

Then there was the biggest gimmick ever – Norman Painting and Ysanne Churchman recreating the notorious Grace Archer Death Scene live on *Pebble Mill at One* – and the biggest party ever, actually held on New Year's Eve. Gallagher had so stunned and mesmerized London with the importance of it all, that the Director-General Sir Charles Curran and Lady Curran and half the BBC Radio hierarchy came trekking up the MI to sing 'Auld Lang Syne' in a Pebble Mill studio with all these whiskery old wireless has-beens. And the has-beens did them proud. Two studios were transformed with shimmering silver foil, and at midnight twenty-five champagne corks were popped in a military salute. Godfrey Baseley – invited, but not present – was quietly toasted by those who remembered, as Norman Painting did, that it was all his doing. Gallagher turned up in a kilt and ran a tombola stall in an attempt to recoup some of the costs. Lady Curran danced, it was reported, until 4am. In the New Year's dawn it was discovered that Norman Painting had got the OBE.

It was all quite wonderful but also quite curious, considering that the only hard statistics that mattered – the listening figures – were still on a remorseless downward trend.

22

A New Ambridge

'**YOU CAN'T REALLY BE FOOLISH ENOUGH** to think the listening figures are ever going to rise,' snapped Charles Lefeaux, irritably, to a young writer in 1976. *The Archers* might once have been the great BBC flagship, but its day was gone and Lefeaux knew this. He was a London drama department veteran, a diplomat skilled in the management of radio's decline.

Quarterly meetings had once been of high importance. In the morning, in the old days, Godfrey Baseley used to meet with his writers and dictate to them the stories he had devised for the coming three months. Before lunch Tony Shryane used to be allowed in, and told of characters he needed to cast. Then there used to be lunch itself – quite a splendid lunch, the BBC 'superior buffet' that featured scampi and smoked salmon rather than the BBC 'working buffet' that featured cold quiche and nasty sausage rolls – and in the afternoon Godfrey used to tell the hierarchy from London and Birmingham what the future held.

Occasionally, in those palmy days, there might have been suggestions, mild criticism even – the hierarchy playing at being programme makers – but nothing serious. Criticism was not what such occasions were about. They were about BBC London – the Head of Light Programme – coming to the Midlands to pay homage to the only man who seemed able to make a successful serial drama.

At some point in the late Sixties, with the listening figures falling, the Controller Radio 4 started to send his assistant up to Birmingham instead of coming up himself, and the *Archers* team found themselves sitting down with a smooth-cheeked young apparatchik who smiled politely as Baseley curtly outlined his plans. The day stopped being a specific '*Archers* Quarterly Meeting', and turned into a general review of Birmingham's radio output, with the actual *Archers* bit cut down to an hour or so in the afternoon.

By now Baseley was long gone, and with him his fertile imagination and calm certainty about future events. In the mornings, when they met under Lefeaux's chairmanship, the writers would discuss the next four weeks of scripts, and Lefeaux would routinely cry out in despair: 'Please, we must have a long-term story. I must have something to tell them about this afternoon!'

The buffet lunch went in 1975. It had been, according to Norman Painting, 'the most enjoyable and often most valuable part of these meetings', but the writers didn't deserve a free lunch any more. Possibly Jock Gallagher and the Controller of Radio 4's chief assistant ate in splendour somewhere, but Charles Lefeaux and his writers made their way to the Pebble Mill canteen, and then, after their apple crumble (famously excellent), descended one floor to the board-room, where they waited for Jock and the young man from London to appear. The young man would solemnly hand round carbon copies of the latest listening figures. And Charles Lefeaux would say: 'Can you tell us if these are in line with the general decline in Radio 4's audience?' And the young man would say, vaguely, 'Yes, just about in line,' and everybody would nod solemnly, as if to say it wasn't their fault, it was the fault of the world.

Each quarter the drop was small but by the mid to late Seventies there were only around two and three-quarter million listeners, which was a far cry from the twenty million who listened after Grace Archer died. The young apparatchik from London was too polite to say so, but the listening figures were not good news at all for a high-cost programme whose existence was only justified if it had popular appeal.

The listening figures were dismal, and audience appreciation surveys dire, but Jock Gallagher's publicity machine continued in full spate. In 1977 a newspaper competition was organized to find the perfect Ambridge and Ashton-under-Hill, a picturesque village nestling under Bredon Hill, was chosen. The choice was partly made because it was the home of country writer Fred Archer, and it was felt that a bit of extra publicity might be garnered by the connection. Either way, Ashton-under-Hill would, in future, be the model for events in Ambridge, and to start the ball rolling Ashton's Jubilee celebrations would be exactly copied in *The Archers*.

In the event writer Fred Archer was cool about having to share his village – the subject of many of his best-selling books – with a family of fictional Archers, and local residents were distinctly unexcited. As a publicity gimmick an entire week's episodes were recorded on location in the village, and to emphasize the youthful image of the programme they were recorded in quadraphonic sound – the first time a BBC radio drama had recorded quadraphonic sound on location. It was a brave publicity effort. Perhaps on Jock Gallagher's hidden agenda (if he kept *doing things* with the programme perhaps they wouldn't take it off) it had useful results, but once the recording was over Ashton-under-Hill was forgotten about by the BBC, and *The Archers* was forgotten about by Ashton-under-Hill. The national press, conservative in so many of its ways, went on insisting that the real Ambridge was Inkberrow, the place where wife-swapping went on.

A new Controller of Radio 4, Ian McIntyre, was appointed. He almost immedi-ately announced a most terrible and dramatic change to the scheduling of *The*

Archers. The evening episode would be moved to 7.05 and the Omnibus to 6.15 on Sunday evening. Fear of the axe petrified the cast yet again. This was the traditional BBC way to kill something off – mess it about in the schedules then announce that it was no longer holding its audience. Tony Shryane, who had never before been known to indulge in internal politics, expressed 'grave disquiet'. Edgar Harrison, the fourth Dan Archer, took up his pen bravely (bravely that is for an actor) and wrote personally to Ian McIntyre, pleading that the move be reconsidered.

McIntyre replied: 'To assume a loss of listeners because of the new timing is to assume that people have only been listening because it's there . . . I believe most people listen because they enjoy it and they will do so at 6.15 on Sunday evening. *The Archers* is healthy and robust and can well stand a bit of movement without suffering much.'

Heartening words – here was a controller who believed in them! A controller, too, who came up to Birmingham *in person* for the first Quarterly Meeting after his appointment, and listened – without saying much, but with an amused glint

Inside the *Archers* production office, with over twenty years of scripts behind him, Tony Shryane prepares to record the first episodes in quadraphonic sound.

William Smethurst

in his eye – to Charles Lefeaux describe the big stories that were pending. Tony and Pat were going to move from Willow Farm to Bridge Farm, Lefeaux announced in a grave portentous voice, and the Tuckers were going to move into Willow Farm. Dan would be chairman of the Ambridge Jubilee committee. Shula would abandon her hopes of a career with horses and become an estate agent – a change that would enable her, as a character, to move round the village and become involved in a wide range of stories.

The writers, taking advantage of the Controller's actual presence, demanded a change in the rules relating to the use of trade names. Under Lefeaux's script-editing nobody in Ambridge could 'hoover' the carpet, it had to be vacuumed. They could not meet in a Borchester 'Wimpy Bar', it had to be a hamburger bar. They could not go anywhere in a Land-Rover – the official BBC-approved term was a 'field reconnaissance vehicle'. 'When did anyone in the real world ever hear a farmer say he was taking the field reconnaissance vehicle to check the lambs?' the writers demanded.

Charles Lefeaux got snappy. He said that the BBC had a duty not to promote commercial products – it was laid down in the BBC charter. Someone mentioned an episode of television's *The Good Life* in which Tom had cried out for brandy for his dying pig, and Margo had asked, 'Courvoisier or Hiné?' Everybody agreed that it was a brilliant line, and that 'Five star or three star?' would not have been anything like as funny. Why couldn't *Archers* writers have the freedom of television writers?

'What television does is nothing to do with us,' said Charles Lefeaux in exasperation. 'There are BBC guidelines and we have no choice but to follow them.'

But the world was moving on. The conceit that a radio drama with less than three million listeners was somehow more important than a television programme with ten or fifteen million viewers, could not be sustained. Ian McIntyre said that the guidelines should be relaxed when it was important for the integrity of the script. Then he got up smartly and left. The meeting was over and Norman Painting was not impressed. The lack of a Quarterly Meeting buffet lunch rankled. He had, in the past, valued the chance to talk informally over the vol-au-vents with the Head of Light Programme, or with Controller Radio 4. He noted that this meeting, which took place after McIntyre's private lunch with Gallagher, was all over by 3.10pm. 'I personally count the slow disengagement of "Bruno Milna" from the writing-team from that day,' Norman wrote in *Forever Ambridge*.

Jock Gallagher did his best to make the move of the Sunday Omnibus into a positive event. The cost of the quadraphonic recording at Ashton-under-Hill was paid by London because the episodes would form the first Sunday evening Omnibus. A new version of the signature tune was recorded by the popular Dorset folk group, The Yetties, and kept just for Sundays.

McIntyre did not attend the next Quarterly Meeting. Instead the chief assistant was again in attendance. He passed round carbon copies of the listening figures.

The Sunday Omnibus audience had been comfortably over a million when it was on Sunday morning. Now it was approximately one-sixth of that figure, at 150,000.

There was a horrified silence.

Somebody asked how many listeners there had been at 6.15pm on Sunday before *The Archers* was moved to that slot. Chief Assistant CR4 said, 'A hundred and fifty thousand.'

There was another horrified silence. Then somebody asked: 'Do you mean that not a single solitary Sunday morning listener decided to listen on Sunday evening?'

'Some may have moved, but they were balanced by Sunday evening listeners who turned off their sets when *The Archers* took over the slot.'

He said there was no chance of Ian McIntyre reversing the decision. He was right. The change back to Sunday morning was not made until a year later, after McIntyre – a man who put more trust in *The Archers* than it deserved – had moved to Radio 3.

23

Sex for Shula

CONTROLLERS COME, CONTROLLERS GO. *The Archers*, it seemed, would creak on for ever, with its declining and fickle listenership, its boring storylines, its poor public image. But changes were being made. Charles Lefeaux had brought in writer Tessa Diamond – the first woman to occupy anything other than a secretarial post on the programme – and during 1977 two previously minor characters came centre stage.

The first was Shula Archer. She became the love interest. She enslaved Neil Carter, the Brookfield farm apprentice, so that he mooned about the place leaving farm gates open and driving his tractor into posts, then she made him join Borchester Young Conservatives, so that he could vote for her as social secretary. On Jubilee Night they sat on Lakey Hill until the early hours of the morning, holding hands as they watched the string of bonfires as far away as Malvern and Wenlock Edge . . . then she dumped him and started going out with Simon Parker, the young editor of the *Borchester Echo*.

Simon Parker, in 1977, sounded on air to be a peculiarly bland and anaemic character. However, Joanna Toye's novel *Shula's Story*, published in 1995, has revealed another side to his nature. He was a man who tore off his tie, Joanna tells us, 'with an animal ferocity'. In 1977, in the programme, sex was not explicitly mentioned, and when Shula lost her virginity to Simon the only clue given to listeners was the way she insisted (in a trembly voice) that they take a car rug with them when they went for a walk in a stubble field. *Shula's Story* deals openly and frankly with the incident. It took place under a hedge heady with elderflowers. The corn swayed softly. Shula closed her eyes and waited to be deflowered. Ears of wheat, we are told, nodded as if in blessing.

They were to nod again – and again. 'When he laid her down on the banks of the Am or on the damp earth of the woods he taught her with lips and fingers the pleasures of her body and how to pleasure him,' we are told, in this BBC-approved book. Listeners knew nothing of this in 1977. Had it been television they would have seen the wheat nodding approval. All they heard on air was an owl that hooted, mockingly, as it watched the couple cavort.

Jean Rook in the *Daily Express* saw it all, though. She knew, eighteen years before Joanna Toye's revelations, what was going on. 'The plot is squelchy and

New characters for the late Seventies. Sara Coward joins the programme to play Caroline Bone, and Richard Derrington joins to play Mark Hebden.
William Smethurst

the dialogue compost,' she wrote. 'Some of the actors who've been in it – man, boy and seed – for twenty-six years, must be withered husks ... but Shula Archer stands out. She is eighteen, blonde, lush, busty and sprouting. The sort of girl every man about town hopes to tumble across in a hay-loft. Recently I've begun to itch with curiosity – like a hayseed in my bra – to see the actress Judy Bennett who plays Shula ...'

And Jean Rook trotted to Muswell Hill to interview Judy Bennett, and wrote: 'She's trimly stacked, with eyelashes like long grass, and any man would climb a loft ladder for her ...'

Jean Rook was pleased with her prose. Several years later, moved to write about *The Archers* for different reasons, she again started: 'The plot is squelchy and the dialogue compost ...'

By this time, according to *Shula's Story*, Shula was having sex with Mark Hebden on Lakey Hill ('Shula was floating high, high over Ambridge, weightless, limitless ... she felt emptied of all worry and utterly, utterly happy') and refusing sex in the woods with Nigel Pargetter, though only because it was November and the bracken was catching her filmy harem trousers. She was truly an outdoor girl, leading an outdoor life.

One person not pleased by Shula's sex life was Tony Parkin. At a script meeting, a writer said it might be wise, in view of all these country walks with car rugs, to put Shula on the pill. There was general agreement that the move would reflect contemporary preoccupations and show how relevant and up-to-date the programme was, but Tony Parkin said that if they did the story he would resign as Agricultural Story Editor. He had three daughters of his own, either in their teens or approaching their teens, he said, and for *The Archers* to give the pill its 'seal of approval' would cause trouble with daughters the length and breadth of the country.

There was a furious debate. The writers thought it would be reckless and irresponsible not to put Shula on the pill. What if she became pregnant? Did Parkin want another illegitimate baby in Ambridge? Or were they supposed to start writing about people slipping into chemists' shops to buy packets of Durex? Even Tessa Diamond thought the pill story was a good idea. But Charles Lefeaux, a worldly, Hampstead man himself, recognized that Parkin spoke for a different, wider constituency. Anyway, he could not afford to lose him.

A compromise was reached. Shula would go on the pill – but nobody would know. Not Phil, nor Jill. Not even the listeners.

The decision to keep the move secret was wise. Only a few months later, a one-sentence reference to the pill by Betty Tucker, a married woman, led to a flood of letters complaining of 'indelicacy' and 'unnecessary embarrassment' and 'offensiveness', and Jock Gallagher had to defend the script in a memo to London. 'The reference to "the pill" was very brief,' he wrote, 'and it was in context of a discussion that seemed to me perfectly acceptable in such a programme, reflecting as it did the embarrassment that many people still have in talking about these matters . . .'

Shula was blonde, busty and sprouting, Jean Rook had said, though this can hardly be the reason why audience research showed her suddenly, out of nowhere, to be one of the programme's most popular characters. She was not a stereotype teenager. She hunted foxes and she helped organize the South Borset Hunt's children's meet (an annual event designed to interest young people in the sport, and featured in *The Archers* by a writer who wanted to goad the anti-hunting lobby). She was a keen member of Borchester Young Conservatives and she actively campaigned to stop Borchester Grammar School being turned into a comprehensive.

After so many desperate attempts to present a believable, credible member of the younger generation, the writers had finally succeeded. In Shula they had created a sexually-active, eighteen-year-old, Thatcherite reactionary.

Neil Kinnock was not happy. His views on Shula's burgeoning sexuality are not known but he was shadow Education Minister at the time, and her campaign to save Borchester Grammar School horrified him. When Sid and Polly decided to send daughter Lucy to the school he wrote a closely-typed two-page letter imploring the writers to present the case for comprehensive education, and let Lucy Perks go to the new High School. It was a good-humoured letter and ended with high praise for the programme and an assurance that he would remain a listener whatever happened.

Whatever happened was that his letter was politely answered, but its advice ignored, and the next thing that happened was that Jock Gallagher received a phone call from the Director-General – one of only two direct phone calls he ever received from the DG, he would later say – demanding to know why *The Archers* was broadcasting blatant Tory education policy propaganda.

Gallagher defended the storyline and refused to interfere. He was a Liberal himself, holding no brief for grammar schools, but he was not prepared to let politicians dictate the contents of drama programmes. Lucy Perks went to the Independent Grammar School, though the education did her no apparent good. The letter from Neil Kinnock started a long association between the Kinnocks and *The Archers* and Glenys Kinnock happily wended her way up to Birmingham for several of the programme's celebrations.

The second character to move centre stage during 1977 was Joe Grundy. The Grundys had lurked around the village for generations, downtrodden tenants of Grange Farm, perpetually skulking behind hedgerows to avoid their landlord, Brigadier Winstanley. They had not impinged greatly on village life. There had been a brief flurry of excitement in 1973 when Joe collapsed from malnutrition outside the Bull, and another when he crashed his lorry into the village pump and demolished it. In 1975 Dan shot his dog, Jacko, claiming that it was worrying sheep, (although Joe will go to his grave swearing that Jacko was innocent), and there was a pop concert at Grange Farm, featuring a group called The Chinese White Bedsock (the writers, at their script conference, thought they were being very witty and contemporary). There was triumph for Grange Farm when Joe won first prize with his marrows in the Flower Show and there was disaster when he was knocked senseless by George Barford's son Terry, who took him for a poacher.

These were minor stories for a minor character. In 1977 Reg Johnstone, the actor who played Joe, died. Only after some hesitation was the character re-cast.

Haydn Jones, who took the part, was one of the most respected radio actors in Britain, and one of the greatest players of comedy in his generation. He instantly brought to the character of Joe a new warmth and humanity and the writers responded. Joe Grundy blossomed. He heard that Shula had danced with Alf at the Young Conservatives (as improbable a storyline as ever there was) and decided that she should become his daughter-in-law, and look after him in his old age at Grange Farm. He gave her a cookery book that had belonged to his wife Susan. He took Jill to one side, and told her that he was all in favour of the match.

Then disaster – something never long absent from Grange Farm – struck. Mary Pound and Shula found him delirious in his farmhouse, suffering from a bad dose of flu. He had been abandoned by Eddie who was cavorting in

Borchester, Joe said, with his tart. His cows were infected with brucellosis and his favourite hob ferret, Turk, was dead in a trap. And there were more sorry tidings, even now – Shula told him, sadly, that she would not be changing her name to Grundy. He said that he fully understood. He was past caring about anything.

Eddie was brought home again and he and Joe agreed to start a turkey venture.

The main characters in the programme were changing, as indeed were the types of story that were being written. There was still the occasional flashback to a former age – Adam bitten by an adder, seriously ill in Borchester General, only saved by a new type of vaccine – but there was now a greater emphasis on social relationships. Walter Gabriel, homeless after his cottage roof blew off in a storm, lodged successively at different houses in the village. Jethro developed gum trouble, and left his denture in unexpected places (Jill forcibly took him to the dentist, who extracted his remaining teeth). Pat, obliged to go back to Wales to look after her mother, left weak Tony to flirt with district milk-recording girl Libby Jones. He even took her to the Cricket Club dance (Jennifer was sure he was having an affair, Brian – an expert in such matters, as the world was to discover – assured her that he wasn't capable). A new barmaid arrived at the Bull – Caroline Bone from Darrington, who had finished a cordon bleu cookery course and wanted to prove to her mother that she could earn her living.

Early in 1978 Paul Johnson, that amazing character who had inhabited the programme for so many years without ever developing a character at all, went bankrupt, disappeared in Christine's car, and was eventually discovered in Hamburg. He said he was never coming back. Frightened, perhaps, that he might change his mind, the writers killed him off in a car crash.

Gwen Berryman was not happy. She was seventy, and her arthritis was causing her a great deal of pain. She had moved to Torquay, and was driving herself to Birmingham every month. Because she only attended alternate recording sessions, Doris could not be given decent storylines and Gwen was distressed. Her part was becoming less and less important. She blamed it on the writers, who, she said, were making Doris seem silly.

The writers were in a quandary. Gwen's scenes were difficult to record. She could only move slowly and had trouble turning the pages of her script. It was evident, listening to episodes, that Doris was far from sprightly. Should they account for this by giving her arthritis – just as Gwen had arthritis? 'We couldn't possibly . . .' a writer said at a script meeting. 'Doris is supposed to be reliable. She's always been the person everyone could take their troubles to. It wouldn't work if Doris needed sympathy instead of giving it.'

They made Doris fall downstairs – which, for a while, accounted for her creakiness – but other writers were in favour of a more drastic solution. Both Dan and Doris were now minor background characters, and Doris, in particular, was very low in the lists of audience popularity.

Agricultural Story Editor Anthony Parkin threatened to resign if Shula was put on the pill.
Harry Smith

Then Gwen had to go into an orthopaedic hospital in Oswestry. Much to Edgar Harrison's annoyance, for he was a working actor, it was announced that both Dan and Doris would be written out of the programme for several weeks. The official reason – told with utter earnestness to Gwen and Edgar and announced with great solemnity to the press – was that a serious experiment was underway to discover if the younger characters were capable of holding the programme together – if, indeed, it could survive without the presence of its two mighty oaks.

'They did not even know if there was any point in considering a future without the Grand Old Couple,' wrote Gwen, trustingly, in her memoirs.

The newspapers were encouraged to follow the experiment with bated breath. 'Can *The Archers* survive without Dan and Doris?' asked a press handout. In fact, everyone knew perfectly well that the programme could survive without them – the experiment would never have been announced if Jock Gallagher had, for one moment, thought otherwise.

The banishment served two purposes. It pleased the writers, who had previously been forced to cast Dan and Doris when they didn't want to, and it allowed the BBC to announce, in triumph, two months later, that there had been 'no significant audience reaction' to the absence of the Grand Old Couple.

Gwen and Edgar – two sensitive artistes, tossed in the storm of life – were deeply distressed. 'As always, it was Tony Shryane who was there to pour oil on troubled waters,' wrote Gwen. But Tony Shryane would not be on hand for very much longer. He was due to retire from the BBC in early 1979, and it was planned that he would leave *The Archers* in the summer of 1978.

There were the inevitable rumours that the programme would be taken off, that the retirement of Tony Shryane would be seen as a fitting finale, but in fact it had survived its years of maximum danger. It had become an institution. It was boring, dusty, not something many people would admit to listening to, but it still had an audience of sorts, and the press – deeply nostalgic – still liked to write about it. The Head of Radio Drama, Ronald Mason, was not hostile to the programme, as many of his predecessors had been – but neither did he value it much. The answer from London, when advice was politely asked about a possible successor to Tony Shryane, was that it might be possible to find a junior drama producer willing to take the job on.

But *The Archers* was in Jock Gallagher's fiefdom. Early in 1978 it was announced that Charles Lefeaux's contract as script editor was not to be renewed. A temporary editor would be appointed, and after that there would be a new, and much more powerful, replacement for Tony Shryane.

24

Farewell to
Tony Shryane

AT THIS POINT, rather like Godfrey Baseley donning the role of Brigadier Winstanley, I must abandon my dispassionate, authorial voice and become a character in my own book.

I had joined *The Archers* writing team in 1974. Before then, as a young journalist, I had often hurried past Gwen Berryman as she toiled slowly up and down those cruel stairs in the Broad Street studios (she had always paused, giving reporters and cameramen a shy, hesitant smile, as if she feared not to be recognized). I had been one of those *Midlands Today* hacks vastly amused when a drunk, enraged reporter threw a plate of cottage pie at another reporter in the canteen and hit several *Archers* actors instead (Bob Arnold, it was said, suffered most). Later, in the newsroom at Pebble Mill, I had seen a beaky little man with an aggressive grin taken to the *Nationwide* studio – Godfrey Baseley, sacked and ready to tell the world all about it. A few months after that we had played the *Coronation Street* theme over photographs of the cast of *The Archers* to welcome Malcolm Lynch from Granada.

Lynch retired to the seaside and it was Lefeaux who asked me to write for the programme. At my first script meeting I learned that Pat and Tony were to have their banns read, Kenton was to go to sea as a merchant navy cadet, and Polly Perks was to have an ectopic pregnancy. It was decreed that I should be the writer to announce the departure of Ralph and Lilian Bellamy from Ambridge – to send the characters off to the Channel Islands, and the actors off into oblivion. In the club bar, that very lunchtime, the actor who played Bellamy, Jack Holloway, heartily welcomed me to the team. I nursed my guilty secret, and thought what fun it was.

Three years later, one evening towards the end of 1977, I was having a drink in the club bar with Roger Pine, the Midlands senior radio drama producer. He told me that the jobs of script editor and producer were to be combined when Tony Shryane retired. The new man would be called 'Editor', so that the London drama department would not be able to get their sticky paws on things (all drama producers, London claimed, were under their artistic control). The new man would report directly through Jock Gallagher to Controller Radio 4.

The job would be advertised and boarded. Did I want to apply? I said I didn't fancy going in for a BBC board unless I knew what the outcome would be. I was told not to worry on that score.

Charles Lefeaux left. I took over as caretaker script editor. The board for Editor was held. I was interviewed. I said that if appointed I would want to bring more social comedy into *The Archers*. A man from administration asked, aggressively, did I know how much comedy writers cost? Jock Gallagher tried to explain the difference between social comedy and the patter of stand-up comedians. Ronald Mason, the London man, looked amiable but bored: this was a Jock Gallagher appointment, and he was wasting his day.

Half an hour later I was told that the job was mine.

I had enjoyed being an *Archers* writer. Keith Miles had patiently explained the basic principles of serial writing – how to leave stories open, how to pick up on other stories, characters and situations. Writing, I had so soon discovered, meant power. It was writers who decided who to cast in their episodes; writers who therefore dispensed episode fees. No wonder the actors were friendly whenever a writer visited the studio.

Writers had favourite characters. Brian Hayles would always want to write about George Barford and Nora, or Martha in the village shop. Bruno Milna had a penchant for Mrs P and Walter Gabriel. My favourite was Shula, so brilliantly played by Judy Bennett. Before starting to think of stories, I would cast her in all five episodes. This irritated Keith Miles, who believed, quite properly, that writers ought to give all major characters a decent number of episodes. On one occasion, knowing that I was following him in the writing schedule, he sent Shula off on a foreign holiday in his last episode.

It didn't make any difference. I brought her back from the airport. If he'd sent her to Hong Kong I'd have brought her back; forced the intercontinental jet into a vast circle over Afghanistan or wherever. The power of the *Archers* writer was global.

Charles Lefeaux was a sound, wise administrator, but he never claimed to be creative. There was rarely any story in the storylines. I made it a point of honour to devise my own stories for my own week. If I was following after Brian Hayles, and the cliffhanger was something to do with George Barford's alcoholism, or boring Welshman Haydn Evans, I would dispose of it in a couple of lines: 'Did you hear about Nora finding George Barford trying to hang himself from the rafters?' 'Yes, but she cut him down all right, no bones broken' – then get on with my own stories.

I scripted one week in four, often following after Norman Painting, whose 'Bruno Milna' scripts I enjoyed. Often my wife Carolynne and I would go for dinner at his Queen Anne rectory at Warmington near Banbury, where he handed over his scripts and stories to me.

Yes, writing was wonderful. I made Shula a leading light in the Hunt and in the Young Conservatives. I set up Joe Grundy and his wayward younger son Eddie in

Re-creating the past . . . *Archers* books at the end of the Seventies cunningly doctored old photographs to give Ambridge a history.

Original photo of bus and pic from *Ambridge – An English Village Through The Ages*

the Grange Farm turkey scheme, and made Joe dream of Eddie marrying into the Archer clan. I gave Eddie his hat with horns. When Jethro astounded the village by announcing that his Uncle Charlie had died and left him a fortune, I made Clarrie give up her cleaning jobs before discovering that the fortune was only £4,000. I introduced Simon Parker, a journalist like myself, as Shula's first lover.

In my last five scripts I introduced what was to become, after Shula, my very favourite character. The episode was broadcast on 5 July 1978. Jennifer was worrying about wildlife conservation, Sid was worrying about his pigeons, and Jack Woolley was alarmed by attacks on his plan to develop 'Glebelands', a tasteful and exclusive development of executive homes. At the end of the episode Jack popped into Home Farm. He had with him a small but solidly-built dog. 'Good boy, good boy, Captain!' he said proudly. Brian asked if the dog was to protect Jack from anti-Glebelands demonstrators. 'Of course he isn't!' said Jack. 'I just wanted a friend . . . a companion.'

And for the next fourteen years, he had one.

It was with a sense of loss that I found that as producer and editor, I could no longer write the programme as well.

'We must be the authentic voice of the English shires,' I wrote in a memo to the writers. 'The programme began as a dramatised agricultural advice service: it has evolved into the story of an English village. It must accurately reflect rural life; if it has attitudes, they must be the attitudes of rural England.'

I went on to say that we should aim, in our grander moments, to write in the tradition of Jane Austen, Laurie Lee and H.E. Bates. 'I don't think this is setting our sights too high. In the day-to-day writing and producing of scripts, there are inevitable scenes and episodes that don't come near the ideal. But we should be *capable* of something very good indeed – and we should, at times, achieve it.'

The writers of which so much was now demanded were Keith Miles, Brian Hayles and Tessa Diamond.

Brian Hayles went on extended sick-leave in June 1978, and died of cancer in October. A teacher and sculptor before he turned to script writing, he had written successfully for television series like *United*, *Dr Who*, and *The Regiment*. In *The Archers* his most notable creation was the character of George Barford, the alcoholic Yorkshire gamekeeper who had left his Roman Catholic wife and two children and was eventually taken up – then abandoned – by Irish barmaid Nora McCauley.

The second writer to leave after a short time was Keith Miles, who said, politely, that life was too short to spend any more of it writing for the same programme.

That left Tessa Diamond.

Tessa lived in a flat in fashionable Chelsea with her husband and children, and worried endlessly over getting her research right. She invested Brookfield family scenes with colour and warmth in a way that a succession of dour, tweedy male writers had never done before. She was utterly modest about her own scripts, and generous in her praise of others. As *The Archers* sailed into new and revolutionary seas, she bravely sailed with it. Her only problem was that in *The Archers* – though not in her other extensive writing – she could not think up names for new characters. They were always Roberts, or occasionally Robertson, or perhaps, in wilder moments, Robinson.

Tessa hosted a dinner for Charles Lefeaux, and his wife Tilly. Then the production team and writing team that had guided the programme since the departure of Godfrey Baseley was scattered to the winds.

In September 1978 the assistant general secretary of the Association of Broadcasting Staffs, who happened to be a Labour prospective candidate, claimed that he had received a number of complaints about 'anti-union sentiments' being expressed in *The Archers*. 'The BBC has a duty to be as balanced in drama programmes as in news and current affairs,' he said, and described *The Archers* as a particularly bad case. Older members of the cast remembered the almost identical fuss in 1954 (also a year before a General Election) when Edwin Gooch, MP, complained about Tory influences in the programme. It was comforting to reflect that a quarter of a century had passed, and *The Archers* was still thought of as a significant opinion former.

There were other comforting signs of continuity. In 1954 teenage girls had written poems to young heart-throb Phil:

> You're breaking our hearts Philip Archer,
> You really are causing us pain.
> By letting Grace buzz off to Ireland,
> You're slipping Phil Archer that's plain . . .

In the summer of 1978 teenage girls were again writing with expressions of love and admiration – though no longer, alas, to Phil. Brookfield's apprentice and pig enthusiast Neil Carter was dangerously ill with Weil's disease, which had turned his skin the colour of custard. Two girls sent a card showing pigs in heaven. 'We wouldn't like to hear you die, and join that Piggy in the Sky,' they wrote.

> To hear you thus we feel quite sick,
> (What a shame it wasn't Nick!
> Or even Shula – stuck up Twit)
> But you're our hero, every bit.
> From our devotion we'll not waver
> ('Spite of sexy birds like Ava).
> We both think you're a dishy fellow
> 'N love you even though you're yellow.
> So chin up, Neil! You must determine
> Not to fall a prey to vermin.

Girls writing poems, politicians complaining of sinister Tory propaganda – were the good times coming back? Many actors from the early days had died

– Harry Oakes, Monte Crick, Bill Payne, and only very recently Gwenda Wilson, who had played Aunt Laura – but many of the original cast were still ploughing their Ambridge furrow. Norman Painting, June Spencer and Gwen Berryman survived from that trial week in 1950. Bob Arnold, Chris Gittins and Patricia Greene were still there, as were George Hart and Lesley Saweard. Ysanne Churchman was also there – young Grace, who perished after the stables fire, now playing Mary Pound.

Anne Cullen was still playing Carol Tregorran, though many and varied were the actors trying, without success, to keep the flame of John Tregorran burning brightly. What do you do with a romantic young college lecturer when he has turned into a middle-aged, well-heeled, well-married antique-shop owner? The writers – Tessa, Norman Painting, and newcomer Alan Bower – decided that he could be nothing other than stuffy, boring, and middle-class. He would have to go off on yet another lecture tour of America.

The cast, in the meantime, were busy saying a long farewell to Tony Shryane, the man who had directed almost every episode since January 1951. Tony was regarded with a warmth and affection that would never again – not, at any rate, to the present day – be given by *Archers* actors towards their producers or editors. Gwen Berryman said: 'He had sheltered me from the more tempestuous outbursts of Godfrey Baseley; calmed my shattered nerves on countless occasions; rearranged recording schedules whenever I had the slightest problem; and, most difficult of all, he had directed me with endless patience. It was through him that I had become Doris Archer.'

The other members of the cast, without exception, expressed similar views.

The actors arranged their own farewell. Nobody from management was involved. They took over a studio one night and recorded a special *Archers* episode written by Norman Painting and directed by the programme assistant Valerie Fidler. They held a dinner and played the tape to him and his wife Valerie who had her own memories of the programme.

The official BBC party took place on Tony's sixtieth birthday in January 1979. The country was covered in snow and swept by blizzards. Denis Norden and Frank Muir could not get to Birmingham, and neither could Gwen Berryman and Bob Arnold, but most of the rest of the cast managed to make the journey. Keith Miles wrote an *Archers* sketch, Ian Wallace sang comic songs, Steve Race played the piano. At midnight it was decided to ring up Bob Arnold at his home in the Cotswolds, linking the phone call into the public address system in Studio 1. When Bob answered the phone it became immediately and embarrassingly evident that he had no idea what Keith Miles was talking about when he said he was 'calling from the party'. After a few moments Norman Painting sprang forward and took the microphone and asked, a twinkle in his voice, 'Bob, whose birthday is it?'

A pause. 'Blessed if I know,' said Bob. 'Is it Gwen's?'

25

More New Men

'WHAT MAKES A GOOD ARCHERS WRITER?' asked *The Archers*, a book published to mark the thirtieth anniversary of the programme, and went on: 'Well ideally he should live in Worcestershire or South Warwickshire (if only so that he can get to script meetings easily, and dash re-writes to the studio quickly in emergencies) and should be able to write with humour and understanding about the countryside and people around him. He should be able to reflect rural society, from a pub darts match to a hunt ball, with perception and sympathy. If he's an officer in the Yeomanry, rides to hounds, and runs the tombola every year at the Conservative Garden Fête, then so much the better.'

One lunchtime in October 1978, Helen Leadbeater, a left-wing, feminist, lawyer's clerk from Islington, who had written a brilliant play for Radio 3, found herself in trendy Joe Allen's in Covent Garden, looking round in search of celebrities and trying to decide if she wanted to script *The Archers*. Tall, sexy, far more interested in defending London's robbers and muggers than in chronicling Ambridge life, she did brighten faintly when she recollected that the Leadbeater family came, a generation or so back, from Chipping Campden. She was fond, she said, of Joe Grundy. She also joined the team.

An unsolicited script came in from a young woman called Mary Cutler, an inner-city Birmingham school teacher. It turned out that she was a friend of Helen's. At school they had both written stories for *Jackie*; they had both been on *University Challenge*. She also joined the team.

Of yeomanry, village fêtes, and hunt balls these writers knew nothing. The sum total of their farming knowledge, as Helen confided, came from looking at cows from the train window. Mary Cutler was astonished to find that grass in fields had to be sown – she had thought it was just, well, *there*. She was amazed to be told that farmers planted different varieties of potato: in inner-city Birmingham a potato was a potato, something a man in the corner shop turned into chips. Mary was punished severely for her ignorance. Before being offered a place on the *Archers* writing team she was told she must go and stay for a week on a farm in the countryside. A nice farmer was found, somewhere down in Herefordshire, and she went, with her daughter Rebecca. She had no car. In the

Jennifer Aldridge (Angela Piper) enters one of her Jacob sheep in the Royal Show, 1979.
Royal Agricultural Society

evenings mother and daughter plodded over the fields to a public kiosk to make wild, desperate telephone calls.

Mary's wit and warmth made her scripts a joy, her anti-Thatcherite sentiments ('Do you realize how many unemployed there are and the mess this country's in, Sid?') were simply blue-pencilled. She is still writing *The Archers*, almost twenty years later, which means that she has written for the programme for longer than any other writer, even Geoffrey Webb, Edward J. Mason, or Bruno Milna. Nowadays she can probably name every potato variety grown in the British Isles and talk for hours about oilseed rape and warble fly. Her political sentiments are probably welcomed by the current regime, unless, of course, time has wrought its magic and Lady Thatcher has become her heroine.

Novelist and Radio 3 dramatist Susan Hill also joined the team. She was particularly interested in the character of Pat – a strong young woman married to a weak if amiable husband. At a script meeting she proposed that Pat should leave Tony for a bit – take the kids back to Wales while she thought things through. This sort of story is generally a pain, and it had been done at least twice (Peggy walking out on Jack, Jill going off to London), but it did give the writers the chance to develop Pat's character, and it provided some comedy with poor bewildered Tony. In the *Daily Mirror* Hilary Kingsley wrote that *Archers* women in the past had been uniformly 'smug, tolerant and cheerful. But that is changing. Reality has struck since the programme took on a batch of women scriptwriters. It was Susan Hill, novelist and mum to a small girl, who got to work on Pat. She knew that life alone with a demanding infant can close in on the most sensible mother and knock her off her footing.'

The public were less confident. 'For some months now I have intended to write to you in order to express my disgust and anger at the state of *The Archers*,' wrote one listener. 'In the past six months it has progressed through weak themes, lousy casting, bad scripts, obvious actor "loss of heart" into rubbish, and now total, indescribable drivel . . .' Another wrote: 'I find no indication of this so-called farming family actually toiling as farmers are known to do . . . instead all I get is the picture of an extremely smug, self-satisfied, indulgent clique whose only problems are the constant greed for food, riches, alcohol . . .'

On the inside, too, there were those less than happy with the influx of writers ignorant of the countryside. Tony Parkin got on very well with the girls – even when they wandered in to script meetings late, from delayed London trains, and then sat watching the clock waiting for lunch – but he complained in private that his job was being made impossibly difficult by writers who knew nothing about agriculture.

Radio Times published a large selection of critical letters. Many of them complained that *The Archers* was no longer about the countryside and country matters. Somebody said it was boring. The BBC replied: 'It is hard to keep agriculture as prominent as it was twenty years ago. A drama about Blossom [the well-loved shire horse] being off her hay is bound to be more riveting than the modern saga of a tractor with an oil leak. Our aim, however, remains the same: to reflect life in rural England, the England of the "shires".'

So why, asked Tony Parkin – and many others – was the writing team being perversely filled with young left-wing feminists from inner-city Birmingham and London?

In fact, there were other writers to balance them – Alan Bower, who lived deep in Kent, Tim Rose-Price who lived in the Cotswolds, and James Robson who lived in a small market town in North Yorkshire. Simply, the programme was looking for good writers. Writers who did not have the dead hand of London's radio drama department upon them.

In July 1979 most of the broadsheet national papers carried the story that *The Archers* was looking for scripts from people who had never written drama before.

'Listen to an episode,' listeners were told, 'then write an episode to follow it!' The qualities needed, the *Daily Telegraph* reported, were 'wit, style and humour'.

Dozens of scripts came in. One was by a person called Debbie Cook. She turned out to be a folk-singer, and composer of the hit song 'The Day We Went to Bangor'. She also turned out to be a splendid *Archers* writer.

It was General Election year. The episode for the day after the election was recorded. In it, Sid Perks commented on Mrs Thatcher's victory. In the studio, actor Alan Devereaux remained at the microphone expectantly, waiting for an alternative script to be given to him. It wasn't. The national press happily ran the story – Ambridge, the only place in England that knows the result of the General Election!

Other press gimmicks were less successful. Jennifer Aldridge entered one of her Jacob sheep in the Royal Show, so actress Angela Piper was sent to the Royal with an actual sheep. A 'topical insert' was laid on for that night's programme, so that listeners would hear the result. Widespread press coverage was expected. In the event only local papers made much of it. Godfrey Baseley had done this sort of thing much better in 1957 when Christine's race horse Red Link was a real horse entered into real races.

A minor triumph was to put George Barford's son Terry into a genuine regiment when he decided to enlist for a soldier. The Prince of Wales's Own Regiment of Yorkshire proved co-operative and in May 1979 they sent a helicopter full of soldiers to Pebble Mill on a publicity visit. The army helicopter circled closely round the building. As it came round for a second time, researchers from *Pebble Mill at One* – the programme that usually got the helicopter visits, the Royal Marine commandos, the charity sky-divers – ran about in confusion, convinced that the helicopter was theirs, and had arrived on the wrong day. Everybody was pleased; the story was re-told endlessly in the club bar. *Pebble Mill at One* was cordially loathed by every other programme in the building.

The Terry Barford link with the Prince of Wales's Own Regiment was important because although most of the Commonwealth had deserted *The Archers*, the British Forces Broadcasting Service still took the programme, and paid around 10 per cent of its programme costs. One of their keen young officers, Julian Spilsbury, eventually left the army and became an *Archers* writer.

The end of 1979 saw a more settled writing team. The infamous 'Quarterly Meetings' had been abandoned. A new tradition was started: every six months the writers went to the King's Arms Hotel at Chipping Campden for a weekend discussion of long-term storylines. Writers talked about characters coming, and characters going; the only fixed rule was that if a new cast character was introduced, then an existing cast character had to go. Many a murder was done in the pink sitting room of the King's Arms.

Sometimes writers would slip across the road and look into the back bar of the Red Lion, startling George Hart as he sat drinking with his cronies.

In the programme, Christine married George Barford in St Stephen's Church, despite the fact that George was divorced, prompting a furious attack on the BBC by the Bishop of Truro and a reproof for the bishop by the *Guardian*, who reminded him that Ambridge was in the Barsetshire diocese, and therefore under the aegis of Dr Proudie. Shula went on a round-the-world trip after accusing Brian Aldridge of being no gentleman (he had shot a vixen that had taken several of his early lambs), and in the pink sitting room at Chipping Campden, the new writers had another look at John Tregorran, the romantic lead of yesteryear now turned into a smug, middle-aged bore. He had been repeatedly dispatched on lecture tours of America to get him out of the way. This would no longer do.

What really did happen to middle-aged, middle-class men who thought a lot of themselves? They had pathetic affairs with younger women, the team decided.

John Tregorran would be re-cast (the excellent Roger Hume, later to play the excellent Bert Fry). After a long-term story, stretching over a year or so, he would fall in love with Jennifer. He would try to kiss her in Leader's Wood. Would she flee, or would the old romancer have his way among the bluebells?

Only time would tell.

26

The End of the Seventies

Paul Johnson had died on a German autobahn early in 1978. Joby Woodford (who had married Martha Lily) had been relegated to a 'non-speaking' part. Gordon Armstrong had been sent off to be keeper of Lord Netherbourne's estate and Haydn Evans, Pat's uncle, was all set to be sent back to Wales. Ralph Bellamy – for so many years exiled to Guernsey – was killed off early in 1979. Actor Jack Holloway told the press: 'I'm really quite hurt. I've been with *The Archers* for twenty-three years and all I got was a polite little note telling me my services would not be required after January 18th.'

New characters had been introduced in the late Seventies. For the most part they made as little impression as the characters they had ousted. Who now remembers Arnold Lucas and Nick Wearing? Or even Simon Parker, the editor of the *Borchester Echo*? Who remembers Shula's chum Michele Brown or Jackie Smith or Libby Jones or Eva Lenz, the blonde nineteen-year-old au pair from Stuttgart (both these latter parts played by Hedli Niklaus, who now plays Kathy Perks), or PC Coverdale, the Ambridge cop (played by Leon Tanner, married in real life to Hedli as Hedli, and in the programme to Hedli as Eva) . . .

The writers tried to make their new characters send roots deep into the Ambridge soil. It didn't happen. They remained bland, two-dimensional, boring. They didn't fit into Ambridge, it was difficult to see where they would fit. They were not real people in a real world, not people you might meet in a Worcester-shire pub, or for that matter in a Soho café. They were cardboard creations, forgotten rejects from *Mrs Dale*.

There had been characters like these before, of course – dozens of them. Andrew Sinclair, the Scottish estate manager brought in by John Kier Cross (the only character able to make sense of all that Scottishness in the scripts). Nora McCauley, the Irish barmaid played by actress Julia Mark. Under the brutal regime that now prevailed, chopping out dead wood from the past was no prob-lem – but it was deeply chastening for the new team to find that their own creations were so dreary, and not a pleasant experience for the actors who had to

166

play them. For the listener it didn't seem to matter: the new characters made no impression when they came in, and nobody seemed to notice when they left. On audience research surveys, they scarcely registered at all.

A meeting at Chipping Campden decided that the new characters were failing because they lacked roots in the Midland countryside. Characters were being invented – generally young, trendy, supposedly handsome or sexy – and were being imported into Ambridge when there was no logical reason for them to be there. In the meantime the team was ignoring Ambridge's own sturdy sons and daughters.

The future, it was decided, lay not with Germans or Scottish people, or with Irish barmaids. *The Archers* was about rural England, the England of the Shires. Its future lay with characters nurtured already on Ambridge soil, with Clarrie Larkin and with Eddie Grundy. It lay with Nelson Gabriel, that eccentric sprig of an Ambridge oak. In a year or two it would lie with Elizabeth Archer (though nobody at this time could foresee quite how much).

Out, in due course, went Simon Parker and Nick Wearing. Out went PC Coverdale and Eva the au pair – the two of them married and dispatched to Portsmouth. Out went Jackie Smith, to a flat in Borchester and a boyfriend called Basil. Back to Ambridge came Nelson, bouncing a cheque at the Bull and being revealed to a horrified Jack Woolley as being quite penniless. Actor Jack May – who had played the young, smooth, mail-van robber Nelson in the programme's early years – slipped effortlessly back as the middle-aged Nelson whose sad ambition was to run a provincial wine bar.

Meanwhile across the Am, across the barren fields of Grange Farm, listeners heard all about the preparations for Eddie's marriage to Dolly Treadgold. They heard Joe put up new curtains in the parlour and prepare the turkey shed for a lavish reception, borrowing the Brookfield flags (not flown since VJ Day) and ordering vast quantities of chicken legs and vol-au-vents from Caroline Bone.

They heard Joe tell Shula how sorry he was not to have her as a daughter-in-law, but she'd missed her chance now, poor girl – and then they heard Eddie call his marriage off, the day before the wedding, declaring that Dolly was too flighty.

To Jethro's annoyance and shame, Eddie started going out with Clarrie Larkin. But what else was the girl to do? She had given up cleaning to work in a travel agent's. She had dreamed of being an air hostess, but had been severely disappointed. 'I told her it was no use,' Jethro confided to Neil Carter, as they ate their sandwiches. 'She's too big-boned is Clarrie, they'll never want to go carrying all that weight about.'

Eddie and Clarrie – created by Trevor Harrison and Heather Bell – had joined Haydn Jones's Joe Grundy and George Hart's Jethro, to start a family relationship that listeners would relish.

Occasional letters began to indicate approval: 'I have been moved to write to you as just lately something has happened to your programme. Today as the episode ended I had a lump in my throat and tears in my eyes . . . recently I have been laughing aloud at Jethro and Neil . . .' Another wrote: 'Since the advent of a fresh team of writers the scripts have improved enormously . . .' and the critic of the *Ipswich Evening Star* said: 'There are definite signs that life is returning to Ambridge . . .'

Philip Garston-Jones, who played Jack Woolley with such distinction and fruiti-ness of voice, was taken seriously ill. In a most bizarre incident, a BBC news bulletin announced that he had died. Nobody doubted that the report was true and tributes were paid, on air, to Philip's great achievement in creating the char-acter. Then a member of Philip's family phoned the *Archers* production office. He asked in a puzzled, rather awed voice, about the news bulletin. He had been at Philip's bedside, he said, only a few hours previously, and Philip had been very much alive. A hasty phone call to the hospital confirmed that Philip wasn't dead at all. He lived for another ten days.

Jack Woolley was re-cast, Arnold Peters (who had played shepherd Len Thomas back in the early Fifties) taking the part.

At the beginning of 1980 Chris Gittins was taken ill. Then, almost immedi-ately afterwards, Norman Shelley, who played Colonel Danby (and was famous for having played the original Pooh Bear on the wireless, and having voiced the speeches of Winston Churchill for wartime broadcast to America) collapsed while recording in the studio. He was admitted to the city's Queen Elizabeth Hospital. Betty McDowall, who now played Laura, sat by his bedside for hours.

When Chris Gittins fell ill there was a huge re-write — stories hacked out of twenty or thirty episodes, new stories and characters inserted. When Norman Shelley fell ill the same scripts had to be rewritten all over again. The misfor-tunes of the cast were becoming common knowledge. After the death of Philip Garston-Jones the *News of the World* had announced: 'After twenty-nine years, time is catching up with *The Archers* . . . many of the leading fictional characters are getting rather long in the tooth. In real life, too, age is becoming a sad prob-lem. To save the show the BBC has had to develop younger characters in what was becoming an everyday story of old folk.'

The *Daily Mail* joined in by listing members of cast in their sixties and seven-ties, and said: 'Ambridge, Radio Four's rural retreat, is a village with a shadow hanging over it . . .'

None of this made Gwen Berryman feel any better. Her arthritis was now causing her great pain. It was difficult for her to get to Birmingham from her home in Torquay — when she came on the train she had difficulty in sitting down and standing up; when she drove her car, the pain in her hands was so severe that she had to take two days to complete the journey. 'While Tony Shryane was there,' she would tell Jock Gallagher in retirement, 'I always knew that, whatever happened, he would sort things out when I eventually got to the studio at Pebble Mill . . .'

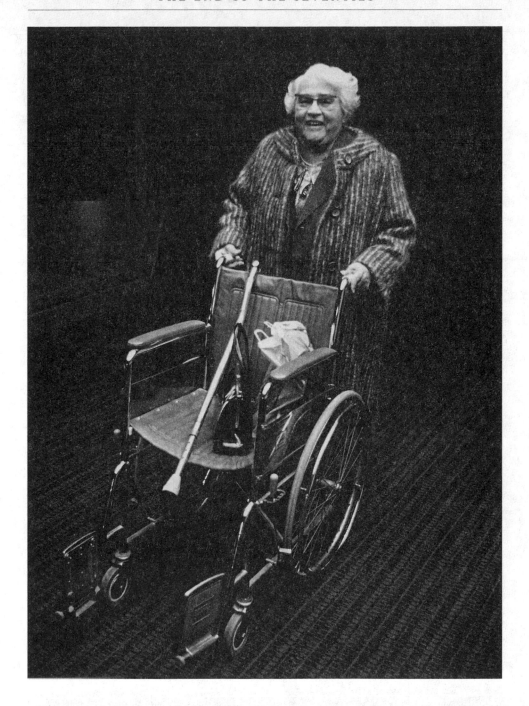

It was 1980, and Gwen Berryman had finally 'handed in her notice'. Leaving Studio 3 at
Pebble Mill she saw photographer Willoughby Gullachsen – known to everyone on the cast as
'Gus' – and called out to him: 'Take my picture, Gus! You won't see me here ever again . . .'
Willoughby Gullachsen

But Tony was gone. The cast were kind and brought her tea and arranged her lunch, and helped her to her car, but they couldn't 'sort things out' and neither, by now, could Tony Shryane have done so. During recordings she sat in a swivel chair, so that by moving her head and body she could move on and off microphone, and thus sound as if she was moving around Glebe Cottage. When Doris had to make an entrance, Gwen's chair was pushed slowly towards the microphone by the studio crew. But her hands were badly affected by her arthritis, and it was difficult for her to avoid script rustle. She started to falter in her delivery of lines, and her scenes took a long time to record, which often meant that later scenes involving major characters and major storylines had to be rushed.

The part written for her grew smaller and smaller. She knew perfectly well what was happening. 'Gone were the days when she had her own chair and woe betide anyone who dare sit in it,' wrote Norman Painting in his autobiography, *Reluctant Archer*. 'Gone were the days when she was Queen of *The Archers*, as absolute monarch. She now hated the studio. She was ill-at-ease with those in charge. She did not like the changes that were being made both in the scripts and the staff . . .'

There was one particularly bad recording session, in February 1980. On the evening of the first day she told Norman Painting that she could not face the studio the next morning. He told she had to go in – she was a pro. Two tears, said Norman, rolled down her cheeks.

The next day, in the studio, she stumbled badly in her speech. Afterwards she said that she wanted to retire – to 'hand in her notice'.

She had 'handed in her notice' several times previously, not meaning to be taken seriously, just looking for comfort and reassurance. Perhaps she was hoping that she would be reassured yet again – told how much she was valued.

This time, however, no attempt was made to change her mind. It was pointless for a woman in her seventies, crippled with arthritis, to go through such pain and trouble to come to Birmingham, every month, to such little purpose.

Her decision to leave the programme was accepted.

On her way home on the train to Torquay she suffered a stroke. 'I had not felt well to start with,' she would tell Jock Gallagher, 'but by then I was quite ill . . . I remember not being able to read the station sign when I eventually arrived in Torquay.'

She had to spend several weeks in a nursing home and it was an anxious, unhappy time for Edgar Harrison. As Gwen's work contracted, so did his. When Doris was sent off to Guernsey for several weeks to visit Lilian, Dan, perforce, had to go with her.

There was no question of re-casting. Jock Gallagher had once made Gwen a promise that she would be the one and only Doris Archer. In any case, Doris was, nowadays, far from being a popular character.

The decision was taken to kill Doris off. It would be very beautiful, and would all be recorded in secret to get as much news impact as possible.

27

The Union that Wouldn't Let Doris Die

THE PART OF DORIS might have become small, listeners might not care much about her these days, but she was a great figure in popular dramatic fiction. Her death was going to make a stir.

She would die quietly at Glebe Cottage. Shula, her granddaughter, would find her. It would be Sunday evening, and Dan would be at evensong in St Stephen's. Shula would go to the church, and quietly tell Christine that her mother was dead. The episode would end as they stood together in the church porch, Christine preparing to tell her father. The congregation would be singing 'The day Thou gavest Lord is ended' – fitting for a woman who had lived a long life as a steady and committed Christian, a farmer's wife who had been baptized here in this church in 1900, and had worshipped here through two world wars, and seen her children and grandchildren baptized here.

The script was written. The scene was recorded in the village of Cherington in South Warwickshire on Sunday, 28 September, with the villagers forming the congregation, and Cherington's own organist playing the music. Almost unbelievably, the secret was kept by an entire village, three hundred people at least, any one of whom could have earned themselves a modest amount by phoning the press.

There was a moment of danger, only a week before transmission. The *Sun* was doing a thirtieth *Archers* birthday supplement, and reporter Bronwen Balmforth was in Birmingham, prowling about and seeking the facts. Fortunately it was sex, not death, that the *Sun* was after.

'Did young farmer David Archer spend the night with his man-mad girl-friend Jackie? Did mother-of-three Jennifer lead on a married man, John Tregorran, hoping that he would fall for her? And what was Shula up to with her boyfriend Mark in a car at night out in the Country Park?'

Bronwen almost got a scoop. 'Jock Gallagher, head of Radio and BBC Pebble Mill where *The Archers* is produced, plans to visit Torquay today to see Gwen in hospital . . .' And Gallagher was quoted: 'We are not at the point where we will definitely have to write her out.'

Jock Gallagher went to Torquay. His job was to tell Gwen that Doris was being killed the following Monday.

Gwen's illness had been widely reported in the press and her nursing home room was full of flowers and cards from well-wishers. The sudden attention had vastly restored her spirits. She was looking forward, she said, to coming back to the studio.

Gallagher was horrified. He found he could not tell her the reason for his visit and set off back to Birmingham. On the way he stopped and phoned the production office, saying the decision to kill Doris would have to be postponed (impossible, as dozens of subsequent episodes – full of Dan the mourning

On 1 January 1981 the programme celebrated its thirtieth anniversary – and Ambridge celebrated the engagement of Shula to young solicitor Mark Hebden. Uneasily combining the two events, the cast were summoned to drink champagne and eat cake at Broadcasting House, London, at the end of December 1980. The photocall was boycotted by the production team because it gave away the following week's storyline. From the left: Patricia Greene (Jill Archer), June Spencer (Peggy Archer), Jack May (Nelson Gabriel), Edgar Harrison (Dan Archer), Sara Coward (Caroline Bone), Heather Bell (Clarrie Larkin) and Charles Collingwood (Brian Aldridge). In the foreground: Judy Bennett (Shula) and Richard Derrington (Mark).

Hulton Deutsch

widower – had been written, and in large part recorded). Before Gallagher was back in Birmingham Gwen's brother, Terry, also phoned the office. He said that Gwen had put on a special effort for Jock. She would not be able to return to the studio again.

The episode was due to go out on the following Monday, 27 October (it was marked 'D Day' in the office diary). On the Friday an Ambridge village folk concert was recorded on a farm outside Leeds, for transmission on Radio 4, which was, as usual and as pointlessly as ever, trying to raise its profile in Yorkshire. In the early hours of Saturday morning the Pebble Mill press office phoned the hotel where the production team were staying to say that the story of Doris's death had leaked. The *Daily Telegraph* not only knew it was about to happen, they knew the details of the death scene, and where the recording had taken place.

A jumble of press statements was put out to try to confuse everybody. 'A funeral service was recorded at Cherington on September 28th and can be used in the programme at any time,' said one BBC spokesman. 'Due to widespread speculation scripts have now been rewritten in order to provide an alternative course of events,' said another. 'Mr Jock Gallagher, network editor radio, visited Gwen Berryman last Thursday to discuss the possibility of recording in Torquay so that Doris could be heard up to the end of *The Archers* 30th Year,' – a cunning one this, containing an element of truth.

I phoned home on the Saturday morning and found my wife had been answering calls from journalists, one of them at 2am. Later I drove with actor Trevor Harrison and Diane Culverhouse, the programme assistant, through the Trough of Bowland. We got out and climbed to the top of the hill overlooking the tortuous road along which the Pendle Hill witches had trundled to their doom. We shouted: 'Doris Archer is dead!' and the sheep looked startled and scurried away.

The impending – though unconfirmed – death was on the main BBC news. The *Sunday Times* carried a leader saying: 'Not since Conan Doyle put Sherlock Holmes, Dr Watson and Mrs Hudson into 221 Baker Street have fictional characters and places commanded such widespread suspension of unbelief . . .' and went on: 'Doris Archer was "born" in 1900, her husband Dan in 1896. Grandparents and great-grandparents, they cannot remain forever, frozen like fossils in a glacier. Though we wish Miss Berryman a return to health and years of content, Doris Archer herself has reached the end of the road. Her passing will be comparable with Trollope's killing off of Mrs Proudie, and much more regrettable.'

The *Sunday Times* headline was 'Alas, Poor Doris'. The *News of the World* headline was 'Bye, Doris'.

On Monday morning the production team was back in the office, busy refusing to confirm anything. Around lunchtime – some seven hours before the death-episode was due to be transmitted – I got a call to go to Jock Gallagher's office straight away. When I got there he said, 'Equity know that you recorded Doris's death scene in a church using ordinary villagers and not Equity members.' I said, 'Godfrey Baseley did it dozens of times and nobody complained.' He said, 'They're complaining this time. I've just had a call to say they've blacked the recording.'

We stared at each other across his desk. We were both filled with rare and inexpressible joy. Jock jumped up. 'Quick,' he said, 'let's go and hide somewhere before they change their minds.'

For the first time in its history, *The Archers* was the front page lead story in a national newspaper. 'BBC's Black Farce' said the *Daily Express* and every other national carried the story. Equity's organizer, Mr Glen Barnham, was reported starkly as saying: 'The recordings made by the villagers of Cherington have been blacked.' The *Daily Express* said: 'We have all heard of restrictive practices but this is ridiculous. Does Equity really believe that the use of ordinary people on this kind of occasion is a threat to their livelihood and their professional pride?'

The Times accused Equity of orchestrating a publicity stunt: 'Its members have had two thousand fewer engagements in radio drama this year than last, according to Mr Peter Plouviez, its general secretary. Are they expected to stand idly by while the scabs who attend morning service at the church of St John the Baptist, Cherington, Warwickshire, supply a funeral rendering of "The day Thou gavest, Lord is ended," always Doris's favourite? Better a gramophone record, on which the Performing Rights Society collects . . . the imaginary mourning of Ambridge has had to make way for Equity's unimaginable talent for farce.' *The Times*, enjoying itself, went on to ask: 'And who is this fellow Plouviez with his made-up name?'

Peter Plouviez responded the next day in a letter to the editor. He claimed that the entire incident of the 'blacking' had been a nonsensical BBC-inspired stunt and he ended up: 'I deeply resent the allegation that my name is "made up". How such a suggestion can be made by a newspaper whose editor we are expected to believe is called Rees-Mogg is beyond me . . .'

The story, rather like Doris, would not die. There were echoes of the death of Grace, when the *Manchester Guardian* had parodied Wordsworth, although the *Guardian*'s wit was not quite matched on Radio 2's *News Huddlines*:

> Eternal Archers strong to stay
> Though days and Doris pass away
> Thy thirty years familiar fame
> Has come from staying just the same
> For thirty years we've sung for thee
> Recorded by the BBC

Solo voice:

> Hullo, is that the BBC?
> Oh no, luv this is Equity
> No amateurs please on the show
> This isn't Songs of Praise you know . . .

The *Daily Telegraph*, the paper that had first leaked the contents of the episode, became irritable. 'We do not express our deep regret at the death of Doris Archer. We refrain from doing so for the reason that she cannot have died since she was never alive. This brutal concession to the literal truth may seem to some to be insensitive and even heartless; but, after the fuss of the last few days, the hazardous duty of placing it on record is surely one which no newspaper, with even a residual concern for the nation's sanity, can properly escape . . .'

Still the story lived on, carried by radio and television stations round the world. A Los Angeles radio station was bemused to find its newspapers full of the demise of a fictional old lady it had never heard of, and astonished to discover that the most successful soap opera in the world was actually on radio in England. Their presenter phoned the *Archers* office at Pebble Mill. 'What's your big story today?' they asked production secretary Joanna Toye (she who would later write a novel revealing the secrets of Shula's love life). Not realizing that her conversation was being transmitted live, Joanna told them quite rightly that the story of the day concerned Aunt Laura's pickled walnuts, which had mysteriously disappeared from the pantry at Ambridge Hall.

The Los Angeles station called back the next day. Its listeners wanted to know how to pickle walnuts. Joanna gave them the recipe. Who, the presenter asked, is Aunt Laura? She told them that Aunt Laura was organizer of the Ambridge Over Sixties, who were currently revolting against her tyranny, and wanted to be allowed to go to London instead of Weston-super-Mare for their annual outing.

The radio station called back the next day. Its listeners wanted to know if the revolt had been successful.

For several weeks Los Angeles phoned every afternoon at a set time and Joanna (her English voice a bit like the Queen's) recounted the daily story of Ambridge life. The broadcasts only stopped on 8 December, when John Lennon was killed and the radio station's schedules were thrown into disarray. They promised to come back, but Joanna told them she had had enough of media stardom in California.

God works in mysterious ways. The 'blacking' of the Doris death episode gave a publicity boost to the church of St John the Baptist, Cherington. There was a great increase in visitors. The vicar, the Rev John Woodward-Court, was able to raise money for church funds by selling tapes ('The Real Doris Archer Tape – £2') of the banned scene.

The actual episode, in the end, was partially re-recorded an hour before transmission. Leslie Saweard and Judy Bennett went to Broadcasting House in London to perform the lines from the scene in St Stephen's church porch (so Equity did get two extra artiste's fees) and in Birmingham the lines were recorded clean and then mixed with the only recording available of 'The day

Thou gavest'. It had been made in a cathedral church, with a professional choir and a thundering, soaring organ.

Several listeners, who hadn't been reading their newspapers properly, wrote to complain about the organ. Gwen Berryman did not complain. She did not hear the episode. Instead she lay in bed and, according to press reports, watched an episode of her favourite television programme, *Angels*. She said later to Jock Gallagher, 'I hated the thought of dying and I hated everyone whom I thought responsible for killing me off. At the time I am quite sure I could not distinguish between Gwen and Doris.'

In the New Year's Honours, she was awarded the MBE. She went to the Palace and the Queen thanked her for the pleasure she had given to so many people over so many years. Gwen wanted to tell the Queen that she had met her mother, and her daughter Anne, and that she liked her dress – but she was permanently in a wheelchair by now, and before she could say anything she felt herself being pulled smoothly backwards.

But she had, as she said, taken her curtain call.

And what, during all this, of Godfrey Baseley? The programme was approaching its thirtieth birthday. One of his greatest fictional characters had passed on. 'If we killed Doris Archer off, we'd be in trouble,' he had said once to *Farmers Weekly*, but it had come to pass. He had fought a hidden war against trade union influences (no member of the cast, even now in 1980, was willing to be *Archers* Equity 'dep', so unlucky was the post in terms of character mortality) and how right he had been proved! He had sneered at the 'hierarchy' all his life. Perhaps that was why they didn't recommend him for an honour, but gave one, instead, to a character that he had created.

He was still living in 'Ambridge', his house near Tewkesbury. He had not been near Pebble Mill for over a decade but just before Christmas, 1980, *Pebble Mill at One* decided to do an item on the programme's thirtieth anniversary. He agreed to take part.

The cast knew he was coming. When he strode into the Green Room several older actors admitted to a feeling of terror ('My heart stopped beating,' said one), while the younger members of the cast wondered who he was. He said 'Hello,' stiffly. Those who knew him said, 'Hello Godfrey.' Then off he went to the television studio where a mock-up of the Bull had been made so that he, and some of the actors, could be interviewed. Godfrey objected. The actors could be interviewed in the Bull he said, but not him – as creator and former-editor he should be interviewed separately.

The television people said it wasn't possible. Three cameras would be on the Bull and their fourth camera would be getting into place for the next item. They explained to him, patiently, how television worked.

Godfrey knew the enemy when he saw it. These were the bright young things who had baffled him so all those years ago in London. He said, 'If you won't

interview me separately I won't appear.' They said, 'All right then, don't appear.'
   Godfrey walked out.

1 January 1981. Thirty years had passed since that first national broadcast, when
Dan said: 'And a Happy New Year to all!' and ushered in yet another year of
rationing and identity cards. Phil and Jill were now the same age that Dan and
Doris had been in 1951. Shula and David were the modern equivalent of Phil and
Christine. Joe Grundy was establishing himself as a lovable rogue, an inefficient
farmer with a tearaway son – very much the part taken by Walter Gabriel in the
early Fifties. There was an attractive, rather posh girl in the village – not cool
Carol Grey, but warm Caroline Bone. There was no question, now, of killing the
programme off. It had become an institution, capable of generating more publicity than the rest of BBC Radio's programmes put together. 'The road lies open!'
said a BBC publication issued to mark the anniversary. 'It only needs a young
college lecturer to come round the corner in a green caravan, and it can all start
again . . .'

28

Ambridge in Liverpool

IT WAS TIME FOR JOHN TREGORRAN, the passionate romantic from the Fifties who had turned into such a desperate bore, to fall in love with Jennifer.

The two characters were thrown together. They would – helped by Caroline Bone and Pat Archer – compile a landscape survey of Ambridge. Week after week they were heard examining Roman remains at Jiggins Field, discovering the lost, deserted village of Ambridge (a bit of a medieval chapel in the barn at Grange Farm), tracing out the line of Aethelwold's Hedge and Eadric's ditch, and collecting bits of old Ambridge wisdom:

> When elm leaves are as big as a shilling
> Plant kidney beans, if to plant 'em you're willing

It was all served up in the scripts, but John was a slow mover, the sexual tension was a long time in coming. Finally they were together in Leader's Wood. It was springtime. Jennifer was getting excited over some English lime trees and Midland hawthorn – 'So characteristic of ancient, pre-Saxon woods, John!' she burbled – when he pounced.

Well, he sort of pounced. He didn't do anything. The writers, when it came to it, chickened out. For several weeks John talked to Jennifer about love in middle age, and Jennifer talked about bluebell and oxlip and wild service trees. Eventually Carol Tregorran got fed up with the two of them forever in a huddle, and spoke sharply to her husband.

The Tregorrans moved to Bristol.

Their labour in the fields and woodlands was not wasted. In September 1981 Jack Woolley's Borchester Press published their research in a book, *Ambridge – An English Village Through The Ages*, and held a launch party at Grey Gables, and a real book by the same name appeared in the shops, published by Methuen. For the real book, the Post Office had supplied Ambridge with a postcode and the Ministry of Transport had given the road through Ambridge an official classification: the B3980. 'Down in Ambridge the Archers and their friends are losing their grip on unreality,' said the *Observer*, and quoted Jock Gallagher saying: 'The borderline between reality and fantasy has disintegrated.'

The book went into three impressions, which for a landscape survey of a place that did not exist was remarkable. 'I admire the wide range of scholarship brought together in one volume,' said a confused Judy Cooke in the *New Statesman*. A French publisher made an offer to print a French edition, in the belief that it was all real.

Those who did not want to read about Ambridge could visit it. The village of Cherington was turned into Ambridge for the day by the *Western Daily Press* which organized a 'coach trip to Ambridge' as a competition prize. The AA changed all the road signs, the brewery turned the Cherington Arms into the Bull, and there was the 'Ambridge Flower Festival' in a neighbouring church, where the Rev John Woodward-Court was pretending to be the Borchester rural

In September 1981 a West Country newspaper turned the village of Cherington, Warwickshire, into 'Ambridge for the Day' and took a coach full of listeners there on a visit. From the left round the bar of the Bull: Clarrie (Heather Bell), Mark Hebden, rather strangely smoking a pipe (Richard Derrington), Jethro Larkin (George Hart), competition winner Mr Ivan Brickell, Mike Tucker (Terry Molloy) and Eddie Grundy (Trevor Harrison).
Bristol United Press

dean and selling his tapes of Doris's 'genuine' death episode. Readers of the *Western Daily Press* had been asked to vote for their favourite *Archers* character, and had given the joint first prize to Dan and to Walter Gabriel.

'The Archers are in revolt,' said the *Daily Mail*. 'The stars have shattered their rural peace to protest about their pay.' The cast were complaining that they only got £44 an episode – while television soap stars in *Coronation Street* got £150. Edgar Harrison was reported as saying: 'We wouldn't strike, so our only hope is to let our listeners know what sort of rates people like myself are on.' Norman Painting said he was only getting £11,000 a year from *The Archers*. 'That's why I've got to sell my house,' he said. The BBC response was curt and unsympathetic: 'With repeat fees and foreign rights they do all right.'

Edgar's hope that listeners would protest at the low level of fees proved unfounded. The public was indifferent, or perhaps thought that £11,000 a year was a good whack for a part-time job reading bits out loud in a nice warm studio.

What could the actors do? They were all so insecure, as *Woman* magazine highlighted. 'We get our scripts on Friday and we record on Monday,' said June Spencer, 'so that's all the notice you get of your death or departure.' She told *Woman* that dark rumours of dismissal were always circulating round the cast: 'People start biting their fingernails and wondering how they're going to pay the mortgage.' Angela Piper confessed to constant paranoia. She had first thought she was being written out when the writers sent Jennifer to live in Borchester. 'I'm so insecure that if the script says there's a strange noise under my car bonnet I quickly leaf to the end to see if it's going to blow up.' It had been a nasty moment, she said, when they sent her up in an aeroplane to photograph Ambridge for the landscape survey.

Edgar Harrison decided to be brave. He felt, perhaps, a certain security. Dan was a popular character, as proved by the readers of the *Western Daily Press*. It would be difficult to kill him off so soon after the demise of Doris. He asked for either a higher fee or the guarantee of a certain number of episode bookings. He was told he could have neither. He threatened to resign. He was told he was free to leave the programme if he wished. 'You don't understand, I'm *Dan Archer*,' he said. 'The third Dan Archer,' he was told, 'and actually you're Edgar Harrison.'

The revolt collapsed. Edgar stayed. Godfrey Baseley would have been proud.

The Tregorrans were gone. There was a character called Alan Fraser, an ex-SAS officer, who nearly broke Tom Forrest's arm (how the malicious young writers liked to make Uncle Tom suffer!) and had a love affair with Caroline Bone. Alan Fraser was a great favourite with writer Alan Bower, but as a character he was not a success. He was a silent, enigmatic type, not a good idea in a radio programme. He lurked around the woods then off he went – mysteriously, like all those secret-service agents and strange French women back in the Fifties.

Then there was Julie Jeavons, the Brummie barmaid at the Bull who jogged in pink running shorts and became engaged to Neil Carter, and even lived with him for a time in Nightingale Farm. A public school master wrote of Julie Jeavons: 'I have had dozens and dozens of critical, heated, furious parents complaining that just as they knew the family could tune in once more to *The Archers* without the usual womanising, illicit, grovelling-in-the-gutter sex activities, it has returned to the low standard that these lazy script writers have reduced this really potentially excellent serial.'

Shula had become engaged to young Borchester solicitor Mark Hebden, whose mother was called Bunty. They bought a cottage in Penny Hassett and started to renovate it. Then Shula was heard having a strange emotional relationship – not to mention implied sex – with an old hippy called Ben Warner who wore a kaftan and lived in a tent. Would she renounce her Conservative-voting fox-hunting former self and live in the woods with a flower-power lunatic? Most of the writing team would have voted 'yes!' – indeed Shula did call off her engagement to Mark – but there were other powers in the land. Shula came through the fire of temptation untouched (emotionally that is) and Ben Warner was revealed as a cat burglar and put in prison. The public school teacher did not bother to write about Ben Warner. Nobody, for that matter, wrote about Ben Warner, or about Alan Fraser.

Characters who had no connection with Ambridge were still being invented, thrown into combat, broken on the rocks of public indifference . . . then written out, sent on their way.

It was resolved that a fight would be made over Mark Hebden.

Mark was not adventurous enough? The writers made him chase poachers in the country park. Mark still not adventurous enough? They made him take up hang gliding. Mark still, even now, a bit wet? They made him defend hunt saboteurs in Borchester magistrates' court, and describe the Borchester bench (Phil was a magistrate) as a high class Mafia. Mark not sexy enough? They thrust him into an affair with Jackie Woodstock, notorious Borchester playgirl and Shula's rival on the committee of Borchester Young Conservatives. Any bloke fancied by Jackie Woodstock had to be a bit special, didn't he?

But it was no use. Jackie said he was wimpish and gave him the push. The writers didn't want her to do it, but she did.

In due course they admitted failure and sent him to Hong Kong.

In November 1982 Eddie Grundy and Clarrie Larkin were married, and *Radio Times* did a big picture feature. They shot the reception in the White Bear at Shipston-on-Stour, where Trevor Harrison chatted up the barmaid (he was irresistible in his hat with horns) and started a love interest of his own, a romance that was to come to fruition a few weeks later after the first *Archers* 'Christmas Revue' was recorded, written by the programme assistant Diane Culverhouse.

Clarrie (Heather Bell) and Eddie Grundy (Trevor Harrison) finally tie the knot . . . photographed at Barcheston church near Shipston-on-Stour, Warwickshire.

William Smethurst

For reasons now lost in the mists of time, but probably connected with Radio 4's ceaseless and hopeless attempts to sell itself North of Watford, the programme was recorded in Crosby Town Hall, Merseyside. The Town Hall was filled to capacity. Ambridge CND turned up with their banners (they claimed that Pat Archer had said it was OK) and distributed 'Nuclear Free Ambridge' stickers. 'It may be cold outside,' said Brian Aldridge, master of ceremonies, 'in fact I can assure you it's very cold, having spent all day harvesting sugarbeet on the far side of Lakey Hill. But we're warm and cosy here in the Village Hall, and Dorothy Adamson [the Vicar's wife] assures me that for once the central heating isn't going to break down . . .'

The revue featured the cast's favourite music hall turns. The Borchester Choir (more generally to be heard in Liverpool Cathedral) sang carols and there were monologues by George Barford, a ghost story by Joe Grundy, and 'our stand-up comic for the evening, straight from an engagement at Grey Gables country club – Jocular Jack Woolley!'

'Here's a good tip for any husband here tonight who's got an over-weight wife,' said actor Arnold Peters, who did not perhaps appreciate the feminist tinge to the programme's new writing team. 'Persuade her to go jogging two miles every morning and two miles every night. By the end of the week she'll be twenty-eight miles away.'

And of course everybody sang 'The Village Pump', that song that has haunted Ambridge life, sung with such gusto by Tom Forrest on so many occasions. The song itself was collected by Bob Arnold when he was a young man, going round village halls in the Cotswolds as a folk singer and entertainer. It needed only minor adjustment to fit into Ambridge life:

> There's a pretty little village far away,
> Where they grows new potatoes, corn and 'ay,
> There's a tricklin' little rill,
> That works a little mill,
> And the mill it keeps a workin' all the day.
> There's a lot of little 'ouses in the middle,
> And two pubs – the Bull and Cat and Fiddle,
> But you make no mistake
> The thing that takes the cake
> Is the pride of all the place, the Village Pump.

For those who have difficulty remembering verse, the chorus, which echoed round the rafters of Crosby Town Hall, runs: 'The Village Pump, The Village Pump, The Village Pump, Pump, Pump, Pump, Pump. The Village Pump, The Village Pump, The Village Pump, Pump, Pump, Pump, Pump.'

When *Archers* scripts in the studio are disastrously short the director generally has two options. One is to stop recording for thirty minutes and write some extra material, and the other is to slow the action by piling in extra sound effects and telling actors that 'this is a thoughtful, relaxed, slow sort of episode'. It is amazing how actors can add three or four minutes by being relaxed and thoughtful. On one occasion in the early Eighties, however, a director had a flash of inspiration. His script was two minutes under. The last scene was in the Bull. He gave a new line to Tom: 'Have you got that new piano for the function room, yet, Sid?' and a new line to Sid: 'It arrived yesterday, do you want to have a look?' and a new line to somebody else: 'Let's all have a look . . .'

And then he just faded down and up again into: 'There's a pretty little village far away . . .' and carried it through, verse after verse, until it was time for 'Barwick Green'.

It was after the recording in Crosby, the next morning in fact, on a Mersey ferry, that Trevor Harrison popped the question to barmaid Julia Cook from the White Bear in Shipston-on-Stour. She had followed him all the way to Liverpool, so great was her love, and it was therefore no surprise when she said yes.

The Ambridge Christmas Revue went out on Christmas Day 1982 on Radio 4, and Trevor and Julia were married the following year.

29

Of Polly, Pinky and a Pargetter

I F TREVOR HAD GAINED A BARMAID the programme had lost one. In 1982 Polly Perks, whose Dad had been a notorious arsonist, who had married Sid Perks and after great difficulty (including a miscarriage caused by post office robbers) had conceived and given birth to daughter Lucy, died in a road accident. Actress Hilary Newcombe had decided to give up acting. It was decided not to re-cast. Sid, left with a small daughter, would provide an onward-going storyline. The scenes of Sid coping with the death of his young wife were written with great power by writer James Robson.

The public reacted with terrible anger:

'No! I am not prepared to accept an explanation that it was a lesson in road safety . . .'

'Oh you mean, nasty, destructive creatures, to get rid for ever of the lovely, endearing, bright as a button, fresh as a daisy, true little English country rose, our beloved little Polly . . .'

'Poor Polly Perks is the victim, the latest in a long line reaching back to Grace Archer. One only hopes the blood lust has been satisfied for another year.'

'For the last few editions having to listen to the "acted" grief has been so painful I have been forced to turn it off . . .'

'Writing out Polly Perks was cruel. Will *The Archers* be better off without her? No, no, no. It would be better off without YOU.'

And there were those who thought it was all real:

'Please accept my sadness on the passing of your good wife Polly,' said one letter of condolence. 'I still cannot take it in. Many sad lives have been broken since the life of *The Archers* started . . .'

One listener sent £5 for a wreath. On the night the funeral was broadcast a member of the production team was in the Pebble Mill bar when he was called to the phone. A man, clearly distressed, identified himself as the sender of the money. The *Archers* director assured him that the funeral had gone well, and that Sid was comforting Lucy, and that, yes, the man's wreath of flowers had been placed by the grave. 'What sort of flowers were they?' the man asked, and the director's mind went blank. It was February. What flowers were there in February? After a terrible moment's hesitation he said chrysanthemums.

The programme was still looking for new writers. Susan Hill had moved on, as had Tessa Diamond and Alan Bower. Two new writers had joined the team. One was Margaret Phelan, a trained midwife who, like Helen Leadbeater, made her living working in London as a solicitor's clerk. The other was Watson Gould. In the Seventies Watson had written a *Play for Today* about a lesbian relationship: in Ambridge she had the vicar light candles in little boats on the Am in memory of Hiroshima, and sent the more thoughtful members of the community to see *The War Game* in Hollerton. In Margaret Phelan's hands, Pat Archer developed strong leftist leanings during 1982 and 1983, attended a 'Women's Studies' course at Borchester Tech, had an affair of sorts with a sociology lecturer called Roger, and changed the Bridge Farm daily newspaper from the *Daily Express* to the *Guardian* without consulting Tony. (Michael Leapman in the *Express* called it a 'perverse decision' and said there was a feminist cell among the writers nobody could do anything about.)

Nobody, the production team told themselves virtuously, could say *The Archers* wasn't keeping up with the times.

In May 1983 Glenys Roberts in the *Evening Standard* let it be known that there were still vacancies for scriptwriters – new, fresh writers who had not, for preference, written radio drama before. This time there came a sour protest from Walter J. Jeffrey, the General Secretary of the Writers' Guild. 'We hope you will agree,' he wrote to the Head of Radio Drama, Ronald Mason, 'that it is regrettable at a time when radio provides a livelihood for so few professional writers that the one surviving daily serial should recruit some of its writers from outside the profession, and boast about it . . . small wonder that *The Archers* sometimes plumbs such depths of banality.'

A writer offered himself from the Falkland Islands. *The Archers* had lost New Zealand – NZ Radio could no longer afford to take it, they said, when BBC's transcription charges were increased – but had been given an unexpected and massive territory in the South Atlantic. In a bleak farming community a young English teacher, sent out from London and hating every minute of it, wrote asking if he could become a writer. He did a trial script, and on his return to England wrote five episodes. They did not, sadly, fulfil his early promise.

Norman Painting wrote in his autobiography *Reluctant Archer*, published in 1983: 'There is almost a score of writers currently producing scripts for the programme. That in my opinion is about ten times too many.'

Norman's book came as a great surprise. He referred again to his belief that the dead writer Geoffrey Webb had influenced his early Bruno Milna scripts from another level of existence. 'One of my new masters was so pontifical in condemning the suggestion as nonsense,' he wrote, 'that I knew him to have the closed mind I had always suspected.' He also said the character of Phil was

At the Royal Show, selling the early Eighties range of *Archers* books, calendars and T-shirts.
From left: production secretary Joanna Toye (who would become an *Archers* writer and
Archers' senior producer before writing *Shula's Story* in 1995) and production secretary
Lisa Ward (who would drink Buck's Fizz in the office every Friday afternoon).
William Smethurst

deteriorating into 'small-mindedness and misanthropy' and that he was frequently unhappy about playing the part. 'If it were decided that I should, for
reasons of plot or policy, be removed from the cast, then I would bow to that
decision without demurring . . .' he said, invitingly.

Jock Gallagher – presumably the 'new master' in question – would have been
happy to take the decision whether Norman demurred or not. For an actor pub-
licly to criticize the part he was playing and the way it was being written was
unheard of. Before the book was even finished, though, Norman suffered a heart
attack and was dead himself. He was possibly preparing, from beyond the grave,
to aid some other struggling *Archers* writer, when doctors in Intensive Care
resuscitated him from his state of ventricular fibrillation by using electric shock
treatment. 'Technically, for some moments, I had been dead,' he wrote, 'it is not
overstating the case to say that I came back from death to write these final pages.'

Norman – recuperating slowly, on no account to be upset or stressed – was
safe, for the moment, from Gallagher's anger.

Edgar Harrison died. He had been the third Dan. Listeners had taken comfort
from his warm tones without noticing, seemingly, his northern accent. He had
loved the character, and his sincerity had endeared him to audiences. In this

instance it was decided to re-cast. A public that had taken three Dans to its heart might reasonably be expected to warm to a fourth. It was announced in the press that auditions were being held.

Godfrey Baseley had been quiescent for several years. There now came a missive from that other Ambridge deep down in Gloucestershire. In a letter to Jock Gallagher he asked if he could play the part. His spirit was admirable but even disregarding problems with Equity – who might well have refused him membership – it was not practical. He was seventy-nine.

Frank Middlemass, a distinguished classical actor, took the role. It was to be an occasional cameo from now on.

In the meantime a new boyfriend was needed for Shula. The script team had tried three times to write strong, manly types – men with personalities, chaps who could stand up to Shula and who would not be reduced to mere accessories. What did they have to do to succeed? They had really given up trying when, in the autumn of 1983, a young man fell off his mount at the opening meet of the South Borset Hunt, and was carried to Brookfield to recover. A week later he frightened Tom Forrest witless by dancing through the country park in a gorilla outfit. Then he turned up at Brookfield in it, to take Shula to a fancy dress ball.

Nigel Pargetter had arrived.

He raced mice in the Pargetter family colours. He drank champagne out of Jack Woolley's Dahlia Society Challenge Cup. He tried to creep into Shula's bedroom one night and crept, instead, into Phil and Jill's. Phil awoke to hear a low seductive voice saying 'Cuckoo!' (Nigel's love call) before Nigel leapt on top of him. A listener wrote to say that he had laughed so much when he heard the scene that he drove his car into a hedge.

Eventually Shula gave Nigel the push. It was at the end of a Friday episode. He sat sadly in the garden at Brookfield, and a new, different voice said: 'Hello, Nigel.' It was young Elizabeth, heard on air for the first time in several years. Out came the gorilla suit again as he drove her back to her boarding school. When she was expelled (men and booze after lights out) he collected her with a bottle of champagne and brought her home.

Audience research, after he had been in the programme only a few weeks, showed him to be the programme's favourite character. When he was sent to Africa by his despairing family his exodus provoked a national 'Bring Back Nigel Pargetter' campaign in the personal column of *The Times* and a flood of letters to the campaign's organizer, Mrs Michael Johnson.

'I miss him dreadfully already and he's only been gone one day – and fancy sending him off without his parents there . . .' said one.

'Nigel, poor Nigel, he does so want to be loved. Well we love him, don't we . . .?' said another.

'Nigel, our gadfly gorilla, his character so sharply etched, should not be lost . . .' wrote a listener in poetic vein.

Another tried to be optimistic: 'Perhaps he will have a holiday in Zimbabwe and come back . . . He need have no fear of the lions as there are very few left.'

He came back from Africa, and gave everybody at Brookfield little wooden elephants.

Another new, also instantly successful character, came on the scene. Village girl Susan Horrobin – innocent daughter of the dreadful Bert Horrobin from the council houses, sister of the awful Clive – won a piglet called Pinky at the fête. Neil Carter helped her look after it, and soon they were walking out together.

Nigel from nearby Lower Loxley, Susan from the Ambridge council houses . . . these were the characters listeners wanted, not incomers from faraway places like Birmingham and Felpersham.

30

The Princess
and the Duke

A ROUTINE LETTER CAME asking for publicity – this time from the NSPCC, which was launching a major fund raising effort. The Duke of Westminster would be attending dinners and receptions in towns all over England during 1984. Could this be mentioned on *The Archers*? Could there, perhaps, be an NSPCC dinner in Borchester, with the villagers of Ambridge heard raising money for the cause?

The request would normally have been turned down. The *Archers* office received at least one letter a week asking for publicity, and the programme had already 'adopted' the Church of England Children's Society and the WRVS. Otherwise it only supported charitable appeals if they provided genuine, entertaining stories. On the face of it, the NSPCC appeal would not provide a story at all.

Then somebody in the *Archers* office had an idea. What, they said, if the Duke himself made an appearance in the programme? And what if he turned out to be a relation of the well-connected Caroline Bone who was now Jack Woolley's assistant at Grey Gables?

The NSPCC press officer was phoned. He said, cautiously, that he was sure the Duke would be willing to take part in the programme. But would he acknowledge Caroline as a relation? Would he say, 'Hi, Caroline,' when she said, 'Hi, Gerald'?

The press officer went away again. When he came back he said the Duke of Westminster was prepared to have Caroline Bone as a relation through his mother's side of the family.

The recording date was fixed. The Duke would come to Pebble Mill on Tuesday, 22 May. Some days later there was another phone call. The press officer sounding bemused. He spoke in a hushed voice – a publicity man scarcely yet believing his luck. The Duke had been to dinner the evening before at Kensington Palace. He had told Princess Margaret – the president of the NSPCC – about his forthcoming appearance on *The Archers* and she had demanded to be on *The Archers* as well.

'The Duke checked again this morning,' said the press officer, 'in case she'd changed her mind. She still says she wants to do it.'

The Queen Mother was known to be a regular listener. The Director-General's office had only recently made discreet arrangements for her private secretary to come to Pebble Mill and sit in on a day of recordings. The Queen herself had told Norman Painting, when he received his OBE, that she listened regularly on a Sunday morning – and later she had told Chris Gittins that *The Archers* was one of her favourite programmes. She had sent Edgar Harrison and his wife a telegram on their Golden Wedding anniversary. Princess Anne had once criticized Shula as 'a ghastly child' and Princess Diana had told us, sadly, that she had had to stop listening after her marriage.

We had not known, however, that Princess Margaret held us in esteem.

Perhaps she wanted to get one up on the rest of her family.

I went and found Jock Gallagher in his office. I closed the door. I said, 'I've just cast a new character.'

'Oh yes?' he said, always interested.

'But nobody,' I said, as hushed as the publicity man, 'must know about it.'

A certain Major Griffin at Kensington Palace agreed that there should be no immediate publicity. Princess Margaret's private secretary, Muriel, confirmed that the Princess did not want her appearance publicized before the event. This gave us the excuse not to tell anybody at all in BBC London for several weeks.

Jock Gallagher and I knew about it, two sound engineers knew about it – they would have to set up a studio of sorts at Kensington Palace – and reluctantly but inevitably, two actors, Sara Coward (Caroline) and Arnold Peters (Jack Woolley), had to be let in on the secret. ('We're recording a little scene in London with a new member of cast who doesn't feel up to coming to Birmingham,' I remember whispering to Arnold, enjoying myself hugely, and why not.)

The recording date approached. Jock Gallagher felt that the Controller of Radio 4, Monica Sims, really would have to be told that the Queen's sister was about to perform as an actor in a BBC radio play. I objected, but Jock had some vestige, not glimpsed hitherto, of a BBC manager's conscience. In the strictest confidence, he told Monica Sims.

The next thing was a phone call from someone calling herself the BBC's Court Organizer. We had not known, until this time, that there was such a thing. Did we not realize – this Court Organizer said – that all contacts between the BBC and the Royal Family had to be co-ordinated through the Court Organizer's office? Could it really be true that we had actually held conversations with Kensington Palace without the Court Organizer being involved? (*Panorama* and the Princess of Wales would find themselves in the dog-house for just this sort of thing in 1995.)

She said that the recording might have to be cancelled – it might not be given BBC approval. She did not comprehend, for a long time, that Princess Margaret was going to act a part in a script. When she did, she demanded to vet it. I refused to let her see it. 'Major Griffin and I have agreed that nobody shall see it but ourselves,' I said. 'Major Griffin,' she said, incensed, 'is being very, very naughty.'

Trouble, trouble. The BBC photographic unit in London heard what was happening and they were hurt at not being asked to take the photographs. We had already commissioned a Birmingham photographer – London said they would pay our man off. Foolishly, we gave in. The result was that the London photo unit accidentally destroyed all the colour pictures during processing.

Trouble, trouble. A call from BBC Contracts and Finance. Why did the Duke of Westminster and Princess Margaret not appear on the episode booking forms? And did I not realize that under the BBC's agreement with Equity, a non-professional actor could only be used if no suitable professional actor could be found to take the part? (Godfrey Baseley's campaign to keep Equity at bay so that he could cast genuine royal princesses, dukes, and plumbers from Ebrington, had been justified yet again.)

We donated two episode fees to the NSPCC.

All this was in late June. In May it was all very secret as we set up our microphone in Kensington Palace. We rehearsed. Princess Margaret rapidly learned how to approach the microphone in such a way as to give the impression that she was walking across a large room (a skill not acquired by some actors after six months). She said her lines. She sounded gloomy and depressed. Taking her on one side to give her notes I said: 'You're being introduced to the organizers of the Ambridge charity fashion show, and everybody's terribly happy, but you sound rather bored.'

She looked at me, puzzled. 'But I would be, wouldn't I?' she said.

On the next take she cheered herself up and laughed a lot.

The Duke of Westminster came to Pebble Mill to record his bit. The episode was due to be transmitted on Friday, 22 June. Early in the week the national press got hold of the story, but nobody would officially confirm it for them. On the Friday morning I gave the details to Keith Wheatley, then editor of the *Evening Standard* diary. I regularly gave him *Archers* stories. He always printed them as a matter of speculation: 'It's the biggest secret in the BBC, but I'll eat my bow tie if Clarrie doesn't get engaged to Eddie tonight . . .' he would write bravely, once we had told him it was definitely going to happen. 'I'll eat my bow tie if Aunt Laura isn't killed off tonight . . .' he would say, and everybody had to listen to find out if it was true. The national papers always picked up the stories for the next day: they were suspicious of publicity stunts, but slavishly followed anything the *Standard* regarded as news. In this case a contrived leak wasn't necessary, but we told him anyway. 'I'll eat my bow tie if Princess Margaret isn't in *The Archers* tonight,' he wrote, claiming to have 'spied the gnome-like Smethurst and two of his regular cast' at a restaurant in the vicinity of Kensington Palace.

A clutch of beer-drinking curates from Cambridge – all members of an Ambridge Appreciation
Society – come to Pebble Mill to meet Caroline Bone (Sara Coward), their favourite barmaid.
Birmingham Post & Mail

At midday there was a press conference deep in the bowels of Broadcasting
House. BBC Television had declined to attend, but ITN sent a reporter and
camera crew along, and ran a story on *News At Ten*.

The tape was played. In the short scene, written by Joanna Toye, Jack Woolley
was heard being at first obsequious to Princess Margaret, then confiding that he
had been born in Stirchley, then being grossly over-familiar with the Duke of
Westminster. 'If there's anything else we can do you only have to get in touch,' he
assured the Princess. 'I was saying that very thing to Gerald here a minute ago,
wasn't I Gerald?'

The tape ended. One bewildered reporter kept saying: 'But who did you get to
play Princess Margaret? I don't understand who was playing Princess Margaret . . .'

The appearance of Princess Margaret was to be regarded by some newspaper
writers as the deciding moment when *The Archers* became fashionable and upmarket, like Sainsbury's or a Volkswagen Beetle. The production team, on the
other hand, liked to think that it was the quality of scripts and stories over the
previous three years that had slowly but steadily changed the programme's profile.

Either way, media interest was now greater than it had been since the Fifties.

There was the first *Archers* Road Show at the Ideal Home Exhibition, where
members of the public were able to act a scene with their favourite character, and

carry the result home on tape. A book came out – *The Ambridge Years* – Dan Archer's memoirs, for the publication of which we were keeping old Dan alive far beyond his allotted span. There was a rush of merchandising offers – a food company that made Mrs Beeton's Christmas puddings planned to launch a range of Ambridge food products, together with Ambridge green Wellington boots and Ambridge Barbour-type jackets. A firm in East Lothian took out a licence to market miniature Ambridge cottages, and a Staffordshire firm made an Ambridge plate which was advertised through full-page colour adverts in the *Sunday Times Magazine*. There was an Ambridge knitting pattern book, using 'Ambridge' brand wool. A film production company got in touch, and producers Kent Walwin and Pom Oliver came up to Pebble Mill. It wasn't a film they had in mind, but a new kind of 'audience-interactive' stage show. The last *Archers* stage show – written by Geoffrey Webb and Ted Mason – had been a disaster. Kent and Pom said that this time it would be different.

Audience research figures showed that the audience had vastly increased over the previous five years. These figures did not lie – but neither, alas, did they tell the truth. The audience had gone up by a third because Monica Sims, the Controller of Radio 4 who replaced Ian McIntyre, had moved the Omnibus back to Sunday morning. Instead of a disastrous 150,000 evening audience, the Omnibus was almost back to its old, traditional million listeners.

At the end of the year an episode was broadcast from Berlin, as we followed a story involving George Barford's soldier son, Terry. It featured the Prince of Wales's Own Regiment of Yorkshire's carol service in a Berlin church. The scene was recorded at 6pm, and the tape then rushed through Berlin with a police escort, to the British Forces Network studio where it was edited in time for transmission at 7.05pm.

In Ambridge, meanwhile, the only village in England unaware of all the media excitement, Jack Woolley had renamed the room used by Princess Margaret as the 'royal garden suite'. Hazel Woolley, the daughter of Valerie Grayson, one-time secret-service agent, and Reggie Trentham, that old Fifties cad and casino owner, had returned home. When he married her mother, Jack had adopted Hazel. He had lavished affection and money on her. He had given her a little dog and a pony. She had loved him in those days. Then she had disappeared off to London.

Why had she come back now? She claimed to be a successful PA in the film industry, but nobody in Ambridge believed a word of that. She seduced Tony and then told him to get lost. When Jack fell off the roof at Grey Gables, and lay in hospital at death's door, she poisoned the goldfish with vodka and kicked Captain. The tabloid press took to Hazel. They called her the 'JR of Ambridge'.

It was decided that Aunt Laura should die. 'Having reviewed the older characters in the programme – there are several well over 80 – it has been decided that one of them must naturally "pass away" for the sake of credibility,' actress

Betty MacDowall was told in a letter. After the distressing experience with Gwen Berryman, the more elderly members of the cast were no longer being told face-to-face that their time in the programme was over. Better that they received the news in private, where they could come to terms with it, pull themselves together, and put on a brave professional face.

Shula started going out with the local vet, Martin Lambert. Three good actors had a shot at playing the part but the public remained quite indifferent, and he remained a character made of cardboard.

The writers decided to bring back Mark Hebden. Mark, after all, was played by Richard Derrington, one of the most impressive actors in the business. If he couldn't develop a credible, interesting character for Shula to marry then nobody could.

Shula was heard pining for Mark. She flew out to Hong Kong to say that she loved him and missed him. He came back to England and proposed to her on Lakey Hill, the spot generally chosen by scriptwriters for such events.

'I think we should get married,' he said, toughly.

'Yes please,' said Shula, eagerly.

'At last,' said the continuity announcer, emotionally, as the strains of 'Barwick Green' brought the episode to a close. 'A million male hearts all over Britain sighed with the cruelty of it all,' said *Radio Times*, 'the painful realization that Shula, the beautiful blue-eyed blonde of Ambridge could no longer be theirs.'

'We tried to get rid of Mark Hebden,' I was quoted as telling Patrick Stoddart of the *Sunday Times*, 'and bring in this chunky vet called Martin. But Shula kept pushing him away in the car. I kept telling the writers this wasn't supposed to happen, but they couldn't make her change her mind. In the end we gave in . . .'

The time had come, as it did in the life of every Archer female, for Shula to settle down. Perhaps it should have happened earlier. Joanna Toye explained to *Radio Times*: 'no one was allowed to marry her for years because she was producer William Smethurst's ideal woman.'

Shula was twenty-six. Some instinct tells listeners and writers alike that the boyfriends are blurring into each other, that for this girl at least there are no more variations left on the courtship theme, that other young females are growing up, having their first boyfriends, demanding airtime for their youthful passions. Shula's shelf-life as the juvenile love interest was running out.

Besides, there was another urgent, critical reason why Shula just had to marry. The programme's thirty-fifth anniversary was coming up, a wedding was needed for the front cover of *Radio Times*, and Lord Lichfield was going to be asked to take the photographs.

31

The Rise of the House of Grundy

THE GRUNDYS, TOO, had a royal connection. It had started in February 1981, when Prince Charles and Lady Diana Spencer announced their engagement. In that evening's episode Clarrie was heard wondering if she, too, might win the man of her dreams, and the episode ended with a recording of 'One Day my Prince will Come' instead of 'Barwick Green'. The following year Eddie and Clarrie became man and wife, just like Charles and Diana did, and just like the Prince and Princess of Wales they had a major photo-feature in *Radio Times*. The ceremony in St Stephen's, Ambridge, did not, perhaps, attract quite the same international media interest, but folk in Ambridge knew which was the most notable Wedding of the Year.

It seemed, too, as if the Grundys' marriage was going to mirror the Waleses in terms of trouble and strife. Eddie disappeared to London for several weeks doing 'gigs' with Jolene Rogers and Wayne Tucson (the singing oilman from Waterley Cross) – a story that eerily reflected the Waleses' known disagreements when it came to musical tastes. Then the Princess of Wales gave birth to a little William – and Clarrie also gave birth to a little William. And Eddie was suspected of dallying once more with Dolly Treadgold, the way Prince Charles was accused of dallying with Camilla.

There the similarities ended. The Grundys' little William was heard being born on air and their second child, little Edward, was born in Great Yarmouth, where Clarrie had gone to look after her sister Rosie. No royal prince has ever been born in Great Yarmouth.

On an earlier visit to East Anglia the *Archers* production team had gone along with her, recording each day in places like Ely and Norwich, and finally on Great Yarmouth beach. How long had it been since the Archer family got this sort of special treatment? In 1983 Eddie was sick in the Bull's piano, and the Eddie Grundy Fan Club (how long was it since any member of the Archer family had a fan club?) went wild with joy. There was a shoal of anti-Grundy letters from disgusted listeners. 'You might as well call it "The Grundys" these days,' they all said – a hundred or so irritated listeners sharing one sarcastic thought.

The Grundys were even getting in on the merchandising. A Staffordshire firm took out a licence to sell 'Eddie Grundy Pork Scratchings'. When Jack Woolley discovered an otter in the Am, and advertised 'bargain wildlife weekends at Grey Gables – Home of Tarka, Otter of the Am' in the *Guardian* (readers opening their newspapers on 7 May found the advert really was there), the Grundys advertised Grange Farm weekends in the *Borchester Echo* ('Come and see "Spot" the otter!'), and Clarrie bought new nylon sheets and condemned Joe to the attic. The Grundys, it seemed, were not only getting all the best stories, they were stealing other people's.

Clarrie was in the *Today* programme's Personality of the Year top ten. When young visitors came to the studio it wasn't the Archer family they wanted to meet – it was the Grundys. 'Who's your favourite character?' they would be asked, and shy young girls would whisper 'Eddie Grundy' when once they would have whispered 'Philip'. Norman Painting, the old heart-throb Phil, could only sit and watch it all with wistful good humour.

The Eddie Grundy Fan Club had influential media members, like Gillian Reynolds of the *Daily Telegraph* and John Peel the disc jockey. There were Grundy sweatshirts, and an Eddie Grundy Christmas card, and regular 'Eddie-ups' at pubs across the country. 'Badger fat!' Eddie fans would say to each other when they met. When Eddie sang in the programme, his songs were released as real records and Terry Wogan played them on Radio 2. 'They say that I'm a no-good,' Eddie warbled, 'They say I'm really mean . . .

> They say my head's a pair of horns
> With nothing in between.
> But I'm a simple country boy
> Ain't got no city side,
> Like the cows in the field and the bullocks in the barn
> And the pig that's gone and died . . .

It was called 'Poor Pig' and was described on the record sleeve as a touching protest song against prejudice, reminiscent of the early Bob Dylan. It topped the charts in Borchester and Felpersham, though not, alas, in London or LA. Undaunted, Eddie wrote 'Clarrie's Song' and premièred it one night at Borchester Country and Western Club before singing it at the Ambridge Concert in Crosby Town Hall, Merseyside.

'The next song I want to sing for you – it's also on ma' latest release – is the song I'm most proud to have written in all the world. As a man goes through this life he finds the most important thing is the woman who's there, standing by his side. In my case, folks, that woman is called Clarrie . . .

'Now I know that my Clarrie's not Venus de Milo,' Eddie sang, 'She's warm and she's tender and besides she's got arms . . .'

Fact and fiction were increasingly blurred. Trevor Harrison had married Julia Cook, the barmaid of the White Bear at Shipston-on-Stour, where Eddie's publicity photos with barmaid Clarrie had been taken by *Radio Times*. Eddie's famous hat with horns was copied from a hat owned by farmer Peter Steel from Willington in Warwickshire, who wore it, and perhaps still does, for nights out at Banbury Country and Western Club. Eddie's friend Baggy (who in the programme lived in a multi-coloured bus with girlfriend Sylvia and children Aslan, China, Sunshine and Buttercup) is called Baggy in real life, and really did live on a bus, and if you want to mix fact and fantasy yourself you can go and buy a pint from him at the White Bear in Shipston, where in 1995 he took over as the landlord. Nowadays Baggy and Sylvia (actually Sheelagh, with a daughter called Maeve, not Buttercup) offer a fine range of beers and barsnacks, and their best bar is called the Ploughman's – which is sad when you think that Baggy in his prime was always a Cat and Fiddle man.

Grundy supporters tend to be young and inclined to revolution. 'Why was everyone so nasty to Eddie Grundy when he lent old fat man Forrest that twenty quid?' a Somerset silversmith complained. 'I hope the sudden interest in the Grundys is only the drum roll before a massive quashing of those Wetlegs of the Western World – the Archers!'

Wetlegs of the Western World . . .

'Archers are the sort of people who know when Harvest Festival is, or Rogation Sunday,' said John Walters cuttingly in the *Evening Standard*, and Neil Kinnock called for the programme to be retitled 'The Grundys and their Oppressors'.

'Where *do* you get your stories from?' people would ask, and one often wondered, particularly during a script meeting that had produced nothing by lunchtime other than *26 Sept, Tom and Pru's wedding anniversary (1958)*.

Stories often come from unexpected sources. The genesis of the sick-in-a-piano story – described by Walters in the *Evening Standard* as the 'highlight of the last decade' – was in the studio at Pebble Mill. Norman Painting was waiting to record a scene, and was idly playing on the studio piano. At the same time the sound recordist was playing pig noises on tape, ready for a forthcoming episode. From the studio speakers, it sounded as if there was a piano being played inside the Hollowtree pig unit.

A production secretary said: 'Wouldn't it be brilliant if that was in an episode?'

At the next script meeting, writers were asked: 'Who wants to write a story of Phil Archer playing a piano to his pigs?'

There followed solid brainwork, awesome to watch, as four writers, an editor, and a production assistant, drinking endless cups of coffee and munching through endless plates of fancy biscuits, managed to extrapolate a single scene into a major story that would run over three weeks.

How could a piano get into the Hollowtree pig unit?

In the end it was decided that somebody must have been transporting a piano

The Archers' chief sound engineer, Alan Mercer, recording scenes on location at Great Yarmouth –
where Clarrie (Heather Bell) and Eddie (Trevor Harrison) had gone to visit Clarrie's sister Rosie.
William Smethurst

on an open trailer. Their car had broken down. They had pushed the piano into the weaner house out of the rain.

Who would do such a thing? Well, whose truck was the most likely to break down? The Grundys'. Why should the Grundys be carting round a piano? Perhaps it was Clarrie's birthday, or perhaps it was for little William.

Gradually the story worked itself backwards . . .

Week One Eddie and Joe are in Clarrie's bad books (writer to invent reasons). Things get so bad they flee to the Bull (no great hardship). Eddie drinks too much. He is sorry for himself. Clarrie is cruel, the world is cruel. Eddie is sick inside Sid's piano. Sid shouts: 'You're both banned!'

Week Two Joe and Eddie pleading to return to the Bull. Joe indignant. It wasn't his fault! Sid unrelenting. His piano is ruined. Joe says it was ruined on VE night. Sid says: 'Out!' Terrible times drinking in the Cat and Fiddle. The beer's dire and the bikers clean their fingernails with carving knives. Despair. What shall they do? Clarrie says: 'You could always stay at home, there's plenty of jobs you could be getting on with.' Another attempt to gain admittance to the Bull. Sid says: 'Get me a new piano or you're banned for life.'

Week Three Trying to buy a replacement piano. (Writer to invent stories – a smooth salesman in Borchester perhaps? A little old lady in Penny Hassett?) Joe unwilling to pay more than a tenner. A piano finally obtained. Truck and trailer break down outside Hollowtree pig unit. Piano moved inside out of rain, which is where a puzzled Phil finds it, sits down, and starts to tickle the ivories.

So far so good. But who will discover Phil playing the 'Merry Widow Waltz' to his weaners? And what will they make of it? The script meeting set about plotting a second-strand story.

Week One Phil tells Jethro do so something daft – dig out a ditch he dug out last week, plough the wrong field or whatever (Tony Parkin to advise). Jethro chortles, 'Plough the Five Acre afore Martinmas? I think you're going a bit weak in the head Master Phil!'

Week Two A second incident. Phil, distracted by his magistrates courtwork or whatever, tells Jethro to do something he's already done the day before. Jethro says to Neil: 'I reckon the boss is losing his marbles.'

Week Three A third incident. (Tony Parkin, help!) Jethro goes on and on about it – much to Neil's irritation. At the end of the week, Jethro has to call in at the Hollowtree pig unit. He finds Phil playing the piano. 'My eye,' he says, 'My eye!' and reels off to tell Neil that the boss has gone totally insane.

Thus, over three weeks, two stories run side by side . . . and only in the final scene, which will be the end scene of an Omnibus, does one story provide the pay-off line for the other.

In the autumn of 1984 scenes by the four actors that had created the phenomenon of the Grundys – Haydn Jones, Heather Bell, Trevor Harrison and George Hart – came to an end. Haydn Jones, perhaps the most accomplished actor ever to play in *The Archers*, died on his way to the studio. His funeral was the following Monday – a recording day. Heather Bell, an old friend of Haydn's, asked to be written out of the script she was in, so that she could attend the funeral. She was told that it would not be possible – the writers were having huge problems writing out Joe Grundy, without having to write out Clarrie as well. Heather recorded her scenes at Pebble Mill, fulfilled her remaining contract dates, and then left the programme.

After several weeks the story was picked up by Sara Bond of the *Daily Express*, and the rest of the media followed. CLARRIE STORMS OUT OF AMBRIDGE said the *Daily Mail*. I QUIT! CLARRIE STORMS OUT OF THE ARCHERS said the *Daily Mirror*. Heather was quoted as saying, 'I couldn't stand working for William Smethurst any more,' and Trevor Harrison was quoted saying, 'I'm embarrassed and shocked by Heather.'

It transpired that Heather had been angry for a long time. She had been upset at not being introduced to the Duke of Westminster when he visited the studios, and further upset when, as she put it, 'members of the cast were "given away" as a prize in a Have Tea with the Archers contest' at the Bath and West Show. She also believed that she had been written out of the programme for a month as some sort of punishment (the accusation was true – it was why Clarrie had had to give birth to her second child in Great Yarmouth).

Fiona Mathieson was cast as Clarrie and Edward Kelsey, a friend of Haydn's, was cast as Joe. Edward Kelsey was able to bring to the part Haydn's warmth and humanity, and quickly made the part very much his own.

32

Wedding
of the Year

BRIAN ALDRIDGE HAD ASKED SHULA TO DANCE at a Grey Gables do, and Shula had replied tensely: 'OK, but just keep your hands to yourself,' thus alerting astounded listeners to something that had been going on in Ambridge for months and months without them knowing about it: an affair between Caroline Bone and Brian.

Caroline, listeners now discovered, had confided all to Shula, her friend.

Tony found the desperate pair kissing in a cornfield, but failed to twig. He found them lunching in the exclusive Mont Blanc restaurant and again failed to twig. But Tony had his own problems in the early summer of 1985: he wanted to go to Crete for his holidays; Pat wanted to go to a caravan at Borth. Tony complained bitterly. He wanted sea, sun, topless lovelies and an endless supply of cheap booze. Could you get all that at Borth? Could you get *any* of that at Borth?

There was an outcry from the Borth tourist office. The chairman of the District Council responsible for Borth told newspapers that Borth was every bit as good as Crete. He said that Tony Archer's gloomy view − cold sea, cold shingle, grey skies and Sunday-suited Welsh Methodists − was a travesty and likely to bring ruin to the bed-and-breakfast trade. Borth folk knew how to enjoy themselves, he said, and invited the *Archers* producers to go and look. Nobody dared.

Geoffrey Baker of the *Daily Star* − an avid *Archers* fan − was persuaded to investigate and Colin Skipp, who played Tony Archer, was sent to Borth with a topless model and a photographer.

On what was indeed a cold shingle beach, Colin was photographed with a can of lager, a bucket and spade, and a girl wearing very little apart from a Borth beach hat. 'While the sun didn't actually shine, local beauty Elaine Dyson provided plenty of sizzle as they strolled on the beach,' said the *Star*.

A story ran round the cast saying that there had actually been not one but two topless girls, and through various misfortunes and misunderstandings poor Colin had been left by the *Daily Star* photographer and had ended up paying both girls' hotel bill.

Encouraging the tabloids to write *Archers* stories was actually pointless. Our listeners did not read the *Sun* or the *Daily Star*. Tabloid reporters listened to *The Archers*, but their readers did not. *The Archers* was increasingly becoming the soap for the middle classes. An audience research survey showed that during the previous ten years the percentage of A and B Social Group listeners had risen from 35 to 40 per cent for the Sunday Omnibus, from 40 to 46 per cent for the midday episode, and from 50 to 58 per cent for the evening transmission. The *Guardian* ran a feature on the programme's new success. '*The Archers* are aiming for – and hitting – a new audience' said writer Robin Thurber, reporting that the new listener was typically a *Guardian*-reading social worker in North London who went to the National Theatre. Thurber admitted that he himself had returned to the fold of loyal listeners after a gap of some thirty years. He printed a letter from a listener in NW6 which, he believed, said it all.

'Today after 12 hours of struggling on the Underground, coping with 30 deprived and confused children in school; talking with a social worker about a mother who is in prison; visiting my bank manager in the lunch hour; shopping; washing; cleaning and cooking, there was Eddie Grundy turning into a Dad, and Clarrie having all the problems that we've all had.

'I know it's all escapism, fantasy – but the sigh of letting go, getting rid of the day's tensions while I peel the potatoes for supper, the tune which my children used to bounce up and down to when they were babies, is very, very real . . .'

In the summer of 1985 Kent Walwin and Pom Oliver presented their *Archers* audience-interactive stage show – *The Archers Live!* – at the Watermill Theatre, Newbury. 'An Everyday story of farmyard theatre,' said a bemused Tim Heald of *The Times*. 'We'd motored down from town and turned off the motorway into narrower and narrower lanes all overgrown with cow parsley and buttercups, and we came into this village which my wife said must be Ambridge. There was a pub and some cottages with roses round the front door and this chap in a tweed cap: Brian Aldridge. "We don't think much of the way you've been carrying on," said my wife. So he looked a bit sheepish, as well he might because although he's married to Jennifer he's been larking about with Caroline Bone, the Grey Gables Sloane Ranger . . .'

The audience sat in the Watermill Theatre, which had been turned into Ambridge Village Hall. On stage, Ambridge's inhabitants were drifting in and out rehearsing a 'Summertime in Ambridge' entertainment. Nigel Pargetter proposed to Elizabeth. Then Jill came in. 'Nigel's such a sweetie,' Elizabeth told her mother. 'He's asked me to marry him.'

'For God's sake,' replied Jill, ashen-faced, 'don't tell your father!'

Then Clarrie rushed in to say there'd been an accident at Grange Farm. The bemused audience were told to leave their seats. They were hurried out of the theatre and were led up a farm track (or, if infirm, carried on a tractor and trailer) to Grange Farm where they found Joe lying, wounded, in a barn. And suddenly there was the sound of an ambulance, a real ambulance! And yes, here it was, coming across the field with its lights flashing, and the audience had to scurry to one side to let it through . . .

Then they all went to the Ambridge fête and had a go at wellie-wanging and bowling for a pig, and dancing round the maypole. Jack Woolley wandered about fretfully (he'd lost Captain) and then they all went back into the 'Village Hall' to watch the second half of 'Summertime in Ambridge'. Elizabeth Archer sang a song – 'I've been to a marvellous party' – and sat on Brian Aldridge's knee, and every night the audience hissed at the rotter. Joe Grundy told a ghost story about Chicken Charlie and the Great Christmas Darts Match of 1932, and Fiona Mathieson as Clarrie stole the show every night with her rendering of 'He's just my Bill' – because everybody knew that she was really singing about her Eddie.

The show was a huge success. Every night the theatre bar heaved with media personalities and television drama executives. What nobody in the media knew was that it had almost been cancelled, a fortnight before it opened, from lack of bookings. Its fortunes had only changed when it received on-air promotion by continuity announcers on Radio 4. Despite its upmarket listener profile, *The Archers* was not proving easy to exploit commercially. The Staffordshire wall plates – beautifully produced – had been a flop, and the miniature cottages made by the firm in Ayrshire had not sold. '*Archers* listeners aren't into kitsch,' somebody remarked sadly.

There were no thoughts of kitsch at Pebble Mill, where the *Archers* office was deep in brochures for posh wedding gowns. Shula and Mark were to be married in September and Lord Lichfield was being approached to take the wedding pictures.

His agent was not hopeful. Lichfield had not done a wedding since Charles and Diana. He'd speak to him and see. He came back and said he didn't for a moment understand what was going on, but Lord Lichfield would be *honoured* to take Shula's wedding photographs.

Lichfield was a fan. Every evening, he delayed leaving his studio so that he could listen to the programme on the way home. For us, he'd even do a day's shoot for a specially reduced fee of £2,000. Plus, of course, expenses.

The normal BBC picture budget for such an event, assuming there was a valid reason to use a freelance, was perhaps £100.

The only way to raise the money was to sell the pictures to *Radio Times*. The editor immediately offered a front cover and a major feature – but there was a problem. He wanted to run the story the week before the wedding took place. We said he couldn't. He said that all *Radio Times* stories were about programmes that lay ahead: that was the point of running them. It was the point of *Radio Times*.

'But how can you show photographs,' I said to the picture editor, 'of a wedding that hasn't yet happened?'

The picture editor looked confused. *The Archers*, he said, was fiction. It was a play. *Radio Times* readers were sophisticated enough to know this.

I said, 'What if Shula runs away with Nigel Pargetter an hour before the church service?'

He said, 'She won't will she?'

'She might.'

'But you've got the wedding photographs.'

'That might not stop her.'

I explained that it was important for listeners *not to know* whether or not the wedding would go off well – or indeed would take place. Half their enjoyment was in listening to find out. Even those who knew that Ambridge was not real liked to pretend that it was, and the line between belief and suspended-disbelief was blurred. Already a piece of wedding cake had arrived in the *Archers* office. It was from a young newly-married woman. With it was a photograph of her wedding, and a six-page letter to Shula, urging her not to delay.

These were the people, I said, who sent wreaths to fictional funerals. It had been going on now for over thirty years. Recently, when the children of Ambridge had taken part in a sponsored sunflower growing competition in aid of The Children's Society, the society's local organizer had written to ask if she could call in at the Ambridge school and give the children a talk about how to grow their flowers.

'Why is it that so many people, otherwise sane and on nodding terms with reality, are willing – even determined – to suspend their disbelief for the sake of a radio programme?' an article in *The Listener* had asked. It had continued: 'Ambridge is a dream world, and the dream is strangely potent . . .'

It wouldn't be potent for long, I told the editor of *Radio Times*, if we went and printed photographs of weddings a week before they happened.

And so, for the first and last time (the picture editor assured me), *Radio Times* agreed to devote its front cover to a programme that had already been broadcast.

It showed Shula, a trifle misty, in her wedding gown from Pronuptia (selected as being far more classy than anything offered by Laura Ashley or Harrods), holding a bouquet of pink and pale primrose roses. 'Shula by Lichfield' said the caption, proudly, and in a brave attempt to be ahead of events, went on: 'Enjoy the big day again on Sunday, Radio 4.'

Radio Times paid £1,500 to use the pictures. A further sum was paid by the *Daily Mail* for a black-and-white exclusive spread. More modest amounts were paid by publishers Weidenfeld for a forthcoming book. All in all, the programme made a profit.

The pictures were taken at Hagley Hall in Worcestershire, home of Viscount and Lady Cobham. Lady Cobham was a friend of Jock Gallagher's. The previous year she had come into Pebble Mill for lunch with the Duke and Duchess of Westminster.

So many people tangentially connected with *The Archers* have found further fame: the *Daily Star*'s Geoff Baker working for Paul McCartney, Lady Cobham, David Mellor's companion.

The wedding invitations were sent out. *Mr and Mrs Philip Archer request the pleasure of your company at the marriage of their daughter Shula Mary to Mr Mark Hebden at St Stephen's Church, Ambridge, Saturday 21st September 1985 at 12 noon, and afterwards at Netherbourne Hall.*

The Archbishop of Canterbury unaccountably failed to reply. The Prime Minister and Denis Thatcher wrote expressing their regrets in a letter quite properly sent to Mr and Mrs Philip Archer, Brookfield Farm, Ambridge, Borchester B57QQ. The Soviet Ambassador's secretary – also replying to the correct address – said that 'since H.E. and Madam Popova are away on holidays and won't be back to London before the mentioned date they will not be able to avail themselves of your invitation.'

The *Archers* office pondered on what might have happened had the Ambassador not been on holiday. Road directions had been included with invitations, for those who had not been to Ambridge before. Would H.E. and Madam Popova have wandered round Worcestershire in their embassy car, desperately trying to find the B3980 to Borchester? Would they have enquired, in vain, for the turning to Waterley Cross?

The week before the wedding a cartoon in *Time Out* showed a man sitting sweating nervously and biting his fingernails in a foreign hotel bar as he waited for a phone call from England. The call arrived. It was his mother. 'Peggy's bought her hat and shoes ... Shula's got cold feet about the whole thing of course but ...' said the bubble of words. The cartoon didn't mention the word Archers at all – even *Time Out* assumed, nowadays, that its readers were familiar with Peggy and Shula.

On the Monday of the wedding broadcast, the *Daily Mail*'s amiable Paul Donovan – an eager *Archers* addict – splashed the story in a double-page centre spread, together with the 'Picture Exclusive by Lord Lichfield'. Readers learned that Shula's wedding photographer from Borchester had broken his leg, and Patrick Lichfield had happened to be staying with his chum Lord Netherbourne, who was, of course, Caroline's uncle. Patrick, a good-natured cove, had been happy to step in ...

The *Daily Express* had lost out in the bid for the pictures. It carried a feature by keen *Archers* fan Maureen Paton.

'All over the land tonight there will be weeping and wailing and a great gnashing of teeth, like the sound of tractor gears clanging together,' said Maureen in fine style. 'Some men may become so distraught that they have to pass through the portals of a public house and take alcohol to calm themselves down. For dithery but delicious Shula Archer, that sacred image of glorious country girl-hood in the Radio 4 soap opera *The Archers*, has finally got married.'

Shula and Mark on their wedding day, photographed by Patrick Lichfield.
Camera Press

Maureen noted that Nigel Pargetter would be best man, 'if he can find his brains in time', and remarked on Shula's string of earlier boyfriends. 'Shula has been pretty successful for someone with the sort of name I always thought you gave to lady horses . . .' she said, recalling the famous scene in which journalist Simon Parker tried to take Shula into a prickly stubble field under a harvest moon and Shula refused to go with him unless she had a car rug. 'The episode faded on an owl,' said Maureen, 'hooting with derision at the thought of being the only one to know whether or not Shula was entitled to get married in virginal white.' (This, of course, was long before the publication of Joanna Toye's searing *Shula's Story*.)

Norman Painting and Patricia Greene were on *Wogan* – the proud, sad parents seeing their daughter go off into the world – or at least to a little flat in Borchester's Wool Market. Trying to ride the crest of the publicity wave, *The Archers* Stage Show opened in a huge marquee in Battersea Park, but the show flopped terribly. Critics noted that the magic of the Watermill Theatre in rural Berkshire on a summer's evening did not transfer to a tent in London in a cold autumn. In fact, it failed because producers Kent and Pom had relied on Radio 4 plugs that on this occasion – through no fault of theirs – failed to materialize.

A book came out, *The Archers – the Official Companion*. It contained the wedding pictures in colour and by October it was number two in the hardback best-seller lists, ahead of *Break In* by Dick Francis and the latest Delia Smith cookery book, and beaten only by John Fowles' new novel, *A Maggot*.

In Ambridge, Neil decided to leave Brookfield and join Bill Insley in a pig venture, David started to go out with fashion designer Sophie Barlow, and the Tuckers went bankrupt at Ambridge Farm. The team of writers now included Graham Harvey, an agricultural journalist, and Simon Frith, a Gloucestershire man who turned up at script meetings in his ancient Barbour, much to the fascination of Helen Leadbeater and Margaret Phelan, who felt they were really getting close to the countryside. These four writers, together with Joanna Toye, formed the backbone of the writing team.

Earlier in the year I had been asked to speak to a European Broadcasting Union media conference (in Tuscany, where else?) about the revived fortunes of the world's oldest radio soap opera. All the other delegates were from television.

I told them: 'We have between four and five million listeners and a very significant percentage of those are middle class, intelligent, and young. Journalists, advertising executives, young academics, social workers – they all seem to have decided that *The Archers* is the soap opera for them. This new popularity has come about, I believe, for one major reason. We have made a large and sustained attempt to improve the quality of the scripts: better dialogue; better stories; better characterization. We have become very much a social comedy about life in rural England. We satirize, very mildly, the ambitions and preoccupations of our characters. Landowner Jack Woolley who waits for Margaret Thatcher to include

By the mid-Eighties the programme's new popularity was well established, not only in London and the big cities but in its old heartland, the English shires. Villages from Cornwall to Gloucestershire started to follow the example of Cherington in Warwickshire and turn themselves into 'Ambridge for the Day'. At Nympsfield near Dursley, four of the cast's stalwarts turned out to add to the illusion. Arnold Peters (Jack Woolley), Mollie Harris (Martha Woodford), Richard Carrington (the Rev Richard Adamson) and Bob Arnold (Tom Forrest).

Bristol United Press

him in the Honours List; Pat Archer, the feminist socialist, with her sociological lover Roger; our rich farmers fleecing the EEC subsidy system for all it's worth; our poor, run-down, stupid farmer trying to claim Common Market money on 40 sheep he doesn't actually have . . .'

This was in June. *EastEnders* had been not long started. Julia Smith, its producer, also freebie-ing in Tuscany, was worried because ITV was scheduling *Emmerdale* against her fledgling programme to try to kill it off.

Another organization interested in *The Archers'* revival was the Women's Institute, whose General Secretary came to Birmingham to find out how it had been done. The WI had the same problems of *The Archers* a decade ago – a declining membership, a 'Jam and Jerusalem' image that many thought was out of date, but no clear way forward. I don't think we were of much help. If we could have loaned them Helen and Margaret as scriptwriters we would have done.

The Americans were back. It was thirty long years since the Department of Agriculture in Washington had wanted to know the secret of *The Archers'* success, and a BBC executive had written a memo saying that in the interests of Anglo-US relations 'we might as well give with a good grace what could easily be taken from us against our will'.

Now the agricultural journalism departments of the universities of Missouri and Illinois wrote a joint letter to 'Dear Director-General Milne' asking to be allowed to come and study *The Archers*, which had been 'recommended to us as a notable programming approach'.

They came, James Evans of Illinois and Delmar Hatesohl of Missouri. They listened to recordings and talked to the production team. Perhaps their visit inspired a deep-South Eddie Grundy, strumming his Nashville tunes as he sat on the porch with his six-pack, or a Brian Aldridge of the northern prairies.

Tony Parkin was the lucky one – he was sent by the Commonwealth Fund for Technical Co-operation to Fiji where he started up an Ambridge of the South Seas (interestingly called *Neighbours*) complete with two Dan Archers, one Indian and one Fijian, and stories of missing pigs and fires in the sugar cane.

33

Goodbye, Dan

WHEN THE *Archers* SHOW OPENED in Battersea Park, in the autumn of 1985, all requests for on-air promotion were met with a blank response from London. The show's producers, Kent Walwin and Pom Oliver, were desperate and indignant: in the summer, at the Watermill, the production had been promoted after every episode for a week. They pleaded for help from the production team in Birmingham. The cast, playing to an empty tent in Battersea every night, also pleaded for help. Jock Gallagher rallied round, brave but unwise, using authority he did not actually have to try to arrange a series of on-air plugs.

Just one plug, that was all we got. The rest were pulled. Jock and I were summoned to London for a showdown.

Relations with London had always been strained. Nobody, it emerged now, had told the current (and quite blameless) Head of Radio Drama, Ronald Mason, that *The Archers* was mounting a stage show in London. Nobody, for that matter, had told the Controller Radio 4. There was a terrible row.

We had gone our own way for too long, said Controller Radio 4, David Hatch. We never told Radio Drama in London what was going on. Books appeared, publicity stunts happened, stage shows popped up in Battersea Park – how did we imagine the Head of Radio Drama felt when people asked him about *The Archers* and he had to admit to total ignorance?

Ronnie Mason, a good-natured man, sat and looked hard done-by. Hatch went on to say that giving licences to commercial companies did not mean giving them free advertising. *The Archers* was a radio drama, not a milch cow to be used to make money from books, stage shows, sweatshirts and records – and who was making all the money anyway?

Well, Jock certainly wasn't, though he took most of the blame. I, at the time, had *The Official Companion* in the top ten, Dan Archer's *The Ambridge Years* (co-written with Tony Parkin) just about to come out in paperback, *The Ambridge Book of Country Cooking* well under way for next Christmas, and percentages, if a profit were ever to be made, on 'Poor Pig' of which I wrote the lyrics and the *Archers* stage show of which I had written the script. With Diane Culverhouse and Joanna Toye I was just about to start on *The Archers Computer Game*.

The dust settled. Afterwards, at a cheese and wine do, David Hatch said to me, with a sombre, beady eye: 'Jock's a pirate.'

And so was I. And the days of pirates, it seemed, were over.

1 January 1986. *The Archers* was thirty-five years old. When it had been ten years old there had been a party in the dusty Broad Street studios, the programme had been mocked by the *Tonight* team as being quaint and fuddy-duddy, and Norman Painting had felt chill winds blowing as the 'bright young telly people' looked in on the old radio folk. When it was twenty-five (with Derek Hart and the *Tonight* team long gone from the screens) there had been a huge party in the new television studios at Pebble Mill, with 'Barwick Green' played on the bagpipes at midnight, and dancing until dawn. The menu had included cold beef, scotch eggs, and hot jacket potatoes, with Black Forrest gateau featuring among the puddings.

In the last decade the programme had moved upmarket, and so had the food. The thirty-fifth anniversary lunch in the Pebble Mill boardroom started with smoked salmon from the River Wye, progressed through Roast Pheasant 'Grey Gables', and then to either Caroline's Old English Trifle (page 156 of *The Ambridge Book of Country Cooking*) or Jill Archer's Sussex Pond Pudding (page 45 – always Phil's favourite). There were English wines from a Worcestershire vineyard.

Mrs Glenys Kinnock toasted 'The Archers of Ambridge' and Mr Nelson Gabriel replied. Dick Francis, the genial Managing Director BBC Radio, made a speech full of glowing tributes – not only to the programme's past, but to its rather strange and unexpected renaissance.

The menu contained a very strange passage from a recent *Yorkshire Post* article:

> While Zola was unashamedly partisan in his denunciation of the rapacity of the French middle class and wickedness of the Second Empire of 1852 to 1870, and did not hesitate to attack the whole French military and political establishment in order to obtain the acquittal of Alfred Dreyfus, the creators of 'The Archers' have to ensure that if Shula is on the committee of the Borchester Young Conservatives, Pat Archer is a member of the Borchester CND . . .

In May, with the birds singing and the blossom on the trees, Dan died. He breathed his last, did old Dan, in the field of farmers Simon and Rita Jones, at Hidcote Boyce, near Chipping Campden. Frank Middlemass and Alison Dowling were muffled up against the cold, because it was actually recorded on 3 February. In the script, Dan was driving to Brookfield with Elizabeth when he saw a sheep lying on its back on the lower slopes of Lakey Hill and he insisted on stopping the car and going to help it. He had always been fond of his sheep – Phil preferred pigs, but Dan had kept up with his flock, even into old age. He tried to pull the sheep to its feet. Elizabeth told him the sheep was too heavy, and

Tony Archer on the beach at Borth. After a story in the programme about Tony wanting to go to Crete instead of Wales, The *Daily Star* took actor Colin Skipp to Borth together with one, if not two, topless models.

Express Newspapers

he was too old. Then (with a sigh, said the script) Dan fell, and listeners heard the big theme of 'Barwick Green', the version that told them that this really was a dramatic event, not just a teasing cliffhanger.

Public reaction to the death was muted. Gwen Berryman had always been Doris, but Frank Middlemass was the fourth Dan, just an actor, although a very good one. Some listeners, perhaps, remembered back to the Fifties, when Dan Archer was not just the head of the Archer family, but in many ways the head of the national family.

Old Dan was ninety. He had been born in 1896 and was two months younger than Walter Gabriel, who would survive him by a further two years. As *Radio Times* said of Shula's wedding: 'Time must pass. However hard it may be for some of us to accept, it was inevitable, and deep down we are glad. The saga goes on.'

Not, though, with the same people running things. For rather more than a year I had been having occasional dinners in expensive Birmingham restaurants with a keen *Archers* fan who liked to meet me first in the bar at Pebble Mill, so that I could point out members of the cast to him. He was Ted Childs, Central

Television's Controller of Drama. He had first wanted me to go and produce *Crossroads*, but eventually offered a job with a wider brief. A couple of years previously, Keith Wheatley in the *Evening Standard* had reported that I had been offered at least twice my BBC salary of around £20,000 a year to join an independent radio company. It wasn't quite true, then. It was true now. I left in May, out with old Dan.

Jock had already got a replacement editor lined up. In future the job would not be on the staff, it would be a contract post. Liz Rigbey, an agricultural journalist, would take up the poisoned pitchfork.

I left with great regret. The *Archers* office had been a friendly sort of place, although others in Pebble Mill accused us of being élitist. Production secretaries on *The Archers*, it was said, didn't only have to have university degrees, they had to have *good* degrees – but this was not so: Diane Culverhouse had only ever been to Southampton, so we couldn't have been that snobby. Most people had writing ability – Joanna Toye was already writing scripts and would successfully write for television before returning to the BBC as a producer and writing *Shula's Story*. Veronica Henry would become a script editor on television's *Boon* and a writer for programmes like *Heartbeat*. Diane would storyline *Coronation Street* and become senior script editor of *The Bill*.

It was a relaxed sort of office, always happiest in those weeks when there were no actors about. There were few days when the production staff did not trickle off to the BBC club bar at 5.30pm promptly; few Friday afternoons when production secretary Lisa Lambert did not bring champagne and orange juice into the office, declaring that at the week's end everybody ought to drink Buck's Fizz. It was quiet and peaceful; a place where Joanna Toye could sit quietly forging the signatures of actors in books and memorabilia sent in by listeners – the actors *would* go off home without filling them in. A place enlivened only by occasional telephone calls from tabloid hacks looking for stories.

For the old team there was one last *Archers* event. An 'Ambridge Weekend' was mounted in co-operation with Trusthouse Forte hotels and a Cotswold tour company. On the first evening at the Gifford Hotel in Worcester there was an 'Any Questions' session. The next morning everybody set out in a coach for a day in Borsetshire. The coach passed a genuine County Council road sign pointed to Waterley Cross and Ambridge. The driver pulled up to ask directions, and there was Eddie Grundy – sitting on a field gate, smoking a fag. He got in the coach and showed them the way to Grey Gables, where they were due to have lunch. And when they got there Jack Woolley said, 'Eddie Grundy, what are you doing here?' and threatened to set Captain on to him. And so the day continued. Eventually the coach wended its way up a lane to a lovely old farmhouse. Production secretary Veronica Henry – pretending to be a Borsetshire Tour Guide – said,

'Ladies and gentlemen, we are now coming to Brookfield Farm, where tea is being provided by Mrs Jill Archer and her daughter Elizabeth . . .'

And there was Jill, running out and looking worried, and shouting, 'Lizzie, they're here!' and Lizzie was looking cool and saying 'Hi,' and Phil had just come in from the farm and wanted a cup of tea himself, and looked just a little bit grumpy about all the visitors, even if it was all in aid of WI funds . . .

Out on location in January 1986, on a photo-shoot to mark the programme's thirty-fiftth anniversary. From left: Arnold Peters (Jack Woolley), Bob Arnold (Tom Forrest), Alan Devereaux (Sid Perks), Angela Piper (Jennifer Aldridge), Charles Collingwood (Brian Aldridge), Judy Bennett (Shula Archer), Tim Bentinck (David Archer), George Hart (Jethro Larkin), Norman Painting (Phil Archer), Scott Cherry (Martin Lambert), Patricia Greene (Jill Archer) and Alison Dowling (Elizabeth Archer).

Bristol United Press

The farmhouse was the one that had been used for the earliest *Archers* public-ity pictures, back in the early Fifties. Among the fans on the coach was journalist Martin Hoyle. He wrote later in the *Financial Times*: 'Tom Forrest, a stout busi-nessman in a suit, signed autographs. The jodhpur-clad Elizabeth excited a youngish man in flared hipsters, an Afro hairstyle and Zapata moustache. His girlfriend, apparently called Poodle, was vociferous in crushed cherry-velvet at the "Any Questions". Of the often referred-to but never heard Shane, the effete wine-bar assistant, she demanded to know if he was a – a – *limp*-wrist. The panel thought she said "linguist" and five minutes of baffling cross purposes ensued.'

The 'Ambridge Weekend' featured on the main six o'clock news on BBC 1. How many other radio programmes ever did that, I asked myself, faintly guilty about the amount that had been spent on costumes and publicity.

Still, there had been a comfortable surplus on the *Archers* budget over the pre-vious three financial years. Each March, the excess had been tucked away in a Pebble Mill internal account, to stop London from knowing that it existed. Only I knew the account number. Weeks after I had left the BBC, Jock was sending messages to Central Television, trying to find out what the number was – he needed the cash, he said, to pay for my lavish leaving party.

The *Ambridge Book of Country Cooking* came out in the late summer, and extracts were featured in *Radio Times*.

34

The New Woman

THE WOMEN'S INSTITUTE HAD WONDERED what lessons it could learn from the revival of *The Archers*. Now another organization, also suffering from a fusty old image, was looking at the programme with interest. 'The Archers have become fashionable,' declared *Marxism Today*, and in a long examination put it down to 'Young fogeyish nostalgia and radical chic' which was all right, except that nobody in the *Archers* office (at least before Liz Rigbey arrived) knew what radical chic was.

Marxism Today looked back to the late Seventies, that time when Charles Lefeaux had stoutly declared that to mention the words 'Land-Rover' instead of 'field reconnaissance vehicle' would breach the BBC charter.

'Ambridge was a strange place where nothing had a price or individual an age, physical characteristic, or financial status. Everyone seemed to pay for their pints in the Bull with exactly the right money . . .' wrote Brian Hipkin, a listener of long-standing. He dated the 'turnabout in the fortunes of Ambridge' to a series of what he called publicity coups. Naturally enough, this being *Marxism Today*, Hipkin was in favour of the conspiracy theory. The press fuss over the recording of Doris's death, he asserted, had been deliberately engineered.

Hipkin credited the 'great attention . . . paid to the style and quality of scripts' but found praise for only one of the new characters introduced in the early Eighties. 'Thanks to the brilliant acting of first Heather Bell and now Fiona Mathieson, Clarrie Grundy has become perhaps the only one of these newer characters to achieve any real depth of character . . .'

He concluded:

As Ambridge enters the late 80s what have we to look forward to? Will Mark Hebden become an SDP councillor and break the hegemony of the Conservatives as the automatic choice of the new Archer generation? Will the character of Hazel Woolley, who has been so closely modelled on Joan Collins in *Dynasty* that one can almost hear the shoulder pads, be brought out again to expose an unknown element of the past of an important member of the Ambridge community? Or will Shane the silent, shadowy and possibly gay barman in Nelson

Gabriel's winebar suddenly come to the fore to provide the swelling number of *Archers* fans with a real taste of soap?'

The cast wondered the same sort of thing. A new editor – only the fourth in thirty-five years – was bound to alter a lot of fortunes. Characters basking in sunshine might quickly be plunged into shadow, and the actors who played them into penury. Characters long neglected might come to the fore, and the actors who played them into sudden prosperity.

Who did Liz Rigbey like, and who didn't she like? Everyone, you could be sure, would be jolly nice to her until they found out.

Liz was an agricultural journalist and had been involved in broadcasting for only two years. She had been made producer of *On Your Farm* – overcoming, as Jock Gallagher said, 'a handful of male chauvinist complaints' – and then, almost immediately, had been offered *The Archers*. She had little experience as a producer, and no experience at all in drama. She was, on the surface, an extraordinary choice to head BBC Radio's most high-profile programme.

Gallagher's overwhelming instinct, however, was to appoint somebody who was not a professional drama department producer. The programme's two longest-serving editors had been journalists. He regarded *The Archers* as a unique mix of contemporary life and fiction that needed a unique talent. Above all, it needed to have a non-metropolitan voice.

Liz Rigbey knew all about farmers and the countryside. She was female, and Gallagher had long since resigned himself to bright, ambitious women taking over the world of broadcasting. 'They're the only ones with any enthusiasm or initiative,' he had said once. 'Where are the young men with enthusiasm and initiative?' I asked, and he looked puzzled for a moment and speculated that they were all in engineering.

Anyway, Liz was young, keen, and energetic. After a short course arranged with the drama department in London she came to *The Archers* possessed of a most fierce determination to make her mark.

Other young women in the world of broadcasting were in no rush to help her. Margaret Phelan and Helen Leadbeater, the two feminist writers, were the first to jump into the Central Television lifeboat. Veronica Henry, the production secretary, was already in there and Diane Culverhouse, the programme assistant, would shortly follow. Joanna Toye, the non-feminist writer, made a more dignified withdrawal, but soon also had her dainty nose in the Central Television trough. Graham Harvey and Simon Frith remained behind. They were men, and it was thought that they would not treat Liz as badly as the girls might have done. They were left, together with Captain Spilsbury, the newest member of the writing team, to make what terms they could with the occupying powers. Spilsbury was an army officer; it was thought that he would know how to conduct negotiations.

In fact, he soon came trotting down the road to Central.

The author of this book, photographed at the last editorial meeting to be held in the sitting room of the King's Arms Hotel, Chipping Campden – the place where a decade of *Archers* stories, from the death of Doris to the wedding of Shula, were plotted.

Harry Smith

When Godfrey Baseley had been sacked, his personal Ambridge character of Brigadier Winstanley had gone with him. With me it was different. My Christian names are William Knowles, and months after I left Pebble Mill a character, Bill Knowles, quietly began to insinuate himself into Ambridge life. He was a farm foreman, was Bill Knowles, not a brigadier; a nasty male chauvinist who ill-treated lovable Ruth, David Archer's girlfriend, and made her do menial tasks, while all the time scheming to defraud Brian Aldridge his employer.

After some months Bill Knowles' roguery was exposed by brave young Ruth. He departed Ambridge, muttering and snarling, and was heard of no more.

35

Storms . . .

'I HAVE NEVER seen anyone adapt to a new job as quickly as Liz,' said Jock Gallagher. 'She was in the office before anyone else arrived and she was there long after everyone had gone. She was absorbing past storylines and getting up to speed with all the complexities of running a daily serial. Within weeks it was difficult to believe she'd had no previous experience of drama production . . .'

On her writing team she had Graham Harvey and Simon Frith, both of whom were experienced, and Mary Cutler was ready to return after writing on other projects. In Peter Windows she had an experienced studio director and Diane Culverhouse had not yet gone to Central – she was regularly directing in the studio and had written several weeks of scripts. Diane also edited the Sunday Omnibus and produced the Tom Forrest narrations – 'I'm off to do my Toms,' she would cry, staggering down the corridor with her arms full of tapes and scripts. Basically the team was set fair for six months, by which time Liz could bring on her own writers and develop her own ideas.

She found Paul Burns, a listener for fifteen years, who had a theatre studies degree from Lancaster University and was in the civil service. He wrote his first *Archers* episodes in the same week that he took his examination as a tax inspector. She took on Rob Gittins, a Manchester writer of some ten years' experience, and Sam Jacob and David Hopkins (a female producer was bringing male writers back to *The Archers*!) and Gillian Richmond, a theatre writer.

Listeners were treated to a spate of press stories about the new, dynamic young lady editor who was going to 'revitalize' the tired old Archers (Jock Gallagher, off with the old and on with the new, ruthless and unsentimental). But nothing terrible happened. Ambridge events remained very much a reflection of life in small-town Worcestershire or Gloucestershire. Elizabeth Archer passed just one A level and tried to set up a fashion business with Sophie Barlow, then had to take a job on the *Borchester Echo* selling advertising to pay off her debts. Phil found that he also had a nasty debt to pay – £50,000 in inheritance tax on Dan's estate. And for anxious listeners, there was still plenty of humour. Walter Gabriel tried to make Nelson queue all night to buy him a heated hostess trolley in the sales. At Grange Farm Joe Grundy put an advert

220

in a Lonely Hearts column and received two replies – one from the dog-woman, Mrs Antrobus, and the other from a certain Sandra who had a twelve-year-old son called Jason.

In 1987 listeners had a wedding – listeners always did like a wedding – when Sid married schoolteacher Kathy Holland. There were tears to shed for troubled Lucy Perks, who left flowers on Polly's grave with the words 'Goodbye Mum' on them. There was a troubled, tortuous romance when Elizabeth fell passionately for an older man – Robin Fairbrother, thirty-four-year-old half-brother to Grace, Phil's first wife, a twist of fate that pleased the writers more than it pleased poor Jill. Robin, in the end, was a bit wet. He abandoned Elizabeth to try to save his marriage to a hospital registrar in London.

Some of the old characters fell quickly from favour. The vicar, Richard Adamson, was dispatched to County Durham, and off with him, perforce, went Dorothy Adamson, played by Heather Barrett (who retains links with Ambridge, however, being the wife of Terry Molloy, who plays Mike Tucker, and the mother of Philip Molloy, who plays William Grundy). Into the village came the Reverend Jeremy Buckle, an ex-Grenadier Guards pacifist who scandalized the village by inviting homeless Clive Horrobin and his pregnant girlfriend Sharon to share the vicarage.

In also came Lynda Snell, all the way from Sunningdale, taking over Aunt Laura's old habitat, Ambridge Hall, and Aunt Laura's traditional role as an irritant in the life of the village. She also followed Aunt Laura in goat breeding, though her two goats were not, as Aunt Laura's was, eaten by a lynx. With Lynda came husband Robert, who had previously been married to Bobo, and who had two daughters by his first marriage called Coriander and Leonie.

Bert Fry, a Brookfield farmworker, and Freda Fry, Jill's cleaning lady, moved into Woodbine Cottage. Bert was a churchgoer and champion at ploughing matches and had a way with words, making up rhyming couplets and getting himself featured on a local television show. Freda was a famous pastry cook. Bert was played by Roger Hume, who had previously played John Tregorran. His voice had last been heard on the Ambridge airwaves as he passionately declared his love for Jennifer amid the bluebells of Leader's Wood, before being carted off to Bristol by his coldly efficient wife.

Liz Rigbey wisely decided that a daffy fashion designer was not what was wanted for the mother to the next generation of Brookfield Archers so Sophie Barlow, played by Moir Leslie, departed, leaving David free to find another fiancée. In the summer of 1987 a nineteen-year-old Northumberland girl, Ruth Pritchard, came to Brookfield as an agricultural student.

No listener in the land could have been in doubt about what was going to happen. After lodging with Martha (who tried to arrange an evening of whist with Colonel Danby and Mrs P for her amusement), Ruth lived with Mrs Antrobus, the dog-woman, to whom she confessed her love for David.

It was the Shula/Neil relationship all over again, only this time the sexes were swapped round, and this time it was for real. In the late Seventies it would have been impossible for a child of the Archers of Brookfield, those *arrivistes* who sent their children to boarding school and mixed socially with the local nobs, to marry a farm apprentice: both Shula and Neil knew that their love was doomed. Even when Christine, ageing, lonely, and able to please herself, married divorced ex-alcoholic Yorkshireman George Barford, there was considerable unease, and weeks of awkwardness as George schooled himself not to ask for a serviette, or to suggest sitting on the settee in the lounge. But at the end of the Eighties all things were possible. Ruth was to be the next Jill, the next-but-one Doris, presiding, at some future time in the twenty-first century, over the Brookfield tea-table, though whether she would bake scones like Doris's, or be comfortingly heard to call, as Jill did, 'One egg or two?' was far less certain.

Ruth was to be a new woman, a feminist, a farmer. She'd be likely, listeners soon realized, to be out at dawn ploughing in the stubble or worming the sheep, leaving David to find his own breakfast.

The decision to cast a Geordie was odd, harking back to those far off days when *The Archers* used to cast lots of Scots and Irish people, irritating the listeners enormously. The script meeting which invented David's fiancée had first toyed with the idea of making her a Scottish lassie called Anne or Heather, or possibly 'Thistle' to indicate her spiky, feisty nature.

'We have to like her,' Liz Rigbey said firmly to the meeting, robbing us for ever of a Thistle Archer. But would listeners, predominantly living in London and the Home Counties, really take to a strong north-east accent? Pat Archer was Welsh when she came to Ambridge, but actress Pat Gallimore, who valued her job, wisely replaced the accent with the more comforting tones of Henley-in-Arden. It will be less easy for Felicity Finch in the late Nineties, and she may find opposition from the management, but she is a skilled actress, and discerning listeners are, perhaps, already noting a softening of the north-east tones.

In 1987 *The Archers* became the first programme ever to win the Sony Gold Award, given normally to individuals for their 'outstanding contribution to broadcasting'. The following year Sony placed the programme on its 'roll of honour'. Also in 1988, a *Daily Mail* readers' poll voted *The Archers* not only best drama on radio, but also best contemporary programme on radio. It was thirty-five years since the programme had received its first *Daily Mail* awards, first jointly with *Take It From Here* as radio's most entertaining programme, and a year after that, in 1954, as outright winner.

To be voted Britain's best radio programme twice – with a gap of more than three decades between awards – is a unique and astonishing achievement.

In the meantime Jock Gallagher had rapidly written three *Archers* novels, the first of which, *To the Victor the Spoils*, was adapted for radio by Peter Mackie and produced as a ninety-minute Christmas special (Trevor Harrison playing Eddie

Sid Perks (Alan Devereaux) who married Kathy Holland (Hedli Niklaus) in April 1987.
Daily Telegraph: Chris Cheetham

Grundy's grandfather). Liz Rigbey had found time to write *The Archers Quizbook* which had been mooted by the old team back in 1986, but had not been written because of all the cookery books and computer games pouring though the system. Liz had also produced an *Archers* 1987 Christmas Special from the programme's archives (a project first developed by *Archers* sound engineer Alan Mercer) which was made into a BBC radio collection double cassette.

In the programme itself, Lynda Snell went to a Dame Edna Everage theatrical spectacular and was invited on stage – and in real life Carol Boyd did the same, and was photographed with Barry Humphries and large numbers of gladioli.

New writers had been taken on. New characters had been introduced. Tony Parkin, who had at first been deeply suspicious of Liz Rigbey's appointment, had become mildly approving and then very enthusiastic. He was at last dealing with an editor who knew something about agriculture and the countryside. He described her as 'terrific'.

Liz Rigbey, though, was not feeling terrific. She was feeling so unterrific that she had told Jock Gallagher that she couldn't cope any longer – that she wanted to resign.

Her troubles had started the previous year, after a lunch at Broadcasting House, given by David Hatch for the cast and production team to mark the Sony Gold Award. After the meal four actors had been taken seriously ill. As the massive job of script re-writing got under way, Peter Windows, the assistant producer, and then Liz herself fell victim.

It was a particularly debilitating form of hepatitis. Even after it was over, when the victims were allowed to return to work, they found it difficult to cope, and for weeks suffered from tiredness and exhaustion. Some of them, though not Liz, began legal proceedings against the BBC.

Liz herself returned quickly to Pebble Mill, but found that the crises were not over, they were only just beginning. 'She had to face the deaths of several members of the cast, two of them in particularly tragic circumstances,' said Gallagher, 'the moving on of two assistant producers, the absence on maternity leave of the programme assistant, and the resignation of a secretary. It was a very difficult time for Liz, made even more traumatic by the serious illness of her father . . .'

George Hart died, robbing the programme of Jethro, one of the listeners' favourite characters. He had been in the programme since the early Fifties, playing first a village policeman and a cricket umpire before being cast as Jethro Larkin. Of *The Archers* he had said, 'It's just like one big happy family, that's the great thing, that's what makes it go.' In the programme, Jethro died of an internal haemorrhage after being hit by a falling tree branch.

Then Chris Gittins died, and Walter Gabriel died with him. Chris had played Walter since 1953. Apart from Mrs P, Walter was the last of the original older generation to survive in the programme. Chris Gittins was himself of the same generation, having been born in 1902. He had spent his childhood summers before the First World War in a lonely cottage in the Shropshire countryside, and like George Hart had been able to bring genuine depth of knowledge of the countryside and country manners to his part.

The inevitability of Walter's demise had already been anticipated. Chris Gittins had been ill for some time and he was so poorly one day back in 1985 that the studio director had got him to record an extra 'Doh! Me old pal, me old beauty!' under the pretext of needing it for a previous episode, so that it would be ready as Walter Gabriel's last words for *The World At One*.

There was no thought of re-casting. Walter was, after all, the village's oldest inhabitant. He was older than Dan. In the programme he had been heard choosing his plot in St Stephen's graveyard and selecting an epitaph, *All the beasts of the forest are mine; and so are the cattle upon a thousand hills*. He was heard having his ninety-second birthday party in the Bull and shouting out that he would go on for ever. Three months later he died quietly of pneumonia. Nelson, in the programme, said, 'He was the sweetest man I knew.'

Two actors committed suicide. They were Fiona Mathieson, who had so successfully taken over from Heather Bell as Clarrie, and Ted Moult who had auditioned to be the fourth Dan and been given, instead, the part of retired farmer Bill Insley. Fiona died after taking an overdose of drugs in a hotel room in Scotland. Ted Moult, whose temporary mental state had been a great worry to his friends and family, shot himself on his Derbyshire farm.

Jock Gallagher had gloried in throwing Liz in at the deep end. It was an axiom to him that people thrown in at the deep end came up swimming like dolphins. And perhaps Liz would have done had not events so conspired against her.

But events had conspired, and she couldn't cope. She was, Jock believed, over-sensitive when episodes were not as good as they ought to have been, when scripts were poor. She was deeply hurt by listeners' letters of complaint. Jock shouted at her in frustration, telling her that at the last change in editor, in the late Seventies, there had been a whole page of letters in *Radio Times* condemning the changes in the programme. He told her she had to learn to delegate, and not work herself into the ground.

But Liz was leading a new team, desperately weak on experience, and it was constantly changing. Peter Windows, her assistant producer, had left both the programme and the BBC – 'If he says "William wouldn't do it like that," one more time I'll scream,' Liz had complained. Diane Culverhouse, the experienced programme assistant, had long gone.

Liz knew that although producers might be expected to work until the early hours, night after night, there is a limit to the extra unpaid effort that production secretaries and assistant producers will put in to save somebody else's career.

She again told Jock she had had enough. She wanted to get out.

36

... and Disasters

JOCK GALLAGHER BELIEVED Liz Rigbey had the making of a long-lasting and influential editor. He was determined that she would not fail now – not after surviving, with considerable credit, the horrors of the past twelve months.

He persuaded her to take six months leave – a sabbatical. He himself went on Radio 4's *Feedback* to answer the flood of criticism that had done so much to undermine her confidence: 'The high point in my radio listening has been spoiled, leaving me with the taste of soap in my mouth . . .' 'The storylines have become more and more inept, and less and less true to life . . .' 'I wonder if it's being made deliberately dreadful so as to lose its audience and then be dropped . . .'

Gallagher responded by claiming a 20 per cent increase in listeners during Liz Rigbey's time in office.

Interviewer Chris Dunkley quoted on, relentlessly: 'Phil has become so stupid. Kenton is totally unreal. Shula and Mark have turned into the most boring couple of the year, and Elizabeth is a spiteful bitch.' And from another letter: 'Elizabeth is a liar, a cheat and a scrounger and a drunk . . .'

Gallagher said that working on a programme like *The Archers* was close to working in a sweatshop. He said the producers were inevitably going to get bored: 'They're going to get slap-happy, they're going to get slapdash, they're going to make mistakes . . .'

Dunkley quoted in full a letter which seemed to pinpoint the most common faults in every bad script that had ever come into the *Archers* office. It was from a Mr Davies of Porthcawl:

> The Archers have developed some irritating ways which make them less true to life than they used to be. One, which might now be on the wane, is their inability to see and find each other, as follows: 'Phil!' – 'Over here, Uncle Tom!' 'Tony!' – 'In the milking shed, Pat!' 'Jill!' – 'We're in the kitchen, Mrs Antrobus!' Having spotted the one they're looking for, they are then surprised to see someone else: 'Oh, hello Elizabeth! I thought you were in Borchester!' David and Tony also seem unable to do any farm work, however light, without gasping for breath between their words in conversation. More recently the series has been hit by an epidemic

of 'Sorry?' and 'What?' indicating a complete misunderstanding of statements. I never hear people speak like this except in serials . . .

Gallagher said he could only throw up his hands and surrender, and promise to sort the scriptwriters out. Perhaps he did, although observant listeners in the late Nineties might still claim to hear: 'Tony?' – 'In here, Pat!' from time to time.

Two short-term producers took over. One was John Scotney, a vastly experienced radio drama producer who had been head of the BBC television script unit. The other was Adrian Moursby, a BBC journalist turned drama producer who had an affection for the programme and had, indeed, written a few *Archers* scripts in the late Seventies. 'Trying to keep a long-running serial ticking over is extremely difficult,' Jock Gallagher said later, adding loyally that 'Adrian and John managed to walk the tightrope without falling off and the programme stayed firmly on course during their time.'

In private, he was to tell a different story, describing the period as a 'total hiatus'.

Letters of complaint continued to pour in. David Blunkett, MP, wrote several grumbling letters to the BBC, then wrote to the *Independent*: 'I have listened to *The Archers* since I was four years old, and I am sad to say it is fast becoming a rather silly soap opera. Unless something can be done to restore the programme to *The Archers* we knew, then I think the time has come to switch it off . . .'

Another letter said: 'David Blunkett is absolutely right about the lamentable state of *The Archers*. With the exceptions of Phil, Jill, Nelson Gabriel, and the cow with BSE which launched the well-timed assault on the increasingly unbelievable Brian Aldridge, it is hard to think of many Ambridge inhabitants whose violent demise would cause anything other than national rejoicing . . .'

Brian Aldridge, in fact, was having a very hard time during the Interregnum. In Liz Rigbey's day he had doggedly pursued Caroline Bone – he bought a share in a horse she rode called 'Two-Timer Tootsie' – and in a terrible lapse of taste and credibility he had made advances on Betty Tucker. Now, after being struck on the head by a crazed cow, he was operated on for a cerebral abscess, and went on to suffer a post-traumatic epileptic fit.

Why the producers wished to punish adultery so severely is one of the programme's great mysteries. It was, however, nothing to what the new radical feminists would do to Brian Aldridge in the future. Had he known what lay ahead he would have hanged himself in Leader's Wood.

Jennifer gave birth to baby Alice (we were told that Brian was annoyed not to have a son) and Mrs Antrobus carried on a spirited campaign against the use of CFC aerosol cans. The Prime Minister, Mrs Thatcher, chastised television soap operas for failing to support environmental causes, and cited *The Archers* as an example of what could be done. Nigel Pargetter had been away for quite a lot of the time – sent to London to work on the Stock Exchange when actor Graham Seed went to play assistant-manager Charlie Mycroft at the Crossroads Motel – but he had returned with a new actor, Nigel Caliburn, playing the part. Nigel Pargetter's father died, and he inherited Lower Loxley Hall. 'The estate, although shrunk by half when death duties forced sale for development, still runs to nearly 2500 acres,' *Stately Homes and Gardens* solemnly reported.

Jock Gallagher went on holiday to Australia. While he was away a sensational story was plotted – a story designed to keep *The Archers* up with the times. Kenton Archer – long since thought settled in the Far East, a merchant seaman plying the China Seas, doing the decent thing for a Borsetshire man with his suspected sexual orientation – was brought back to Ambridge in order to have Aids.

It would reinforce *The Archers*' claim to be relevant, contemporary drama. It would illustrate vividly the shock to a middle-class English family when both homosexuality and the dreaded virus were suddenly discovered in its midst. It would point up the ability of *The Archers* to deal with real tragedy – the light and the shade of human existence – an ability that had saved it in the past from the fate of *Mrs Dale's Diary*.

Scripts were written and recorded. On air Kenton began to show symptoms – tiredness, vagueness . . . there was something the matter, Jill could tell, as she fretted over her world-wanderer son, but what could it be?

Jock came back from Australia. He caught up with current storylines and saw that Kenton was about to be revealed as having Aids. 'I have long resisted the temptation to ask an editor to change a storyline and instead have relied on a mutual understanding about the nature of the programme and its listeners . . .' he said later, claiming that the production team picked up a gentle hint of his displeasure – expressed to a third party – and amended the storyline without him having to say anything directly.

Other reports say that it was not like that. They tell of orders being issued – whether through a third party or not – to alter the storyline radically and instantly, despite the fact that scripts had been written and recorded and Kenton's ailment was on the point of diagnosis.

Kenton was discovered to have an over-active thyroid – something his Mum ought to have recognized, having suffered from something similar back in the mid-Seventies.

For some listeners it was a terrible anti-climax. '*Archers* fans I know are fed up and angry at such a pathetic cop out,' wrote a listener from Bath. 'We 25 to 40-year-olds have amused ourselves with speculation on the mystery illness. Could it be AIDS, a dark legacy of Merchant Navy life? What about cocaine, the champagne drug of the city yuppies? Or even ME, that unexplained new syndrome affecting hustling young go-getters? Nope, just a thyroid problem. Yawnsville.'

But the weight of opinion was firmly behind Jock Gallagher, a man who knew his audience after all these years.

A new Clarrie joins the cast. At the end of 1987 Rosalind Adams took over the role that had been played so successfully by Fiona Mathieson. Fiona had committed suicide whilst suffering from depression after the birth of her son Thomas. Also in the picture are Ted Kelsey (Joe Grundy) and Trevor Harrison (Eddie Grundy).

Mirror Syndication International

'I really think that if you had given Kenton Aids I would have thrown the radio out of the window,' said a Mr Merrington, writing from exile in Denmark. 'What kind of insane, warped logic could ever have come up with the idea that people can be entertained by listening to other people moaning on about imaginary "real life" problems . . . people like Lynda Snell (and now this absurd vicar) are merely badly drawn caricatures motivated by an implied common social prejudice. We are supposed to think that they are "just like ———— " and then supply the name of our own personal offending bugbear. It doesn't work . . . people who, in real life, exemplify such undiluted manic traits as many of the current Ambridge folk are usually found in psychiatric hospitals . . .'

A Mrs Taylor from Lancashire wrote: 'In my opinion you are allowing too much aggravation to creep into *The Archers* lately . . . I did not like today's episode one bit.'

She added a note of advice: 'If I were you, I should not engage any scriptwriters who have themselves been in the abyss of divorce, since I think they would have a natural tendency to let their own misfortunes stray into the storyline.'

A lady from Alcester wrote: 'I know it's just a story but we do listen for plea-sure and not to have the worries of the world rammed down our throats. Oh, for the old days of the Tregorrans.'

In the spring of 1989 Liz Rigbey told Jock that she would not be coming back. 'She simply decided that enough was enough,' said Jock Gallagher. 'We accepted her resignation with sadness. She had done a remarkable job in livening up the programme . . . I have no doubt that time will show she has made a lasting impression on *The Archers*.'

He said later, 'She was too nice, that was the trouble with Liz.'

37

The End
of the Eighties

THE NEW EDITOR was Ruth Patterson. She was in her late twenties, and had trained in radio features before moving to television to direct the Sunday lunchtime agricultural programme *Countryfile*. 'I was confident she was right for the job when I appointed her, but even I couldn't have expected her to show so much strength so quickly,' said Jock Gallagher – words ominously reminiscent of what he had said when Liz Rigbey had arrived. The *Daily Telegraph* commented that Ruth had arrived at a time of trauma, but was well equipped to cope: 'She has degrees in English and film, a remarkable amount of TV and radio experience packed into her three years with the BBC, and the gritty determination associated with the natives of Yorkshire.'

Ruth had worked on *The Archers* when she was training at Pebble Mill. Nevertheless it was a difficult start. She had to take over from the acting-editor, ('unruffle ruffled feathers in the production office,' was how Gallagher put it) and help a new continuity assistant to settle in. The programme was approaching its 10,000th episode, which meant that press interest was very high. 'Dum dee dum dee dum deesaster!' screamed a magazine called *Riva*. 'Stand by your wireless. Ambridge is in turmoil. A VIP is coming to town and Elizabeth hasn't got a thing to wear! . . . Is it Joan Collins? Mick Jagger? Or will Prince Charles follow Auntie Margaret's lead and drive down from his Cotswolds pile for a jar of Pru Forrest's WI-beating jam? Give us a clue, Jock. "Nope. And I'll chew the balls off anyone who tells you," says the charming Scot.'

Nigel Andrews wrote coldly in *The Listener*: 'There has been a frankly terrifying report that some sort of link is to be forged between *The Archers* and *EastEnders* . . . This (if true) is sheer insanity: in Ambridge, television doesn't even exist. I hope this has nothing to do with the newly appointed editor, Ruth Patterson.'

It hadn't. The idea had come up during the previous year. One of the residents of Albert Square would turn out to be the daughter of an old friend of Mrs P, and would come to visit her. There was nobody, seemingly, on the production who recognized that the vast majority of *Archers* listeners liked to believe –

for fifteen minutes each day – that Ambridge was a real place, and that the aura of reality was being threatened by these merry pranks.

Perhaps they should have appointed Nigel Andrews as the new editor. 'The Archers got where it is, not by publicity stunts but by being true to itself, week in, week out . . .' he lectured Ruth Patterson, severely and unfairly. 'It has nothing to prove, and no need to lower itself, least of all in the quest for a younger audience – of which it already has a bigger share than almost any other Radio 4 regular. I sincerely hope that once the hype has died down, things will get back on course and we shall again hear the "Tum-ti tum-ti tum-ti-tum . . ." without instinctively cringing.'

The media hype for the 10,000th episode was only just starting. Suddenly, London journalists all wanted to make personal appearances, either as characters or as themselves. In the old Godfrey Baseley days, when a newspaper reporter had been needed for an episode, realism had been maintained by rousting one of the newsroom hacks out of the Broad Street BBC club bar. BBC Midland Region reporters like Geoffrey Green, or Barney Bamford, would drift into Studio 2, saying, 'How are you Gwen me love, how are you getting up those awful stairs?' before doing their bit and going back to the club bar.

Now half the hacks in Wapping wanted to be on The Archers, and write a breathless feature about it. Esther Rantzen even got herself into the studio to do the sound effects.

Esther had been keen on The Archers for a long time. Back in 1980, That's Life had wanted to film Archers characters travelling through London on an open-decker bus humming 'Barwick Green' and giving Esther Rantzen a cheery wave. The That's Life researcher had been astonished and resentful when the idea was rejected. He had been unable to understand that the inhabitants of a Midland village would not, naturally, travel on an open-topped bus through London humming the signature tune of a radio programme and shouting 'Hello Esther'. And if they did such a peculiar thing, they would, at the very least, be heard to talk about it the next day.

The researcher had brought up the big guns, Esther herself, on the phone, honey-tongued and persuasive, saying how harmless it would be, and how everyone would have a laugh . . . but the request had been turned down all the same.

She remained, however, a loyal fan. Baulked in 1980, here she was for the 10,000th episode, darting round the Archers studio opening creaky doors and clinking knives and forks. Other media celebrities, too, were falling over themselves to take part. Terry Wogan made an appearance ('Golfer Joins Archers' said the cover of Radio Times) and Judi Dench played Pru Forrest, which must have given the actress who really played Pru, Mary Dalley, a good laugh when she found out.

'The Archers is at its best when it is left to trundle along under its own momentum, without sudden lurches into high drama and low comedy, without contrived situations and publicity-inspired gimmicks,' cried Nigel Andrews,

Wedding bells for Jack Woolley, married to Peggy Archer on 1 January 1991, the fortieth anniversary of the programme. Actor Arnold Peters (*left*) first joined the cast of *The Archers* in 1953, playing Len Thomas the Brookfield shepherd.

Jack May (*right*) has also been in the cast since the early Fifties, playing the suave mail-van robber and winebar owner Nelson Gabriel – consistently one of the listeners' favourite characters.

Universal Pictorial Press & Agency Ltd

speaking for all those believers who listened nightly in cold, austere bedsits, but at the time of the 10,000th episode his was a lone voice in the wilderness.

At Euston Station the cast turned out for the naming of a new train engine: *Royal Show.* Norman Painting and the chairman of the Royal Agricultural Society unveiled a plaque. An American TV team turned up at Pebble Mill, its reporter confiding to his viewers that he was in Birmingham 'to unravel the mystery of how, in the age of television, a radio programme can capture the minds and hearts of the British nation'.

Mrs Thatcher pronounced from Downing Street that the reason for *The Archers'* success and longevity 'has been the strength of its main characters and the rich continuity of family life which they represent'.

Friday, 29 May 1989. The Ten Thousandth Episode. The Royal Mail franked every letter in the land with the historic date. There was a party – yet another party in such a long line of parties – in the Pebble Mill studios, and this time it was an undisguised media event. Even Gillian Reynolds of the *Daily Telegraph* – not averse to reprimanding the programme makers for stunts and gimmicks and inspired press leaks – was there, happily joking about whether or not Joan Collins would soon be hired to manage the Bull.

June Spencer made a speech. She and Norman Painting were the only members of the cast surviving from that first trial week in 1950 – and although she had not, like Norman, been in the programme continuously, her time away was being gallantly ignored. 'It doesn't matter how many miles are on the clock, it's the state of the engine and the bodywork that matters!' she cried, and the cast thumped the tables and shouted 'Hear hear!', even those with dicky hearts and rheumatic joints.

'Barwick Green' was performed by singing group Cantabile. Barry Norman was there (he'd just made a Radio 4 programme about *The Archers*) and Glenys Kinnock, and the editor of *Country Living* magazine Francine Lawrence. Francine had been a fan of the programme for years and years – as she moved about from magazine to magazine so Ambridge features kept popping up all over the place. There was a celebrity called Zandra Rhodes that a distressingly large number of the actors had never heard of.

The 'hierarchy' were on full parade – David Hatch, now managing director of network radio, Michael Green, Controller Radio 4, David Wayne, Head of Pebble Mill Network Centre. Representing the sad and sorry makers of *Mrs Dale's Diary*, *Waggoner's Walk* and *Citizens*, was the London drama head John Tydeman, come to smile and clap as best he could when Barry Norman announced that *The Archers* now held 'the trophies not only for the best drama but also for the best contemporary programme on British radio'. It was the old hierarchy in force, the successors to the old chiefs of the Light Programme and Home Service who had irritated Godfrey Baseley over so many years.

And Godfrey was here himself.

He had been brought back at last, so that the media people he so despised could pay homage to the grand old man who started it all. He – and Tony and Valerie Shryane – were given a standing ovation.

He was eighty-five. Even if he wanted to say something cutting, and get in his car and drive home, he was no longer able to do so. He no longer lived at 'Ambridge' near Tewkesbury; he had returned, when his wife died, to his home town of Bromsgrove, and lived alone in a small bungalow. He had no BBC pension and the BBC was not paying him a penny for having created, unpaid and in his own time, its most famous radio programme, still running, five nights a week, after nearly forty years.

But they all stood up and gave him a round of applause.

Earlier he had been taken into the studio to watch the new editor, Ruth Patterson, directing an episode. 'I feel sure you have a winner in her,' he said, kindly, afterwards. 'We found we had much in common about the basic principles of the programme.'

Perhaps he was thinking of the basic principles, of the happy days when Doris Archer was president of Ambridge WI, and Dan's shorthorn dairy herd had just become attested, as he enjoyed John Walters' vigorous performance of his 'Ambridge Rap'.

> We're in the Cat and Fiddle knocking back the beers,
> We're bored with the Archers and their 'opes and fears
> We Grundy fans couldn't get much fanner
> But you still make the Archers lords of the manor.
> When are the writers going to write,
> That episode that sets the wrongs to right,
> That raises the programme to that wondrous height,
> Of that magical moment and that glorious sight,
> When Eddie was sick in the piana!

In the meantime readers of the *Guardian* (not asked to the party, that privilege having gone, strangely enough, to six readers of the *Daily Mirror*) were obsessed by Pru Forrest. 'I am telling you that the Pru we heard just recently was a fraud,' wrote Michael Parker from Tonbridge. 'Thirty years ago when Tom Forrest was courting and marrying her, she sounded more like Martha Woodford. Last month's Pru sounded more like Judi Dench!'

Like several scriptwriters, Michael Parker believed that Pru lay at the bottom of Tom's deep freeze, in amongst the frozen pheasants. 'It is highly significant,' he went on, 'that the only people she spoke to last month were a stranger to the place, Terry Wogan, and Jack Woolley who, let's face it, is not very bright.'

The *Guardian* has always worried more over Pru Forrest than over many a political prisoner of distant, hated overseas regimes.

'Some believe she has not said a word these 30 years,' said a *Guardian* editorial, back in the last days of Liz Rigbey's editorship, when the correspondence page had been full of Pru letters for a week. 'Others have detected expletives like "shush" (a rebuke to her husband for speaking in church) or "aargh" (an instinctive reaction when confronted on her eightieth birthday with a cake she had not expected). Three readers in London WC2 allege that Pru is so drunk that she cannot get to the microphone. This may be the sort of condition which is commonplace in WC2 but it would not have gone unremarked in Ambridge. Only one of our correspondents claims to have heard a whole sentence. Asked some time ago if she felt proud to have won a jam-making competition, he alleges, Pru replied: "Yes, I am proud, very proud."'

Well, the truth can now be told. It wasn't 'Yes I am proud, very proud,' it was 'Fine, my dear, just fine,' and it was the last line of a script by Margaret Phelan, *circa* 1985.

Aware of the theory that Tom had murdered Pru (but occasionally dressed in her clothes to make brief, fleeting appearances round the village), Margaret Phelan had, some years before, devoted an entire week to situations where Pru was about to speak but didn't. 'Here's Pru,' somebody would say on the village green, and then call out: 'Pru, I meant to ask you – oh, she's gone into the shop, dang it!' The last script of Margaret's week ended in somebody saying 'Hello, Pru, how are you keeping?' and then faded into 'Barwick Green' before Pru could reply.

It was felt, in the *Archers* office, that this was rather a weak Omnibus ending. It was felt that there might be those – in Humberside, perhaps, or in Wales – who would not share the joke. It was felt that it would be more dramatically satisfying if, at the last, when everybody expected a cop-out, Pru actually said something.

One line of dialogue was inserted. The actress, Mary Dalley was booked. This, I have to say, was the only thing in my editorship I am really ashamed of. Booking an actress – raising hopes of a return after years in the wilderness – bringing her all the way to Birmingham for one joke line . . . on the day of the recording I asked Peter Windows to direct the episode and went and hid somewhere.

38

Goodbye, Captain

O NE RESPONSE TO THE CONFUSION and hiatus of the past three years had been to add more staff. In 1986 there had been an editor, part-time director, programme assistant, and Tony Parkin. There was now:

Ruth Patterson	*Editor*
Anthony Parkin	*Agricultural Story Editor*
Niall Fraser	*Producer*
Julia Parker	*Assistant Producer*
Jane Froggatt	*Senior Production Assistant*
Gillian Powell	*Continuity*

and the programme had also acquired a team of specialist experts:

Dr Fiona Kameen	*General Medicine*
John Pogmore	*Gynaecology*
Rev. J. Martineau	*Religious Affairs*
Edward Allsop	*Land Management*

With her enlarged staff and her special advisers Ruth Patterson settled down to rule over Ambridge and its inhabitants. During the short rule of the two temporary male editors there had been a flood of complaints about the coarsening of Ambridge life, and in this area, it seemed, little was going to alter. Kathy Perks had sex with drunken village policeman Dave Barry. Then she had fish-and-chips and sex with him on the way home from First Aid classes. Then she was heard telling Sid she was tired, just to avoid sex in the proper marital bed. Some listeners, traditional types, found all this tacky, and not what they wanted to hear. But they must have felt that the old *Archers*, the old Ambridge, was truly doomed when Pat Archer arranged for Kathy to have counselling.

She was an adulteress who had betrayed poor, kind Sid Perks. But this was the Nineties, and Kathy, it turned out, was a victim.

Ambridge was to be full of female victims. What had started under Liz Rigbey continued under both Ruth and her successor. Caroline Bone would be a victim when Cameron Fraser, the wealthy, sophisticated estate-owner, romanced her, charmed her, and then revealed his devious, callous nature. Elizabeth Archer would be a victim when Fraser picked her up, had an affair with her, made her pregnant, then abandoned her at a motorway service station. Shula would be a victim of 'domestic violence' from Simon Pemberton, another man to reveal a weak, nasty nature. Betty Tucker – already a victim of predatory sex-fiend Brian Aldridge – would be a victim of her husband's self-pity and evil temper.

Males, on the other hand, would now be recognized as oppressors, and dealt with accordingly. Fraser the ruthless Scot would be exposed and banished. Barry, the drunken cop, would get into a brawl with Grey Gables chef Jean-Paul – after passing smutty remarks about Caroline Bone – and would also be banished (sent off to St Albans, a sad day for actor David Vann). Brian Aldridge, who had been kicked by a cow and given post-operative epilepsy, would have to watch, drugged and helpless, as Jennifer – who in the past had been unable to look after a very small flock of Jacob sheep – showed herself able to manage the farm and business with total competence. Roger Travers-Macy would return, and Jennifer would start sleeping with him. Money troubles would come down on Brian's head. ('It's really impossible for a man in Brian Aldridge's position to have serious financial problems,' Tony Parkin had firmly insisted in the past, but money troubles would come now.)

Strong or victimized women . . . weak or brutal men. It had been there in the past with Tony and Pat, of course, and before them with Jack and Peggy. All soap operas are supposed to create strong women characters and weak males – there have been MA theses written on the subject – but never before had the men of Ambridge been punished so severely for their sex. Phil Archer may have been spared – Godfrey Baseley's dashing, impetuous young hero was now an old chap with a hip replacement – and David Archer may have been grudgingly allowed a sort of equality with the forceful Ruth, on condition that he ran her bath and cooked her supper now and then (she showed her feminist mettle early on, demanding a woman priest for her wedding and grumbling about having to take the name Archer), but the rest of the men were clearly inferior to their clever, courageous, or forceful wives. Benign but idle Eddie was paired with hard-working, long-suffering Clarrie; not-very-intelligent Nigel with very clever Elizabeth; rather stupid Jack Woolley with capable if unlikable Peggy; weak, wet Tony with strong, sharp Pat; quiet, unforceful Robert with forceful, get-things-done Lynda; and weak, mentally-unstable Mike with courageous and hard-working Betty.

There were promises that things would settle down. 'I knew in my heart of hearts that radical change was not what anyone wanted,' Ruth Patterson told the *Daily Telegraph*.

And there were, indeed, tales of a traditional nature. Peggy and Jack were married on New Year's Day, 1991 – the rough-diamond Brummie businessman at last securing the hand of the genteel widow of Blossom Hill Cottage (although

Jock Gallagher, who guided the programme for over twenty years before leaving the BBC
to form his own production company. He wrote several books about *The Archers*, including
Doris Archer's Diary and four novels.
Jock Gallagher

Peggy was a working-class London girl when *The Archers* started, a tough little
thing from the ATS with a cockney accent that had somehow gone, over the
years). The wedding, by the Bishop of Felpersham, marked the fortieth anniversary of the programme, and there was a reception in Broadcasting House,
London. Arnold Peters and June Spencer stood by the door welcoming the press
as guests.

Ruth Patterson's true nature, however, can perhaps best be revealed by the
terrible story she allowed while Jack Woolley and his blushing bride were on
honeymoon.

She killed off Captain.

Captain, it must be admitted, was an elderly dog. It was thirteen years since
his snuffle had first been heard (Wednesday, 5 July 1978, episode 7158), and bull
terriers are not long-lived. His had not been a life of total happiness. Hazel
Woolley had kicked him. In 1988, when his master went into hospital to have a
pacemaker fitted, he had been handed over to the untender mercies of George
Barford, who had turned him into a leaner, fitter dog, cutting out the profiteroles
and introducing long walks instead of fireside snoozes.

He was buried in an oak coffin, in a spot next to the golf course. His tomb-stone said 'Well done thou good and faithful servant.' Jack made a speech at a memorial service, and bought drinks for mourners in the Bull. One can only hope – though without too much confidence – that the writers and their young editor did not laugh and make jokes as they plotted Captain's end.

Pauline Seville died. She had played Mrs Perkins since 1951 – an unassuming, invariably cheerful actress, who remained aloof from the politics and grumblings and jealousies of the cast – if, indeed, she ever noticed them. As a student in the Thirties she had trained at RADA and had spent much of the Second World War touring with ENSA before marrying a Leicestershire businessman. Her only problem, particularly in the early Fifties when Mrs P was one of the most important characters, was that she was a good twenty years younger than the part she was playing. In cast photographs she was heavily disguised to look something like Grandma out of a Giles cartoon, but personal appearances were more tricky.

Mrs P was one of the originals, Walter Gabriel's old flame. There was no thought of re-casting the character. On 3 May 1991, listeners discovered that she had passed away quietly in her chair, just as Doris had a decade ago. She was found by her daughter Peggy, and granddaughter Jennifer, when they arrived for lunch.

Among the cast, the only survivors from the Fifties were now Norman Paint-ing, June Spencer, Bob Arnold, Jack May, Leslie Saweard, and Patricia Greene.

The Archers now suffered two more blows. First, the most forceful influence on the programme for the last twenty years was removed. Jock Gallagher left the BBC. No longer would he be available to fight the programme's corner against the indifference of London, promote it in the press at every opportunity, and ter-rorize cast and production team alike with his passionately-held views and his enthusiasms. *Archers* actors generally let their bosses depart without showing undue emotion, usually, indeed, with no more than a muttered invocation: 'Please let the next one be no worse than the last.' But, as with the retirement of Tony Shryane, this departure was different. There was an *Archers* promotion event at Bewdley in Worcestershire, close to where Jock and his wife Sheenagh live. Afterwards the actors went to his house and thanked him for everything he had done for the programme. They gave him a sculpture – and an umbrella, which was the only thing they could find big enough to take all their signatures.

Then came the second drama – Ruth Patterson resigned as editor. Jock – busy setting up his independent television production company 'Broadvision' – had known for some time that she was unhappy. The BBC had sought his advice and asked him to talk to her. They had gone together to the funeral of Pauline Seville in Leicester, and in the car had talked through her worries, both personal and professional.

Like Liz Rigbey, Ruth had had enough.

For the inexperienced producer, a daily drama can be a nightmare that does not end. One crisis is over, one more set of scripts recorded – but then it's another day, and another set of scripts are being prepared for the studio, and another set are being written, and perhaps an actor can't be reached (because his agent is boxing clever hoping to pick up a television booking on the date *The Archers* wants him) and so the writer can't write, and the next writer can't write because he doesn't know what the first writer is doing, and they're both on the phone complaining – and in the meantime the scripts that have just arrived are at least a minute under in length, and are actually *no bloody good* but there isn't time to get re-writes, and so you have to try to do it yourself.

And the new writers you've taken on aren't doing what you want them to do.

And the stories aren't working the way you wanted them to work.

Then an actor is taken ill, and the scripts you edited last week and the week before all have to be brought back out of production and pulled apart, and the writers contacted, and new stories devised to fill the gap, and new actors booked . . .

And the listeners, who know nothing of all this, send in streams of sarcastic, unpleasant letters, and each day you have to read them and answer them.

Gallagher, who talked to both Liz and Ruth during their times of crisis, would later say that it was the public spotlight, the media attention, that was the greatest problem. That they took their responsibility far too seriously. That they lacked the insouciance of those who went before them. That they cared too much.

The job of editor was advertised. The new editor would have to be somebody who was experienced, it was said, somebody who was *tough*. The men who applied – several young radio producers who had worked on the programme – were again passed over. Again it was a woman, this time Vanessa Whitburn.

Would Vanessa be a toughie?

39

Another New Team

V ANESSA WHITBURN had worked on *The Archers* in the late Seventies, as one of a series of assistant producers. At that time she was young, enthusiastic and jolly, and invented the slogan CULTIVATE THE ARCHERS that was printed on the first *Archers* T-shirts. She left *The Archers* after a year and in due course she went off to television, producing *Brookside* in Liverpool.

She was back freelancing at Pebble Mill when the *Archers* job came up in the summer of 1991. It says much for her affection for the programme that she turned her back on television and returned to the quiet backwaters of Radio 4.

Ambridge in the mid-Nineties. To people out for a Sunday afternoon drive – turning off the A1999 at the Pedlars Rest, Edgley, perhaps, and drifting through the late autumn countryside down the winding B3980, with Lakey Hill and its bronze-age burial mounds on the left, and Blossom Hill on the right – it might seem a typical village of South Borsetshire; not as pretty as Penny Hassett, but very much an enviable community, a place where people might well look for a Rodway and Watson 'For Sale' sign on a thatched cottage, and contemplate a peaceful retirement.

They would be making a terrible mistake.

Blossom Hill Cottage – as thatched and pretty as they come – was until recently used for illicit drinking, smoking and false imprisonment, by a local teenage gang, and is now occupied by a Hindu woman who has been subject to racist threats and had acid thrown in her face by local fascists.

Beyond Blossom Hill Cottage – just to be seen through the trees of the country park in all their splendid autumnal colours – is Grey Gables Lodge, the place where Jack and Peggy Woolley live, Jack having to take things quietly after collapsing during an armed robbery at the village shop.

And going down into the village our Sunday afternoon motorists would find themselves passing the house of the armed robber's sister, Susan Carter – Susan having been in prison herself for shielding her brother from justice, and having been released only to find her best friend Maureen 'Mo' Travis trying to seduce her husband Neil.

Then they would drive past the Bull public house, where mine host Sid Perks not long ago threw his wife Kathy out because of her adultery with the drunken village policeman – and on the green they might espy two nice, middle-class girls: Shula Archer who had suffered 'domestic violence' and her cousin Kate who over-dosed on alcohol and drugs.

Leaving Ambridge by the bridge, past St Stephen's with its trendy lady vicar, our motorists would pass the field where failed-farmer Mike Tucker tried to commit arson. And heading south they would pass Grange Farm, and would very likely tut-tut at the broken-down squalor of the house that holds the only family with tranquillity and peace of mind in the entire village.

And they would go on their way remarking what a quiet sleepy place Ambridge is – a bit of England where time has stood still – and would not real-ize for a moment what a ferment of greed, sexual passion, family discord, racial hatred, and rampant radical feminism they were leaving behind them.

'It's a good thing we're not really like our characters,' June Spencer told the *Archers Addicts* newsletter in September 1995, 'or we'd be a bunch of drunks, junkies, nymphomaniacs and racists!' A letter to *Radio Times* in the same month

Norman Painting (Phil Archer) rehearses a scene with Alison Dowling (Elizabeth) and Patricia Greene (Jill). When the programme started, Phil was a young, aspiring pig farmer. Now he is a magistrate who likes to experiment with Thai cooking.

Wolverhampton Express & Star: Paul Turner

complained, 'For the last year or so, the insidious word processor of the politically correct has spelled doom and depression to the majority of listeners . . . this is supposed to be light entertainment, remember?'

Well, no, the present producers probably don't remember. But has anything really changed? A couple doing the same Sunday afternoon journey back in the early Fifties, following the same route in their little Austin car, would have found Blossom Hill Cottage occupied by Dachau concentration camp escapee Mike Daly, and would have driven past the Bull public house where Bill Slater had recently been killed in a drunken brawl, and the woods where young Phil Archer had been involved in a desperate midnight fight with ironstone drilling saboteurs, and the cottage where weak, alcoholic Jack had just been abandoned by his wife Peggy.

And in the Sixties they would have found themselves in a village where teenage arsonists on motorbikes had beaten Walter Gabriel unconscious, and criminals were blackmailing John Tregorran, and young Adam had been kidnapped in broad daylight.

In the Seventies – dear me, George Barford would have been in the Lodge trying to commit suicide, and burglars would have been viciously assaulting Jack Woolley at Grey Gables, and at Brookfield Farm (had they turned east towards Ten Elms Rise and Traitor's Ford) burglars would have been viciously assaulting Doris Archer, and they would have passed the very spot (had they then branched off towards Penny Hassett) where Harry Booker's postbus had been held up by masked gunmen.

Only during the Eighties was the programme different, attempting to engage listeners' interest with stories of the ghostly Hob Hound of Edgley (that terrified Tom Forrest and ate Laura's goat); Eddie Grundy's singing career; Nigel and Lizzie's love life; and the saga of the Over-Sixties missing tea money.

In many ways the programme in the Nineties has moved back to its origins. Even the media gimmickry – Anneka Rice saving the village hall, radio disc jockey John Peel popping into the village production of *Aladdin* – has been a throwback to the Fifties when Rank Organization film stars like Richard Todd came to open the Ambridge fête. Otherwise it has been the old mixture of violence, melodrama and sensation mingling with the eternal round of births, marriages and deaths.

Ruth and David Archer had a daughter in 1993 – Philippa Rose, known as Pip – and everyone was very excited in the production office about the bold dramatic decision to feature the actual birth scene in the programme, quite forgetting Clarrie Grundy's on-air delivery of little William Grundy (yet another example of the Archer family stealing the Grundys' credit). In February 1994 Mark Hebden died in a car crash after swerving to avoid Caroline Bone, who was herself unconscious after being thrown from her horse (the writers did not miss a trick on this story).

In 1995, Caroline Bone was married to wealthy sixty-five-year-old estate-owner Guy Pemberton and there was a big cast photograph in *Radio Times*. (If the picture showed a slightly surprising selection of characters, it was because *Radio Times* was being mean about money, and some regular members of the cast had refused to attend the photo-call.) In the accompanying article actor Hugh Dickson, playing Guy Pemberton, confessed to having been surprised to find his character in love with Caroline. 'We only know what's happening six weeks before transmission,' he said, bewildered. 'Until then I was paired off with Marjorie Antrobus.' Only in a soap opera can an old-age pensioner so effortlessly be parted from an old lady in her seventies, and find himself wed to a cool, attractive sprig of the aristocracy.

Springtime, 1993, and a new *Archers'* stage play was on a national tour. *Murder at Ambridge Hall* was by former *Archers* scriptwriter Andy Rashleigh and featured several of the programme's newer members of cast. From the left: Carole Boyd (Lynda Snell), Felicity Finch (Ruth Archer), Richard Derrington (Mark Hebden), Terry Molloy (Mike Tucker), Graeme Kirk (Kenton Archer), Rosalind Adams (Clarrie Grundy), Trevor Harrison (Eddie Grundy) and the show's stage manager Catherine Yates. It was widely thought that the play saved Mark Hebden's life for several months, as the deadly deed at Pebble Mill could not proceed until *Murder at Ambridge Hall* had finished its tour.

Bristol United Press

'She's been a bit of an easy lay,' actress Sara Coward said unfeelingly about her character. 'She's been known as the Ambridge bicycle.' This was a distressing comment on a girl of Caroline's breeding: listeners' letters, later, often called her Bowen or in one instance de Bohun, showing appreciation of her classy background. After only a few months with his vigorous young wife, old-age pensioner Guy was to die, alas, of a heart attack.

The decision to write in an 'ethnic' character, solicitor Usha Gupta, introduced in 1991, was predictable – though, as with the on-air birth of baby Pip, not quite the bold and fearless move that the production team believed. The first coloured character in *The Archers* was cast in 1972. She was a West Indian girl called Rita, who was invited to Grey Gables for Christmas by Hazel Woolley. 'The trouble was,' Tony Shryane said in embarrassment later, 'that nobody listening knew she was coloured, and if we had people mentioning it all the time it sounded terrible.'

Rita had quickly gone. The following year, in 1973, the Community Relations Commission received a complaint that *The Archers* failed to portray Britain as 'a multi-cultural and multi-racial society'. In the *Guardian* Barry Norman pleaded that *The Archers* should be left alone. 'Let them carry on with their caricatures of indigenous country folks,' he wrote nastily, 'and far from clamouring to have coloured people represented, offer a fervent prayer that no immigrant should ever be so unfortunate as to end up in Ambridge.' (The treacherous Norman would later win himself a place at the 10,000th episode banquet by calling *The Archers* 'a fascinating chronicle of British life over nearly four decades'.)

In the Eighties, whenever the demand for a black or Asian character was raised at script meetings, Tony Parkin would point out, tiredly, that 'in the entire country there's only one black member of the Agricultural Workers Union'. But the issue would not go away. Letters regularly asked that an 'ethnic' character be introduced. In 1982 one correspondent received the following reply: 'We already have a coloured immigrant in Ambridge. We are delighted to find, from your letter, that our character is so well integrated that you did not guess their ethnic origin. We thought we had given the game away when Colonel Danby was discovered cooking a Madras curry . . .'

The original letter, and reply, were sent to the magazine *Spare Rib* which printed them under the headline 'Smug Racist'.

The problem of identifying a well-spoken coloured character on radio remains. Unless Usha Gupta keeps telling us that she is a Ugandan Asian, we might easily forget and think she is a middle-class English girl with a cool name and pleasant accent. In recent years the writers have found an answer to the difficulty. 'We want you to be godmother to little Pip,' says Ruth. 'I can't, I'm a Hindu . . .' says Usha. 'I'm not supposed to do a menial job like chambermaiding,' says Mrs Snell. 'My father was a professional person in Uganda but had to do all sorts of menial jobs when he first came to this country . . .' says Usha.

And, of course, Usha gets threats from racists, and acid thrown at her. Not an everyday story of countryfolk, perhaps, or townsfolk for that matter, but it's certainly a story that hasn't been done before. And it is part of what is new in *The Archers* in the mid-Nineties: urbanization, feminist propaganda, and political correctness.

'At least I'm not going out with a racist!' cries one Aldridge daughter to another, whereas forty years ago she would have cried, 'At least I'm not going out with a teddy boy!' In July 1995 John Walters – Radio 1's *Archers* iconoclast and founder member of the Eddie Grundy Fan Club – told the *Evening Standard*: 'I can think of almost no other BBC situation where people just light up a joint – that's Kate, who went off with New Age hippies and lived in a squat. And people being beaten up by neo-Nazis? I do bemoan it . . .'

In the *Sunday Telegraph* Ian Irvine pursued a similar theme: 'A succession of racist attacks on Asian solicitor Usha Gupta blighted Ambridge's reputation as a rural idyll. A couple of biker fascists called Spanner and Craven brought brutality . . . Greed, promiscuity, narcotics, racial hatred, violent criminality – these are deep waters. I can recall a time not long ago when the progress of a Gloucester Old Spot pig would occupy the programme for weeks.'

Well, indeed. And if Brian Aldridge ever thought that the feminist Gods had forgiven him his affair with Caroline, he was very mistaken. What with his epilepsy, and Jennifer sleeping with Roger Travers-Macy, and Debbie sleeping with her university lecturer Simon Gerrard, and all his money troubles over the fishing lake, and Kate getting a criminal boyfriend called Warren . . . he was finally expected to attend 'family therapy' sessions recommended by Kate's educational psychologist. He refused – a last attempt by the old, sane, human being caught in a mad world – and Kate promptly ran away from home.

'He still twirls his vocal moustache when he meets a pretty woman, but it has become a habit rather than a danger . . .' said the BBC's official *The Book of The Archers* published in 1994. The feminists had done for him. And the feminists had also done for Mike Tucker, the other Ambridge arch-chauvinist, whom you'd think they'd have spared, him being a former union representative and man of the people.

Poor Mike Tucker – failed farmer, failed everything really, blinded in one eye – took to drink and got involved in a fight with his only chum Tony Archer. He attempted arson, and was only stopped by Eddie Grundy. He threatened to beat up Betty, and she walked out on him. On Christmas Day he was found, alone, broken, sobbing uncontrollably for his wife and children.

When faced by trouble Mike had become 'unpredictable, depressed and aggressive' noted the perceptive writers of *The Book of The Archers*, just as they noted that Brian Aldridge had become 'aggressive and unpleasant to others' when things got sticky.

Trouble, on the other hand, has had a very different effect on the womenfolk of Ambridge. Betty Tucker has come through the family's frightful problems a lively member of the WI, a parish councillor, and a member of the ladies' football team. Jennifer Aldridge showed herself competent to run the farm when Brian was being pathetically ill, and faithfully attended the family therapy sessions 'showing unexpected courage and tenacity'.

What Tony Parkin has made of all this political correctness, neo-Nazis and radical feminism is not known. In his book, *My Life On Your Farm*, he severely criticized *Archers* writers who were 'more interested in changing the face of Ambridge to conform with their own concepts of society than in understanding what makes a rural community tick; in campaigning for rape crisis centres or one-parent families or women's rights rather than getting to terms with what is involved in growing a good crop of sugarbeet or rearing a bunch of calves.'

And that was in 1982, when the word feminist had scarcely been heard in Ambridge, and its first exponent had yet to sneak across the Am.

The programme is changing with the times, the producers will say, and indeed it is pointless to complain about radical feminism and neo-Nazis in Ambridge. If the storyliners had the ability to tell a tale of the English countryside they would be doing so: rather blame the people, Godfrey Baseley's old 'hierarchy', who hired them. A more damaging complaint has been against the quality of the scripts. *Financial Times* radio critic Martin Hoyle wrote in 1995: 'Pasteboard characters mouthing inert dialogue semaphore every unco-ordinated spasm of plot to an audience of potential imbeciles. Stereotypes . . . reeking of patronising artifice from every pore. *The Archers* is the Barbie doll of radio drama: sleek, oddly mid-Atlantic, lifeless.'

It is a depressing charge, and one wonders what all those editors and producers and assistant producers in the production office (five at the last count, including an archivist) are doing with their time. An independent production company that put in a bid to make *The Archers* in 1991 promised to save the BBC over £200,000 a year – reckoning to account for at least 25 per cent of the sum by sacking everyone on the production team except for the admirable Jane Froggatt who ran the office.

But *The Archers*, overmanned or not, goes on. How many cups of tea have been poured in Brookfield Farm kitchen since January 1951? How many pints of Shire's bitter have they pulled in the Bull? The Pebble Mill press office will tell you, just as they would have told you ten years ago, and ten years before that, and will be able to tell you in another decade – when a new editor and team of writers will perhaps be taking the programme back to country matters, and farming stories, and Vanessa Whitburn will be complaining about the programme betraying its commitment to social justice in the inner cities. To say that the scripts in the mid-Nineties are sometimes desperately poor, and the script-editing frequently lazy and amateurish, and the stories no longer reflect anything of life in the English shires – well, it is only to say what Godfrey Baseley would have said about the 'new people' who had taken over his programme in 1971.

So, even in this there is continuity of sorts. And continuity – forty-five years of continuity! – is what this extraordinary programme is all about.

APPENDIX

Selling the Archers

I N THE EIGHTIES there were Ambridge calendars, and books, and computer games, and a range of Ambridge wools, and a knitting pattern book, and little sterling silver pigs, and hats with horns; and there were cottage miniatures, and an Ambridge plate, and sweatshirts for the Bull, and the Cat and Fiddle, and – earliest, rarest, and most prized of all – a sweatshirt for the Hollowtree Playboy Club.

Playboy was Phil Archer's prize boar at the Hollowtree pig unit. To launch the sweatshirt in 1980, and as part of Radio 4's unending campaign to raise awareness of its existence in Yorkshire, a plan was devised to get four Bunnies from the Playboy Club in Manchester to lead a pig through the streets of Leeds. There was no problem getting the pig. The Manchester Playboy Club – sensitive to charges of male chauvinist piggery – not only refused to supply any Bunnies, but threatened to sue if the words Playboy Club were ever published over a pig's leering face.

Playboy Club sweatshirts are, alas, no longer available, and neither indeed are Playboy Clubs. But in 1996 you could buy a Grey Gables bathrobe and a Grey Gables bath towel. You could, if really dedicated to the Archer family, buy a matching set of six limited edition Daniel Archer Hebden christening mugs for £24.99, or for a more modest £3.99 a herb wellie complete with peat and seeds, that would enable you to 'grow herbs just like Bert Fry'. You could purchase a bone china 'Fallen Archers Mug' showing the gravestones of Dan, Doris, Walter Gabriel, Mrs Perkins, and – appalling bad taste, this – of Captain. For Christmas 1996 you can buy a Borset County Council traffic cone (£1.75), a tee-shirt with Dum Di Dum on it, an *Archers* cookery book and a range of preserves that includes Brookfield Breakfast Marmalade and Auntie Pru's chutney.

Archers-related products are being sold on a far greater scale than ever before. It all started in 1990. The programme itself was in chaos with new editor Ruth Patterson trying to get to grips after Liz Rigbey's six-month sabbatical. The decision was taken to let the cast organize their own roadshows, promotions, and personal appearances.

With the hour came the woman. Hedli Niklaus, graduate of Manchester University and the University of California, the only member of the cast to have married the same man twice (once in real life to RSC actor Leon Tanner, and once to him in the programme when she was playing Eva Lenz and he was playing PC Coverdale) emerged as the Borsetshire Businesswoman of the Year. A limited company was formed, and Hedli became managing director. There followed an explosion in promotional activity and merchandising. There have been four 'conventions' for fans, and two major theatre tours. In the summer of 1995 Stephen Pile in the *Daily Telegraph* asked: 'Is any fair, fête or festival complete without an appearance from employees of *The Archers* telling cheery anecdotes about themselves and explaining how soap operas mould modern society . . ?' The fan club, *Archers Addicts*, has 13,000 members and issues a quarterly newsletter containing letters, merchandising offers, a Lynda Snell gossip column and discount vouchers for products like Interflora and *Country Living* magazine. In 1996 you could buy a weekly programme story synopsis for £1.20 (expensive, but well worth taking the worry out of your holiday: neighbours might promise to tape the Omnibus for you, but would they remember?). You could go on an *Archers* cruise on P&O's new liner *Oriana*, and enjoy 'exclusive insights into the world of *The Archers*' with Lynda Snell, Joe Grundy, and other characters deft enough to clamber aboard. The BBC rule that *Archers* characters cannot promote commercial products – Norman Painting can open a supermarket, but Phil Archer cannot – has been abandoned. A return has been made to the libertarian days of the late Fifties, with commercial products being joyously and profitably linked to *Archers* names. P&O's advertisements, and indeed *Radio Times*, promised Ambridge residents Pat Archer and Mike Tucker on the *Oriana*, not actors Patricia Gallimore and Terry Molloy.

The latest *Archers* recipe book, *Jennifer Aldridge's Archers Cookbook* is at least the fifth such book to be published since the programme started, not counting various recipe leaflets and collections of recipes by Ambridge WI. The first was *Doris Archer's Farm Cookery Book* published to coincide with the 2,000th episode. Then there was a Peggy Archer cookery book – when Peggy was landlady of the Bull – which relied heavily on Ministry of Food type recipes. In 1977 came *The Archers Country Cookbook*, written by Mollie Harris who played Martha Woodford, wife of Joby the woodman, and who would go on doing so for another eighteen years, until her death in 1995. Mollie's book had wholesome, no-nonsense recipes for rabbit stew, and bacon and egg tart, and liver in batter, and leveret casserole. It told you how to make beestings custard – beestings being the rich, golden milk a cow gives just after she has calved, thick with nourishment and nutrients for its offspring. It had notes, based on Mollie's own Oxfordshire childhood, on the changing of the seasons in a Midland village.

It wouldn't do now. Mollie's account of Jethro calling in the village shop, covered in brown March dust from the planting at Brookfield, would not be

The fortieth anniversary of the death of Grace Archer in 1995 might have been a reflective time for some older listeners and members of cast (Ysanne Churchman and Norman Painting had a quiet dinner together in a restaurant where the old Broad Street studios had been) but Patricia Greene had almost four decades of playing Jill to celebrate – and she had written an *Archers* book together with Hedli Niklaus (Kathy Perks) and Charles Collingwood (Brian Aldridge).
Bristol United Press

approved by Pebble Mill in this day and age. 'You'd a laughed other day, Martha,' says Jethro. 'I go's indoors for me dinner and my Lizzie hardly recognized me, I was as black as a tinker; 'course our Clarrie was thur and her started singing "Mammy" . . .'

Mollie's book was written long before political correctness, long before the programme had been adopted by *Country Living* and by celebrities like Glenys Kinnock and Zandra Rhodes. When the next cookery book, *The Ambridge Book of Country Cooking*, was published in 1986, there was a different kind of listener out there: trendy young journalists and social workers in Notting Hill who wouldn't know a leveret if it jumped up and bit them, who would think it cruel to eat a little calf's beestings, and who called bacon and egg tart a 'quiche'.

It was written ostensibly by Caroline Bone, who had, readers were told, learned her cookery in Lausanne, and who believed that 'the best cuisine in the world is good English cooking with a French flavour'. Like Mollie's book it had country notes, but as befitted a romantically inclined young woman, the prose was more extravagant: 'Poor, sad August! Her withered hedgerows full of the dying glories of June and July; the green leaves of summer turning dull and dusty; all that glorious, foaming cow parsley reduced to gaunt dry stems . . .'

The recipes were largely designer Sainsbury's: chestnut soup, crispy roast duck, and brown bread ice cream, but it contained, for the first time, the recipe for Philip Archer's favourite Sussex Pond Pudding. For forty years, every time Phil said wistfully to Jill, 'I don't suppose you're making a Sussex Pond Pudding?' listeners wrote in asking for the recipe. Here it is:

SUSSEX POND PUDDING

8 oz suet crust pastry	4 oz demerara sugar
4 oz butter	1 large, thin-skinned lemon

Reserve a quarter of the pastry, and line a buttered 2-pint pudding basin with the rest. Press the cuts firmly to seal. Grate the butter and put half of it, together with half the sugar, into the basin. Prick the lemon all over and put that too into the basin. Cover with the rest of the grated butter and sugar. The basin needs to be full. Wet the pastry edges, fit the reserved pastry as a lid, and seal well. Cover with buttered greaseproof paper and foil, and steam for 2 hours, adding more boiling water as necessary to maintain the level. Turn the pudding out on a shallow dish, and cut open at the table.

Jennifer Aldridge's Archers Cookbook came out in autumn 1994, published by David and Charles and lavishly illustrated with watercolours by Sally Maltby. Nobody was in any doubt that it was the best, and most original recipe book ever done in connection with the programme. It was written by Angela Piper, who has played Jennifer since the early Sixties. Previous recipe books had followed the changing seasons, but Angie's book was themed round Ambridge events like the Summer Fête and the village Bonfire Night party, and took us out and about to the cottages and farms. 'Brookfield has been a haven and a sanctuary for me ever since my childhood,' says Jennifer, leading us up the farm track. 'With my satchel bumping on my back, my sandalled feet would race along the dusty lane from school . . .' Reminiscences over, she goes on: 'I'll step inside the porch now, tug off my wellies, hang my Barbour on the peg and grab a clean tea towel – there are plenty in front of the Aga – and help dry up while Jill tells me all about Christmas dinner at Brookfield.'

And tell us she does, with recipes for lemony forcemeat stuffing, creamed celeriac, and a special Christmas pudding.

As entrepreneurial as Hedli, Angie Piper also took out a licence to market *Archers* food products. There is now a range of jams and preserves that includes an Apricot and Ginger chutney by Pru Forrest, and Mrs Blossom's Blackcurrant Jam. Auntie Pru's chutney is to be expected – old Tom has been praising it over a good many years – but it is astonishing the hold Mrs Blossom's cookery has had over the eating habits of Ambridge. In the Sixties she was housekeeper to Brigadier Winstanley, and was famous for her Easter biscuits, lettuce and onion soup, and asparagus omelette. When the brigadier died she went to work for the Bellamys, only to fall out with James Bellamy's nanny, Mrs Beard. She had been silent since the mid-Seventies, and killed off, for the sake of tidiness, in 1986.

There is also a Bridge Farm Autumn Chutney. 'My environmentally friendly sister-in-law Pat Archer swiftly and efficiently chops and peels her earthily wholesome fruits and vegetables . . .' says Jennifer Aldridge on the side of the jar. Jennifer adds that Tony likes his chutney with homemade bread, cheese, and a pint of Shire's Best Bitter – a shock to those of us who thought Tony attached with the strength of superglue to his six-pack of Asda's own-brand lager.

Giftpacks of 'The Archers Pantry' preserves can be had by mail order from: Garden of England Preserves Limited, The New Oast, Coldharbour Farm, Wye, Kent TN25 5DB. Telephone 01233 812251; Fax 01233 813326.

Archers Addicts live at: 1–117 The Custard Factory, Gibb Street, Birmingham B9 4AA. Telephone 0121 772 3112; Fax 0121 753 3310.

Index